Professional Aquatic Management

Second Edition

Robert D. Clayton, EdD
David G. Thomas, MS

Human Kinetics Books
Champaign, Illinois

Developmental Editor: Sue Ingels Mauck
Copyeditor: Bruce Owens
Proofreader: Pam Johnson
Assistant Editors: Robert King, Holly Gilly
Production Director: Ernie Noa
Typesetter: Sandra Meier
Text Design: Keith Blomberg
Text Layout: Denise Mueller
Cover Design: Hunter Graphics
Printed By: R.R. Donnelley and Sons

ISBN: 0-87322-217-2

Library of Congress Cataloging-in-Publication Data

Clayton, Robert D.
  Professional aquatic management.

  Bibliography: p.
  Includes index.
  1. Swimming pools—Management.   2. Aquatic sports—
Management.   I. Thomas, David G., 1924–
II. Title.
GV838.53.S85C58   1989   797.2'068   88-8221
ISBN 0-87322-217-2

Printed in the United States of America

10 9 8 7 6 5 4 3 2 1

Human Kinetics Books
A Division of Human Kinetics Publishers, Inc.
Box 5076, Champaign, IL 61820
1-800-DIAL-HKP
1-800-334-3665 (in Illinois)

CONTENTS

PREFACE

Our goal in this book is to provide information so that, insofar as material and human resources permit, a total aquatic program can be organized and managed to the benefit of everyone. Throughout the text, we will discuss how to design such a program on the basis of the interrelationship between resources and management. Specifically, we will discuss the facilities and equipment needed, facility operation, safety and legal considerations, lifeguarding, budgeting, staffing and managing, program development and promotion, and specific details concerning various recreational and instructional aquatic programs.

We will describe both the theoretical and the practical aspects of each of these areas and provide a list of excellent specialized publications and organizations.

Our underlying purpose is to develop truly professional aquatic workers who have received advanced education in their chosen specialities. Until at least one professionally educated person is employed in a community, it will be difficult to establish a total aquatic program for its patrons.

ACKNOWLEDGMENTS

This is the second revision of this text. The contribution of John A. Torney is still a major factor in the body of knowledge it addresses. Although he is deceased and did not aid in this revision, we wish to acknowledge his part in its creation.

Our developmental editor, Sue Mauck, has worked diligently to keep us focused on the subjects we proposed to address. Our thanks for her effort and support.

Appreciation is expressed to Dr. Stephen Langendorfer for his comments on "Aquatic Programs for Preschool Children" in chapter 11 and to Louise Priest, author and consultant in adapted aquatics, for suggestions on the section "Programs for Disabled Swimmers" in chapter 12.

We have borrowed liberally from the works of others in an effort to bring together in one place the information needed for the proper organization and administration of aquatic programs. Each of our sources is identified within the text, and their work is used by permission. We must acknowledge that their contribution to this text is vital.

Robert D. Clayton

David G. Thomas

Chapter 1

DEVELOPING A TOTAL AQUATIC PROGRAM

Typical Community Aquatic Programs

A Total Aquatic Program

Professional Leadership

Supplemental Learning Activities

"There's a love affair between the American people and water" (Hertig [cited in Keith, 1987, p. 14]). The evidence is plain. According to the National Sporting Goods Association (1987), approximately 73 million Americans swam at least once in 1986, 26 million took to motor boats, and 12 million water-skied. Keith (1987) reports that each year about 2 million Americans float down rivers, about 11 million kayak or canoe, and millions of others choose to sail, snorkel, scuba, surf, parasail, jet ski, and fish. Currently, there are 10 million competitive swimmers, plus 400,000 triathletes (United States Swimming Association [USSA], 1987). Or, consider that in the three summer months alone, 22 million visits will be made to the 29 miles of lakefront and two inland lakes in Chicago—and this does not count the visits by patrons of its 90 swimming pools (Pecoraro [cited in Lynch, 1985]).

Youth have always participated in aquatics, but the recent boom in aquatic sports has been fueled primarily by adults. *Sports Illustrated* (1986, pp. 39-44) surveyed 2,043 Americans aged 18 and older. Various water activities dominated the list of participant sports: Swimming was first (48% swam at least once a year), fishing was third (35%), boating (not including sailing) was twelfth (20%), waterskiing was nineteenth (10%), sailing was twenty-fifth (5%), and snorkeling/scuba was twenty-eighth (3%).

Swimming is considered to be especially valuable to adults from a health standpoint. Reported benefits range from reducing mental stress and anxiety to increasing cardiovascular health and a sense of well-being (Stern, 1980) to building strong bones (Orwell, 1987). The USSA (1987) estimated that there are 30 million fitness swimmers in the United States.

More leisure time and increased personal incomes have also contributed to interest in aquatic sports. Power-boating and small-craft sales increase each year. Scuba diving, spearfishing, and snorkeling groups vacation in waters throughout the United States. Parasailing, bodysurfing, white-water canoeing, and rafting show annual gains in popularity. As the workweek shrinks and the time and money spent on recreation increase, participation in all types of aquatic activities by persons of every age will continue to rise.

To accommodate these people, aquatic facilities abound throughout the United States and Canada. By 1976, the United States had more swimming pools than the rest of the world combined (Conrad, 1976), and there is nothing to suggest that this will soon change. In addition, through ecological efforts even more outdoor aquatic sites are being reclaimed and created. Both outdoor and indoor facilities are used for much more than swimming. Activities range from below the surface (scuba) to above the surface (waterskiing) and include all ages, from infants to senior citizens.

TYPICAL COMMUNITY AQUATIC PROGRAMS

Practically speaking, it is difficult for any aquatic facility to accommodate all who wish to participate. One facility cannot provide the space or the time for the typical aquatic program (swim lessons, recreational swimming, and swim-team practice and meets) while simultaneously providing aquatic safety education for fishermen and duck hunters, deep water for scuba divers, 60 feet of clear water for fly-casting practice for fishermen, therapeutic exercise for the disabled, and so on. Yet almost every community has numerous aquatic programs, many more than most people realize. These programs, which usually focus on only one or two activities, are conducted by either private or public groups that act independently. For example, patrons of an outdoor pool that is operated in the summer by a neighborhood home-owners association have no interaction with the sailing club on the city lake, nor does the fishing club have a kinship with the year-round U.S. Swimming (USS) age-group team. Yet all are part of the community's aquatic program.

How did all these programs originate? Their development serves as a guide to the creation of new programs and also points out the need for coordinated community action. A typical scenario follows.

In the past, a group of persons felt the need for a new (or better) aquatic program or facility. They became an informal "special interest aquatic group." The group may have focused its efforts on one particular goal, for example, recreational instruction for the physically handicapped, winter meetings of wind surfers, or providing adults the opportunity to swim in a Master's competitive program. Or, perhaps the city recreation department concluded that a new facility (pool, marina, beach, etc.) was needed.

To broaden its base of support, the special interest aquatic group began to survey community groups and aquatic facilities. What were the present facilities? Where could this activity be done? Who else is interested in this activity? The survey, coupled with newspaper, radio, and television requests for citizen input, provided information about the conditions and availability of local facilities as well as names of people with similar interests.

To pursue its goal, the interest group became more formally organized. Volunteer and part-time leaders were chosen, mostly those who were original group members. Because space and time were at a premium at every facility, the group had to convince at least one local facility manager of its need. When the management was satisfied with the leadership and acknowledged the merit of the activity, one more program became a part of an already-crowded facility.

If the goal was related to a new facility, then funding became the task. Formal organization was done to provide a power group to lobby for public tax money or private funds. Eventually, sufficient funds were obtained and the facility improved or built.

Once the activity was housed, financial support to provide leadership and space became the problem. A sponsoring group was thus formalized, and short-range (1 year) or long-range (3 years) goals were developed, over which time the sponsoring groups became more conservative and continued to offer the same programs.

A TOTAL AQUATIC PROGRAM

The typical scenario just described shows that communities often have many independent aquatic groups that each use the water (and sometimes the same water) for their special interests. Table 1.1 lists the potential sponsors of such programs.

Table 1.1
POTENTIAL AQUATIC SPONSORS AND THEIR FACILITIES

Sponsor	Probable facilities
Parks and recreation districts	
Neighborhood	Wading pool, pool
City	Pool, beach (lake, river, ocean), small-craft ramps, marina
County	Beach (lake, river, ocean), small-craft ramps, marina
Agency and church	
YMCA, YWCA	Pool, camp waterfront (swim, small craft)
Red Shield, CYO, YMHO	Pool, camp waterfront (swim, small craft)
BSA	Camp waterfront (swim, small craft)
Red Cross	Pool, lake, river

(Cont.)

Table 1.1 (Cont.)

Sponsor	Probable facilities
Schools and institutions	
Elementary, junior, senior	Pool
Community colleges (2 years)	Pool
Colleges and universities (4 years)	Pool, camp waterfront
Hospitals	Therapeutic pool
Penitentiary	Pool
Centers for special population	Therapeutic pool, camp waterfront (swim, small craft)
Private groups	
Non-profit-making	
Home-owners' association	Pool
Fraternal (Elks, Kiwanis, etc.)	Pool, camp waterfront (swim, small craft)
Single-interest clubs (scuba, power boat, sailing, spearfishing, waterskiing, synchro)	Pool or open water
Profit-making	
Schools (swimming, diving, waterskiing, power boating, sailing, scuba)	Pool, open water
Motels, apartments	Pool
Specialty (wave pool, casting pond, marina)	Pool, pond or lake, open water

Note. Joint programs, especially between park departments and schools, are common.

Theoretically, a community could have an ideal aquatic program if enough special interest aquatic groups were active and worked together. This would be acceptable if the entire effort continued to meet the needs of the community. But frequently the initial leadership wanes, the facilities become outmoded, the financial burden becomes too great to maintain a quality program, and a once-accepted aquatic site or program is no longer adequate.

Ideally, a total aquatic program involves coordinating all enjoyable, meaningful aquatic experiences desired by the community while ensuring the safety of the participants. It is not enough to serve separate parts of the public well; instead, within reasonable limitations, an aquatic program must do something for each segment of the public. In theory, this means that people of all ages, interests, and abilities must be provided for.

PROFESSIONAL LEADERSHIP

How is a total aquatic program developed? Facilities are important, and so is funding. But the most important element is professional leadership. One or more leaders must be knowledgeable about aquatic budgeting, staffing and managing, and programming. Although knowledge in these areas can be enhanced through informal learning situations (e.g., visitations, conferences, and trial and error), a more formal approach is recommended. For example, there are numerous aquatic courses taught throughout the country by both local and regional health departments. Courses on various aquatic subjects are conducted by professional groups such as the National Spa and Pool Institute and the YMCA of the USA. Furthermore, many colleges offer aquatic courses on the organization and administration of aquatics, water chemistry, and aquatic programming as well as numerous skill classes. Certain colleges have identified a series of courses that provide a broad professional background in aquatics. Ideally, professional aquatic leaders should have competencies equal to those of the graduates of such an "aquatic emphasis" curriculum. For further information on such programs, see the resource list at the end of this chapter.

There are at least two local resources that can aid the professional aquatic leader. The first, the community aquatic council, serves as a vehicle for uniting each special interest aquatic group and each facility into the total community program, thus providing a forum for the exchange of ideas. The second, the computer, can provide information about virtually every aspect of past and current efforts and can also make projections about the future.

The Community Aquatic Council

To ensure the best possible community aquatic program, it is suggested that a coordinating group—a community aquatic council, such as described by Friermood (1976, p. 107)—serve as a liaison among all special interest groups. The community aquatic council would have three main purposes, the first of which would be to serve as a united "voice" for all aquatic interests (recreation, instruction, and competition) in the community.

The second purpose of the council would be to support each independent aquatic group by fostering interaction among the member organizations. This would aid understanding and perhaps lead to cooperative efforts to achieve a particular goal.

Because a total aquatic program is usually too broad for one sponsoring group to undertake, the third purpose of the community aquatic council would be to aid groups in periodically defining and refining their goal and objectives. The sponsoring group would set a broad goal, such as "to provide a safe environment for wind surfing," "to sponsor an age-group swim team," or "to build and operate a wave pool." Although some goals are not attainable (e.g., not all children can be taught to swim), they nonetheless serve as a constant reminder of the main purpose of the effort. The community aquatic council can help unite all aquatic interests by sharing information—goals, needs, and problems—among all the members.

Membership should go beyond the obvious (swim-team coach, county Red Cross water-safety chairperson, president of the scuba club, etc.) to include representatives from fishing and duck-hunting groups, local sailing/yacht clubs, bodysurfers, wave-pool operators, teachers of adapted physical education in schools, and so on. Although some groups might not consider themselves to be aquatic groups, their participation will ensure a broader base of support for the proposals that are made.

There is no need for regular meetings of the community aquatic council, but a master list of the following should be continually updated: (a) all aquatic sites, (b) contact persons for each group, and (c) contact persons from the public sector (e.g., health department, county commissioners, etc.). City park and recreation departments tend to have the broadest programs and at least one full-time aquatic specialist, who is the logical choice to be the coordinator. The best source of qualified persons is the city or county health department, which maintains a list of pools, beaches, lakes, and other aquatic sites.

Computer Assistance

The development of a total aquatic program requires that many decisions be made by the sponsoring group, the facility manager, and the staff, and these decisions will affect all aspects of a total program: which activities will be offered, who will conduct them, how much should be charged, and how they can be improved. Good decisions are based on information, and the computer is invaluable in providing data for such decision making. "It has been estimated that administrators spend 80% of their time on information transactions" (Naisbitt [cited in Stotlar, 1987, p. 117]),

thus the need for computers, now found in almost all organizations.

In some cases, the aquatic facility is placed on-line with a large computer, thus providing instant access to information from a central location. In other organizations, microcomputers (called personal computers, or PCs, and including such brands as Apple, IBM, and Tandy), are on-site. In either case, the printouts and on-screen information greatly aid management in such areas as budgeting, staffing and managing, scheduling, facilities and equipment management, time management, and data security.

The primary use of computers in aquatic facilities is to make pertinent data instantly accessible. Class details (rosters, lesson plans, etc.) are usually the first items computerized, but, as Table 1.2 shows, there are many other uses.

An aquatic manager's most important consideration with computers is the software (i.e., the program that tells the computer what to do). If the sponsoring organization is large (such as a city recreation department, college, or regional headquarters of a sport-club chain), it probably already has computer capability, and the local aquatic site can usually be tied in to the computer system. Qualified technicians and programmers can install and adapt the necessary hardware and software.

If the facility is developing its own computer capability independently, software is still the most important consideration. A list of expected computer tasks is developed: reports, word processing, bookkeeping, projection analysis, label generation for mailing lists, and so on. Software programs are evaluated on their ability to perform the tasks. There are dozens of commercial programs on the market as well as free-lance programmers who can easily make adaptations to meet every need.

Table 1.2

EXAMPLES OF COMPUTER USAGE IN AQUATIC FACILITIES

Safety
- Details of past accidents
- Roster of qualified lifeguards: name, address/phone, certifications, expiration dates
- In-service training sessions attended: when, where, topic

Programming
- Registration: process payments, class rosters (past, present, pending)
- Classes: scheduling, locating unused teaching areas
- Mailing list: special interest aquatic group members, sponsors of programs, advertisers
- Course descriptions: lesson plans, audiovisual aids
- Personnel records: certifications held, schedule of classes taught

Budgeting
- Income and expenses: current, year-to-date
- Projections of future income/expenses based on past data
- Payroll

Sanitation/maintenance
- Equipment and supplies: vendors, past costs
- Water-quality records
- Supplies used
- Inventory lists
- Repair/replacement data
- Roster of maintenance personnel at other aquatic sites

SUPPLEMENTAL LEARNING ACTIVITIES

1. Using Table 1.1 as a guide, develop a list of all aquatic sites (indoor and outdoor) in a particular community. Sources of information might include managers of known pools and beaches, local health department records, and the Yellow Pages of the telephone book.

2. Visit a local aquatic site. What assistance, if any, does the manager receive from a computer?

REFERENCES AND SUGGESTED READINGS

Conrad, C. (1976, June 11). *Statement to the President's Commission on Olympic Sports.* Unpublished manuscript.

Friermood, H. (1976). Community organizations for improvement of aquatics. In B. Empleton (Ed.), *Aquatics for all*

(p. 107). Indianapolis, IN: Council for National Cooperation in Aquatics.

Keith, S. (1987, February). Messing about in boats. *Friendly Exchange*, pp. 14-15.

Lynch, L. (1985, August 9). Who is the best on the beach? *USA Today*, pp. D1-2.

National Sporting Goods Association. (1987). *Sports participation in 1986*. Mt. Prospect, IL: Author.

Orwell, E. (1987, August 16). Swimming laps good for bones. *Fort Collins Coloradoan*, p. D6.

Sports Illustrated. (1986). *Sports poll*. New York: Lieberman Research, Inc.

Stern, S. (1980, June 1). The new wave in swimming. *The New York Times Magazine*, p. 86.

Stotlar, D. (1987). Managing administrative functions with microcomputers. In J. Donnelly (Ed.), *Using microcomputers in physical education and the sport sciences* (pp. 117-134). Champaign, IL: Human Kinetics.

Thomas, D. (1986, Summer). A survey of aquatic education in 140 colleges and universities in the United States. *National Aquatics Journal*, pp. 10-14.

United States Swimming Association. (1987, July). *Sporting Goods Dealer* [Advertisement], p. 13.

RESOURCES

Over a dozen institutions in the United States offer a series of aquatic courses that provide an "aquatic emphasis" or "minor in aquatics" to their students. For a current list, contact the Aquatic Council of the American Alliance for Health, Physical Education, Recreation and Dance (AAHPERD), 1900 Association Dr., Reston, VA 22091.

Chapter 2

EVALUATING LOCAL FACILITIES

Evaluation Criteria
Gathering Information
Decision: Rent, Renovate, or Construct a New Facility
Supplemental Learning Activities

Chapter 1 provided an outline of the typical procedures followed when developing an aquatic program. One of the first steps is to search for adequate facilities. This chapter will present specific criteria and procedures for surveying local facilities and then help aquatic professionals and special interest group members make decisions as to where their programs could prosper best.

EVALUATION CRITERIA

Although each aquatic interest group expresses a need for "adequate" facilities, members of the group too often have only a rudimentary knowledge of what this means specifically. Therefore, before beginning any survey, members of the group should be knowledgeable about two areas: (a) the desirable features of a pool and/or

beach waterfront and (b) the needs of specific programs (i.e., exercise programs, springboard diving, etc.). It is advisable to develop check sheets for use by the evaluators so that all pertinent items are noted.

Desirable Features of Swimming Pools

1. All decks and floors in the pool and locker rooms should be nonslip (preferably 1-inch nonslip tiles).
2. Storage space should be easily accessible and adequate for all types of equipment.
3. Relative humidity should be controlled (70% to 80%).
4. Indoor acoustics should be controlled by the acoustical treatment of at least two walls and the ceiling.
5. Lighting should be at least 90 to 125 footcandles at deck level.

6. Air temperature should be 5 °F above water temperature up to an air temperature of 85 °F.
7. Water temperature in outdoor pools should be kept about 5 °F cooler than indoor pools for each activity.
8. Water clarity should be such that a 4-inch black disk can be seen on the pool's bottom at the deepest point.

Desirable Features of Beaches and Waterfronts

1. Lakes, natural or man-made, should have pollution-free water and a continuous flow that protects the area from pollution resulting from stagnation.
2. The watershed that feeds the area must be pollution free.
3. The beach or waterfront should be protected from violent erosion or wind damage.
4. Periodic damage from ice or changes in water level should be minimized by the proper construction of piers and docks.
5. The usable beach area should extend at least 50 feet from the water edge, though many waterfronts operate successfully with less.
6. The waterfront should be positioned to obtain maximum sunlight but should provide areas of shade nearby.
7. Offshore depths must be commensurate with the program being planned for the area. Swimming, boating, and canoeing areas require depths of 2 to 12 feet, and scuba-diving areas should have depths of 4, 20, and 40 feet.
8. Optimum water temperatures in the area during the operating season are between 65 °F and 75 °F.
9. The water at swimming beaches should be clear enough that a large object on the bottom in 15 feet of water can be seen easily.
10. The bottom slope should be gentle, without drop-offs or holes.
11. The bottom should be sand or gravel, and there should be no mud, marine weeds, barnacles, or submerged objects in the portion of the waterfront used by swimmers.
12. Boundaries must be clearly indicated by restraining lines, booms, cribbing, or solid walls, and depths in the dock areas should be prominently noted by signs.

Requirements for Specific Pool Activities

Each pool activity also has its own special facility needs.

Swimming for Disabled Persons

Special means of access such as ramps and handrails will be necessary. Storage is needed for wheelchairs and crutches. Other required features include hydraulic lifts, deck-level overflow troughs, and wheelchair-height "transfer" steps, which facilitate the transfer of a patron from a wheelchair to the pool. There should be no curbs, and drain trenches should be covered with nonslip grating.

Filters should be designed for a turnover of 3 or 4 hours, and water temperature control should be possible up to 95 °F. For sanitation it is preferable to use an ozone generator in conjunction with the use of bromine or chlorine.

The area should be large enough for lap swimming (at least 45 feet by 45 feet), and the depth should be from 0 to 4 feet, with a gentle bottom slope (1 inch in 12 inches). A movable floor, which permits easy alteration of water depth, is desirable.

Aquatic Exercise

Aquatic exercises require a depth of 3 to 4-1/2 feet and a water temperature up to 85 °F. Handholds on the pool's perimeter are necessary. The pool can be of any shape.

Children's Play and Instruction

A depth of 0 to 2 feet (a movable bottom facilitates this) is desirable, with a water temperature of 83 °F to 85 °F.

Control of the pool chemistry is vital and should be accomplished by an automatic chemical control unit. A filter turnover rate of 2 hours is required by health department regulations in many states. Some states require draining the pool daily. Dual pool drains with an area of at least 1 square foot and with a firmly fixed grating at least four times the area of the drain pipe are necessary for safety.

Sprays or fountains are desirable but, if used, should be installed only in a "flow-through" pool, through which new water is continuously passing but not being recirculated. It is difficult to hold a chemical residual in pools with sprays and fountains. Colorful, attractive designs or sea animals may be painted on the pool bottom.

Leisure Recreation

Most (90%) of the people who enjoy aquatic recreation are seeking passive relaxation (Wong, 1982). They like to lounge and watch other people having fun or to cool off or soak in the water with an occasional splash and frolic. They bat a beach ball around, swim through underwater rings, and then retire to a towel or blanket to relax again. They do not care for deep water because most of them are poor swimmers. These people can make the difference between a profit and a loss for an aquatic complex, so a leisure area should be included in plans for aquatic recreation.

The leisure recreation area should range in depth from 0 to 4-1/2 feet and should contain areas designed for both adult and children's water play. Fountains, sprays, underwater benches, playground equipment adapted to water use, and pool-bottom murals should be surrounded by a large deck area that need not have a defined shape or size. However, its theme should be variety and innovation. Water temperature should be 82 °F to 84 °F.

Teaching Swimming (Mixed Ages)

The water depth should be from 6 inches to 4-1/2 feet and the water temperature from 82 °F to 85 °F. The teaching area should be at least 45 feet by 45 feet and rectangular. A deck-level overflow is preferred, as it permits easy exit from the water.

Competitive Swimming

The minimum water depth should be 4 feet, but the desired depth is 6 feet. Constant water depth is preferred. A water temperature of 78 °F to 82 °F is best for competition.

Pool size should be a minimum of 75 feet, 1 inch by 45 feet, or 25 meters plus 2.54 centimeters by 45 feet. A more desirable size is 50 meters plus 2.54 centimeters by 75 feet, 1 inch. Pools 50 meters long should have one or two bulkheads. Increase the pool length by the width of the bulkhead(s).

A rectangular shape is necessary, and there should be no ladders, water inlets, or underwater lights in the end walls. Underwater windows must be below the 4-foot-depth level. Minimal deck space is 10 feet on both sides and 25 feet on the ends.

Lane lines and end-wall targets should meet the specifications of governing bodies such as USS, the National Collegiate Athletic Association (NCAA), and Federation Internationale de Natation Amateur (FINA). Lighting should be 100 footcandles at the water surface, and pools should have exceptional acoustic and humidity control.

Locker space for the visiting team is needed. For comfort, adequate spectator seating and dual temperature-zone controls in pools are desirable.

Springboard Diving

The minimum pool depth should be 12 feet (1-meter boards) to 18 feet (10-meter platform). Depth must be maintained for sufficient distance in all directions from the end of the board or platform (see the official rules of the NCAA, FINA, and the U.S. Diving Association).

The minimum width should be 8 feet times the number of boards, plus 16 feet. A wider pool is required if platforms are used. The minimum length should be 45 feet, or 50 feet for a 10-meter platform. The diving well should be rectangular in shape, with vertical walls to within 6 inches of the bottom.

Ceiling height must be 16 feet over the boards and 11 feet over any platform. Adequate lighting requires 100 footcandles at the water surface and on the takeoff. Water temperature should be 80 °F to 85 °F.

Scuba Training

A body of water in any shape will be adequate, but different depths (4 feet and 12 feet) are necessary. An area with a depth of 15 to 18 feet is desirable. Pool size should be at least 45 feet by 60 feet. For classes, water temperature should be 82 °F to 84 °F. Water may be cooler if wet or dry suits are available. Underwater lights, windows, and speakers are desirable.

Synchronized Swimming and Water Shows

The area can be any shape, but most routines are planned for rectangular pools. Ample spectator seating is desirable.

There must be some shallow water (5 feet), but most of the area should be 10 to 12 feet deep. The minimum size should be 45 feet by 60 feet.

Provisions for total blackness and for rheostat control from 10 to 100 footcandles at the water surface are desirable, as are a theatrical spotlight system and underwater lights with versatile controls. Provisions must also be made for the hanging of backdrops and drapes on walls and ceilings. An exceptional sound system and acoustical treatment must include underwater speakers. Underwater windows are helpful. Multiple entrances from locker rooms are desirable.

Water Polo

The minimum pool size should be 75 feet by 45 feet (NCAA) or 30 meters by 20 meters. (U.S. Water Polo Association). A rectangular shape is necessary, with vertical sides to within 6 inches of the bottom. Ample spectator seating is desirable. Constant water depth is a minimum of 2 meters (6-1/2 feet), with desirable water temperature being from 76 °F to 82 °F. Markings on the pool's sides and bottom must conform to NCAA and U.S. Water Polo Association rules and specifications. Lighting must be a minimum of 100 footcandles at the water surface.

GATHERING INFORMATION

Once evaluative criteria have been developed, information concerning facilities and programs can be gathered from four sources: local facilities and programs, other facilities, publications, and professional consultants.

Evaluating Local Facilities

The survey should not be confined to the obvious pools and swimming beaches but should include rivers, streams, ponds, creeks, lakes, private pools, or any body of water that could serve anyone's aquatic needs. An often-overlooked facility is the private pool. For years the San Diego Red Cross Chapter has conducted successful learn-to-swim campaigns in such facilities.

Survey of Other Facilities

At this point (if not before), members of the special aquatic interest group must determine what other groups have done with their own facilities and programs. Small groups should contact (and, if possible, visit) the aquatic facilities and groups that are sponsoring programs similar to those being considered. Group members can gain worthwhile information by observing

and by talking with the workers and patrons of the facility being studied.

Publications

Every member of the group should be responsible for other methods of gathering information. Reading and then discussing the sources in the reference lists at the end of this chapter and chapter 3 is highly recommended. At least one member of the group should read each of the listed sources.

Professional Consultants

Consultants are persons who, through experience and training, are qualified to offer advice. A consultant should have experience in the specific area under consideration and should be able to supply a list of past clients who can verify his or her competence. Most important, the consultant should work exclusively for the aquatic special interest group and should not have financial ties to any company that could profit from the programming or from the renovating or building of a facility. Some consultants are associated with such companies; and, although their advice may be sound, it may also reflect a bias toward the abilities of their employer.

The importance of this principle can be illustrated by the case of a midwestern country club that did not hire a consultant because a contractor assured the club that he had built many satisfactory pools. The consultant was aware that the contractor had planned to use an inappropriate filter in the club pool, and he warned the club's building committee of the error. The building committee ignored the advice, and a type of filter was installed for which the water supply in the area was inadequate. Two weeks after the pool opened, it was shut down and a new filter ordered.

In another case, a pool architect was advised by a pool consultant that the locker-room floor was a safety hazard. The advice was ignored because the contractor assured the architect that it would be satisfactory. Two accidents in the first month of operation forced the pool owner to dig up the floor and replace it. To repeat, the pool owner should hire a professional consultant.

DECISION: RENT, RENOVATE, OR CONSTRUCT A NEW FACILITY

By the end of the information-gathering phase, the group will have found out that the features of a facility determine the scope of the activities that will be conducted in it. For example, the total water area and depth will be a limiting factor; that is, a small pool accommodates only a few swimmers at one time, shallow water rules out springboard diving and water polo, cold temperatures at an outdoor site require adjustments in the length of instructional periods, currents and drop-offs limit the number of programs offered at beaches, and so on. The group will find that the general design of the facility affects the ability to provide for the safety and security of its patrons. Finally, certain goals of the group, such as large membership, adequate practice time, sponsorship of championship events, and so on, may need to be adjusted to the facility, not vice versa.

A preliminary decision concerning the location of the program can now be made.

Possible choices include renting a present facility, purchasing and renovating a present facility, or constructing a new facility.

Use of a Present Facility

The simplest decision, although not necessarily the best long-term solution, is to rent space in a pool or to secure permission to use a beach or waterfront site on a part-time basis. Although this may not be a desirable permanent solution, almost all aquatic programs began this way.

If the decision is to rent facilities, it is customary to divide the costs among the members of the special interest group. But remember that funds must be raised for expenses other than rent (see also chapter 7 on budgeting).

Renovate

The concept "new life for old sites" implies that it is less expensive to upgrade older facilities than it is to build new ones and that, if done with foresight, the undertaking will be cost efficient.

Normally, renovation is considered an option if the size of the water area is adequate for all planned programs and, in the case of an indoor pool, if the walls and roof of the building are in good condition. A key limiting factor to remodeling is facility location. If patrons cannot (or will not) travel safely and easily to the facility, an otherwise suitable renovation plan should be rejected. Many existing pools and beaches are inappropriately located because of population shifts or economic or transportation demographics.

Because the cost of constructing a new pool is high, enclosing an existing outdoor pool is often considered. However, unless this remodeled facility can meet the previously determined needs, this option is not practical.

If renovation seems feasible, a consultant should be employed who can consider the economic aspects of selective, or complete, remodeling. The existing heating and lighting, water filtration, locker rooms, deck/storage space, and spectator seating must be carefully analyzed to determine whether alterations are necessary.

Shropshire (1984) cited three ways to improve pools inexpensively:

1. Cosmetic changes: colored murals on walls, subdued (but still adequate) lighting, background music, hanging plants, hanging sound panels, and appropriate air and water temperature
2. Accessories: personal-challenge facilities (tarzan ropes, innertubes) and sensation facilities (slides, underwater mirror, videotaping swimmers and then playing the tape back, inflatables, parachutes, earth ball, water hockey)
3. Amenities: food, lounge chairs, sun deck, live entertainment, fitness classes, babysitting, pro shop, picnic area in adjacent land, and so on

An example of extensive remodeling of a 27-year-old rectangular pool was presented by Giles (1987). The project group (representatives from the recreation staff, senior aquatic staff, pool users, and community members) first looked at programming. They were instructed to develop three lists: a "must-do" list, a "should-do" list, and a "could-do" list. The must-do list that was developed for the instructional program called for adult, family, and fitness programs to be more varied. The same list for the recreational swim program had plans to add leisure-pool accessories and to increase general recreation time, and the general programming list called for increased contract rentals to specific target groups such as birthday parties and business groups. Facility management lists were also constructed, with the major recommendations being to develop marketing plans, avoid program duplication, and provide for a staff training program.

Next, a design group (with a budget restraint of no more than half of what it would cost to build a new pool) developed a plan to (a) modernize the locker rooms and pool office; (b) add a solarium with such amenities as background music, whirlpool, and tanning areas; (c) brighten the pool interior with new windows, lighting, graphics, slides, and background music; (d) provide access for disabled persons; and (e) enclose and air condition half of the spectator gallery. It cost $500,000 to make these changes, less than half the cost of building a new pool.

Construct New Facilities

The impetus for constructing new facilities usually begins when the special interest group members decide that they need more water time and space than the existing facilities can provide and that renovation of a facility is not possible. (The construction of new facilities will be discussed in the next chapter.)

SUPPLEMENTAL LEARNING ACTIVITIES

1. Using the list of desirable features given in this chapter, evaluate a pool or open-water facility for its

suitability for one of the following activities: swimming lessons, recreational swimming, diving, scuba, or water exercise.

2. Draw an outline of a pool and keep changing the shape and dimensions to see how many activities listed in this chapter you can fit into a single pool without sacrificing any of the desired features. Use movable bulkheads and movable floors. (Remember that you cannot change the temperature quickly.)

REFERENCES AND SUGGESTED READINGS

Giles, R. (1987). Updating the image: New life for old pools. In C. Wilson (Ed.), *The world of lifesaving* (pp. 29-31). Toronto, Ontario, Canada: The Royal Life Saving Society Canada.

National Recreation and Parks Association. (1979). *Evaluating water-based recreation facilities* (Management Aid Series, Bulletin No. 70). Arlington, VA: Author.

Shropshire, D. (1984). Innovation, not renovation. In J. Bangay (Ed.), *Aquatic programming* (pp. 28-31). Toronto, Ontario, Canada: The Royal Life Saving Society Canada.

Wong, H. (1982). Humanizing the multipurpose pool. In R. Clayton (Ed.), *Aquatics now* (pp. 2-17). Indianapolis, IN: Council for National Cooperation in Aquatics.

Chapter 3

DESIGNING POOL AND OPEN-WATER FACILITIES

Designing the Ideal Swimming Pool Complex
Pool Equipment Needs
Designing the Ideal Open-Water Facility
Funding Aquatic Facilities
Planning and Constructing an Aquatic Facility
Supplemental Learning Activities

This chapter presents the ideals of pool and open-water facilities and equipment and then offers suggestions for their funding and construction.

Assuming that a special interest aquatic group decides to renovate or construct a new facility, it is important that each member knows the features of an ''ideal'' facility. Members representing different aquatic activities should know exactly which features they want incorporated into the facility. Because the ideal can be expensive, conflicts among group members concerning desirable facility features must be resolved by compromise. For example, children need shallow water, divers need deep water, handicapped persons need ramps and lifts, and competitive swimmers need clean pool walls with no ramps or ladders.

DESIGNING THE IDEAL SWIMMING POOL COMPLEX

Because there is no ideal single pool, a pool complex that is built to serve a total aquatic program should include several pools. Although conflicts can persist, (e.g., over the relative placement of the pools in relationship to one another), the overlapping requirements for each aquatic activity (see chapter 2) provide guidance to some workable compromises. The goal is to use the least number of pools in which to conduct the greatest number of programs.

An ideal pool complex would contain a main pool, a diving pool, a therapy pool, and a leisure pool. The main pool would be 52.46 meters (172 feet plus 1-1/2 inches) long by 75 feet wide, allowing for a 50-meter (plus 1 inch) race course and two bulkheads, each 4 feet wide. It would range in depth from 2 to 3 meters and have a movable floor that is capable of providing an area of 75 feet by 45 feet ranging from 0 to 4-1/2 feet deep.

This main pool, with its movable floor and bulkheads, could serve as a training pool, a children's pool, a water polo pool, a synchronized-swimming and water-show pool, a water exercise pool, and a competitive pool. It could also accommodate boating, canoeing, and kayaking.

The diving pool would be 75 feet by 60 feet and 18 feet deep, sloping to an area 60 feet by 15 feet that is 4 feet deep. It would serve for springboard diving and for scuba instruction.

The therapy pool would be 45 feet by 45 feet, with a movable bottom that allows any depth and slope from 0 to 4-1/2 feet. This would be a warm-water pool and would serve as an instructional pool for children, an aquatic exercise pool, and a therapy pool.

The leisure pool would be most appealing to the recreational swimmer who likes to rest, swim, and play in the water without the restrictions of organized or competitive activity. It would probably be the feature attraction of the complex. The leisure pool has neither defined dimensions nor a specific shape but should be large, ranging in depth from 0 to 4-1/2 feet. It should contain as many odd and attractively shaped benches, fountains, sprays, slides, playground toys, and "relax-and-soak" areas as can be safely arranged in it. Maximum deck area should surround the leisure pool for relaxing and socializing between water sessions and for parents who wish to supervise their children from the deck (see Fig. 3.1).

However, it is possible for one pool to serve more than one specific program. Figure 3.2 illustrates a Toronto, Ontario-area pool, which includes a 50-meter competition water area, shallow water area, water playground, greenhouse, therapeutic pool, wading pool, beach area, and a terraced spectator gallery. The shallow end of the pool is 3 feet, 6 inches deep and gently slopes up (1 in 35) to 3 feet deep at the middle of the pool. From the 3-foot deep area the pool bottom slopes up again at 90 degrees to the swimming lanes toward the beach, where it goes to zero depth. The transition is gentle from the beach through the shallow water area to the middle of the pool and then beyond to the deeper end. The deeper half of the pool is designed to accommodate diving, synchronized swimming, water polo, and swimming competitions. The pool is fitted with a movable bulkhead that can be used to divide the water area for 25 meters or 25 yards for competition or training. The bulkhead slides to the deep end of the pool for use in 50-meter competition.

Play equipment includes an animal slide, rocks and water sprays, another slide from the mezzanine level, ponds, bridge, island, lumberjack's log, and ring swing. For dry play, there is a room full of small balls for young children to use. Skylights and low level windows admit sunlight into the pool without creating direct and reflected glare from the water. Subtropical plants grow in a greenhouse so that when the pool is shut down the greenhouse can still be heated independently to keep the plants alive. The greenhouse also functions as an expanded solar collector, which supplies a heat exchange system for heating the pool water (Wong, 1982).

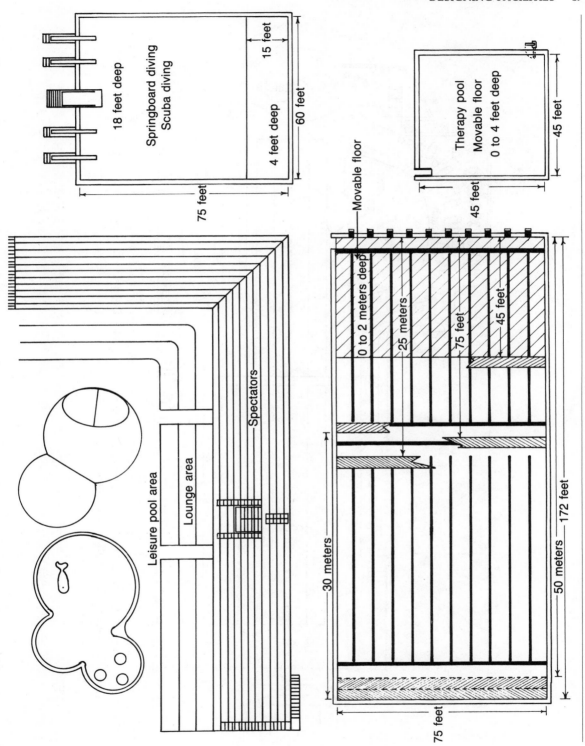

Figure 3.1.   Multi-use pool complex.

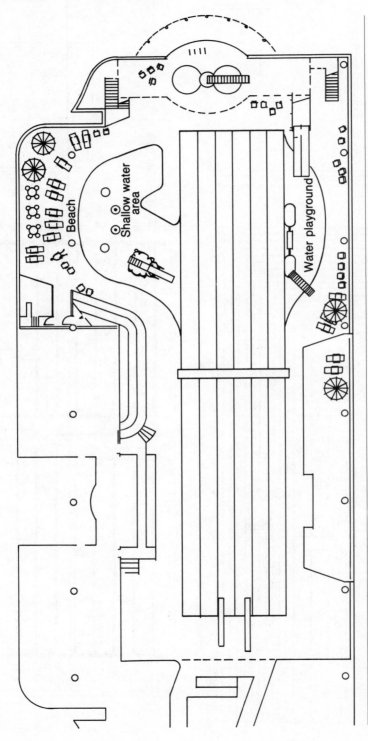

Figure 3.2. 50-meter leisure pool, Toronto, Ontario. *Note.* From "Humanizing the 'Multi-Purpose' Pool" by H. Wong. In *Aquatics Now* (pp. 15-16) by R. Clayton (Ed.), 1982, Indianapolis: Council for National Cooperation in Aquatics. Copyright 1982 by Council for National Cooperation in Aquatics. Reprinted by permission.

POOL EQUIPMENT NEEDS

Pools are not complete without equipment. Individual items of equipment may be classified as either essential or desirable, depending on the situation. An item that is deemed essential in a sophisticated program may be deemed desirable in a simple one. In a simple program, improvisation often is necessary. For example, kickboards placed in an overflow trough may substitute for water polo goals, a megaphone may be used as a public address system, and flashlights may be used as a communications system during swim shows. Consequently, the designations in Table 3.1 of items as essential or desirable serve only as guides and are subject to modification, depending on individual situations.

Table 3.1

AQUATIC EQUIPMENT FOR POOLS

Instruction

Essential: Restraining lines and lines for demarcation of areas, flotation devices, kick boards, rubber bricks, masks, fins, snorkels, pull buoys

Desirable: Diving boards; stroke charts, diagrams, loop films; slide and movie projectors and screen; videotape recorder and monitor; blackboard and chalk, bulletin board

Recreation

Essential: Water is the only essential component of a recreation program. Many items used for the instructional and competitive program may be used for recreation.

Desirable: Water balls, goals, nets; diving rings, pucks, and bricks; beach balls, whiffle balls; foam mats, air mattresses; skin-diving items

Competitive swimming

Essential: Starting blocks, starting gun, timing devices; lane lines, backstroke flags, recall line, whistles; diving flash cards; diving and swimming score and entry forms; pace clock; score book; kick boards, pull buoys, hand paddles

Desirable: Scorer's table, press box, radio and television phone lines; public address system, recording of national anthem; typewriter, copy machine, computer, meet software, record board, scoreboard; electronic timing device and printer, touch pads; stretch cords, swim benches, weight-training equipment; videotape equipment; underwater windows, pace lights, underwater mirrors; blackboard and chalk; water-surface agitators for divers

Water polo

Essential: Balls, goals, officials flags, caps, poolside markings, whistles, score books

Desirable: Underwater windows, videotape equipment

(Cont.)

Table 3.1 (Cont.)

Special events, shows, demonstrations, clinics, and exhibitions

Essential: Portable blackboards, seating accommodations, projectors (movie, slide, opaque), videotape equipment and monitors, public address system, underwater speakers, music records and players

Desirable: Scenery, theatrical lighting system, underwater windows, costumes, underwater lights; separate zone air conditioning

Scuba

Essential: Tanks, regulators, underwater pressure gauges; buoyancy compensators, masks, fins, snorkels, alternate air supply units, weight belts, weights; depth gauges, diving watches; boots or socks; compressed-air source (*Note.* Some equipment can be rented.)

Desirable: Boots, gloves, hoods, wet (or dry) suits, compasses, diving knives; chain vice, large wrench, visual inspection lights, tank tumbling facilities, compressor

Safety

Essential: Ring buoys with line, heaving jugs, reaching poles and/or shepherd's crooks, rescue tubes, rescue buoys; whistles, megaphones or bull horns, guard chairs or stands, masks, fins, snorkels; posted regulations, depth markings, warning signs, boundary markers, lines or booms to define safe areas; equipment suited to site (surf boats, rescue boards, vehicles, etc.); emergency lighting; spine board, stretcher, first-aid kit, blankets, resuscitator

Security

Essential: Sturdy locks on gates and doors (keys identified and restricted); bars on accessible windows, trap doors, and air vents; locks on storage areas (to prevent persons from hiding until after closing time); fencing around outside water areas

Desirable: Outdoor floodlighting, night lighting; security alarm system to warn of trespassers when facility is closed

Sanitation and maintenance

Essential: Pool vacuum cleaner, wall brush, leaf skimmer; filters and chemical feeders, chemical test kits; scrub brushes, mops, brooms, squeegees; materials for repair and upkeep (tile pieces, grouting, adhesive), paint, thinners, brushes; water and air thermometers; ammonia and gas masks (if chlorine gas is used); hoses

Desirable: Automatic electronic chemical monitoring and feeding system; pool cover (for security or heat conservation); special nonskid treatment of tile decks and locker room floors

Administration

Essential: File cabinets, desk, chairs, telephone, wall clock, locker keys, key board, safe, first-aid room

Desirable: Desk lamp, private lockers

DESIGNING THE IDEAL OPEN-WATER FACILITY

Some design features relate specifically to the open beach and camp-type waterfront areas. These areas may be natural or man-made, and they may be protected saltwater shores or on lakes or rivers. Surf beaches have special problems that are not discussed in this text.

The beach layout must be both safe and efficient. Ideally, it consists of a complex of floats, docks, and restraining lines arranged in a pattern to define specific areas for several aquatic activities and for different ability levels. Piers and docks should lie perpendicular to the shore.

Certain activities (boating, sailing, scuba diving, waterskiing) should be limited to the outer areas of the complex to minimize danger to swimmers. Boats must not be permitted to pass into areas reserved for springboard diving, lifesaving, swimming, and skin and scuba diving. Likewise, swimmers must be forbidden in the boating or diving areas, and skin- and scuba-diving areas must be marked by buoys and "diver-down" flags to signify the presence of divers below the surface. The waterskiing or boat racing course must be large, clearly defined, and separate from all other activities. (If this cannot be done, specify that both can use the same areas but at different times.) Figure 3.3 offers a sample layout design for open-water areas.

Specific Area Design Features

Boating

Boating areas should be separate from other activities, protected from the wind and violent water, and large enough so that boating instructional classes can maneuver easily. Adequate dock space for all boats should be provided and equipment storage buildings should be nearby.

Boat docks should be wide enough to accommodate boaters carrying oars, anchors, and lines when passing on the dock. Small sailboats, if docked, require more room because of the equipment required for rigging them before and after sailing. Boat docks should be designed to accommodate the type of boat most commonly used, should be equipped with adequate cleats for tying boats fore and aft, and should allow for changing water levels where appropriate.

Sailing

A large triangular sailing course should be planned in accordance with prevailing winds and should be prominently marked with corner buoys at the turning points. If sailboats are to be moored rather than docked, a mooring site must be selected that is protected from severe weather.

Mooring buoys for sailboats must be far enough apart to prevent the boats from swinging into one another in wind shifts and should have large, easy-to-reach mooring rings. They should be constructed of sturdy material (steel, aluminum, heavy-duty plastic, or wood) and painted for easy recognition. They must be anchored securely to withstand the greatest foreseeable storm.

Bathhouses

Bathhouses are seldom necessary at camp waterfronts but are a necessity at open beaches. Local or area health department regulations will specify the size of the locker room; the number of toilets, urinals, and sinks that must be provided; and other similar elements of design. The design

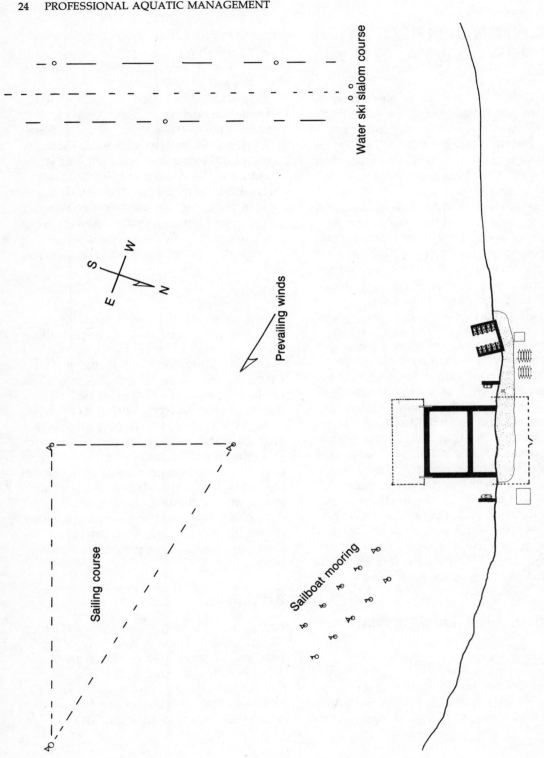

Figure 3.3. Open water activity areas. *Note.* From *Alert: Aquatic Supervision in Action* (p. 31) published by The Royal Life Saving Society Canada. Adapted with the permission of the publisher.

should exceed the minimum requirement for ventilation. The bathhouse should be built for maximum safety (nonslip floors) and for ease of cleaning.

The facility operation office is often included in bathhouse design and, if so, should contain a first-aid room. Facilities for a first-aid room are listed in chapter 5, Table 5.1.

Springboard Diving Areas

For each diving board the area for springboard diving must have a minimum depth of 12 feet in an area at least 21 feet by 16 feet and be free of all obstructions such as weeds, large rocks, and tree stumps.

Instructional/Recreational Swimming Areas

Areas for competitive swimming, swimming instruction, springboard diving, and recreational swimming must be carefully planned for safety and utility. Waterfront dock configurations for these areas and their placement in regard to other activity areas make up the heart of waterfront planning. A suggested beach waterfront layout for such areas is depicted in Figure 3.4.

Alternate configurations that may be better suited to a particular open-water site are the result of many years of practical experience among camp waterfront directors. Some of the layouts that have been successful are shown in Figure 3.5.

Docks and Piers

Types of docks and piers vary greatly with both the intent of the sponsor and the requirements of the geographic area and environment. Wind direction, bottom contour and consistency, changes in water level, and possible ice damage from sea-sonal changes will dictate whether the dock system will be the floating type, the bottom-supported type, or the temporary, portable type. The construction details of each type of structure are beyond the scope of this text, but a few design details should be mentioned.

Dock tops (decks) should be of nonslip material, and planks, if any, should be laid across the dock rather than along the length. Small spaces should be left between planks for adequate drainage and to increase traction. Ladders from the water must be easily accessible for egress in each area. Wherever possible, the under-dock area should be fenced or walled to prevent swimmers from going under the dock. Swimmers are more visible when the docks are low to the water.

FUNDING AQUATIC FACILITIES

In most cases, funds for the renovation or the building of a new facility are raised through tax money. Unless there is money earmarked specifically for recreation needs (as, e.g., all state lottery profits in the state of Colorado), the appropriate governing body avoids the stigma of raising taxes by putting the measure to a vote. At this point, a special interest aquatic group can make a serious mistake by failing to realize that most voters are neutral when they first hear about the proposal to renovate or build an aquatic facility and that neutral voters do not usually vote for tax increases.

Typically, a spirited pro-pool campaign ensues. However, unless all potential users of the facility are consulted beforehand, it is possible that the planned facility could alienate one or more aquatic groups. For example, the kayaking club may need more water space and dock area, the scuba group

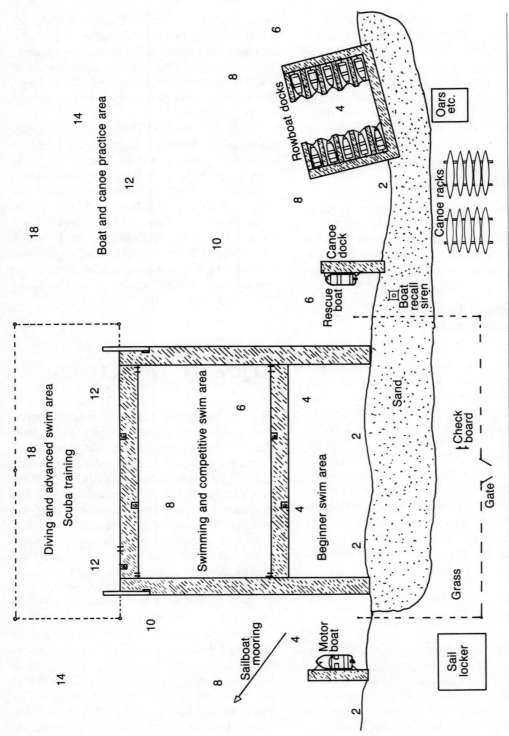

Figure 3.4. Beach waterfront layout. *Note.* Numbers indicate water depth. From *Alert: Aquatic Supervision in Action* (p. 31) published by The Royal Life Saving Society Canada. Reprinted with the permission of the publisher.

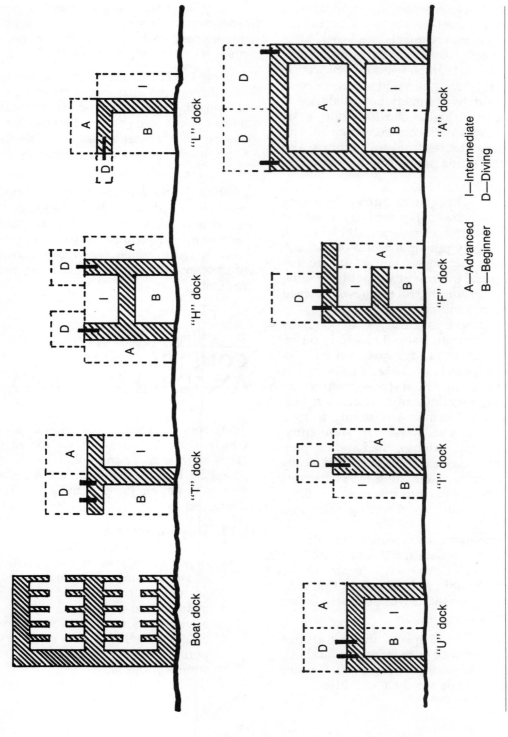

Figure 3.5. Waterfront dock systems.

may need deeper water in the pool and a safer area in the lake, and the surfers may need beach improvements and jetties. Thus the support of every group is necessary.

Cooperation can be fostered by forming a citizens' steering committee composed of a representative of every potential user of the facility. A logical starting point is the community aquatic council, which already has representatives from such groups. The sequence of this new group's meetings is as follows.

Meeting 1. This general citizens' meeting is held after newspaper publicity about the facility and after telephone calls have been made to every potential group of users. A temporary chairperson should ensure that every special interest group at the meeting has a representative on the newly formed steering committee.

If the proposed facility is a pool, the steering committee should include representatives from groups involved with instruction (preschool, K-12, adults, senior citizens), competition (age-group swim teams, high school teams, Master's teams, synchronized teams, and diving teams), recreation (scuba, kayaking, snorkeling, sportspersons, sailing), the handicapped, and aquatic exercise. If the proposed facility involves open water, then the committee should include persons involved in sailing, snorkeling/scuba, wind surfing, canoeing, and fishing.

A permanent chairperson should be selected and a date for the next meeting (3 to 4 weeks away) set. A report of the meeting should be circulated so that anyone not represented will be aware of the project.

Meeting 2. Small special interest groups should meet once or twice and should list, as essential or desirable, the special features or facility needs for their activities.

Meeting 3. This is a large-group meeting (anyone can attend) in which a representative from each special interest group presents the group's "wish list."

Meeting 4. The chairperson and one representative from each special interest group should meet with a professional consultant if at all possible to present the wish list. In some cases, representatives of architectural firms might attend either meeting 3 or meeting 4.

Meeting 5. At this meeting, the special interest groups, as a whole, decide on the essential features of the facility. If a consultant (or interested architects) can report on what appears feasible for various amounts of money, the decisions can be more realistic.

PLANNING AND CONSTRUCTING AN AQUATIC FACILITY

A 12-step procedure for planning and constructing a pool follows. Not all the steps apply equally to pool or beach construction, but the sequence of the steps is worth examining. (Steps 1 and 2 have been discussed in chapter 2.)

1. Determine the need.
2. Study similar facilities.
3. Select a pool consultant. Retain the consultant early so that he or she can perhaps help in the selection of the architect and engineer as well as give advice on general facility features.
4. Select an architect who has had experience in designing at least two similar projects.
5. Select a site in consultation with the

architect and pool consultant. Although a facility can be developed to fit the site (e.g., size, shape, depth), the determining factors for site selection are accessibility (e.g., public transportation, population in the immediate area, and population age), physical features (e.g., direction of sun and wind, size, subsurface water level, streets, and landscaping requirements), and utilities (e.g., availability and adequacy of storm drains), all of which must be considered by the architect, engineer, and consultant. Too often the local planning group overlooks these factors and considers only the facility itself. Differing opinions on where a site should be located often cause community dissension and alienation among the affected groups.

6. Prepare a functional description that is consistent with program requirements and specifications. Speaking as an architect, Junker (1987) has said that the architect's hands are tied until the functional description has been drawn up. What will the pool be used for? What will the building be used for? Describe the space needed, then consult frequently with the architect and consultant to ensure mutual understanding. Crucial topics to cover include program objectives, filtration and water treatment preferences, size and shape of the facility, underwater lighting and observation preferences, overall structure, security requirements, storage space, office and first-aid rooms, and deck or dock space.

   Often these conferences can become strained and the practical limitations of space and money restrict the adoption of some of the ideas of the aquatic group. However, group members' wishes should be considered seriously. Assuming that the consultant is employed by the sponsoring group and not the architect/engineer, he or she is probably the most objective person involved and is perhaps the best source of guidance.

7. Commission the architect to prepare preliminary drawings and cost estimates.

8. Meet with the architect and pool consultant to begin the process of compromise. Ideals and realism clash when the first estimates are submitted by the architect. Invariably, the planning group is enthusiastic about a facility that will meet all the needs expressed but has no idea of its cost. The group usually has a general idea of an amount of money it believes could be raised. Initial estimates are shocking, and the process of compromising ideals to the reality of price begins. Second, third, and fourth estimates on scaled-down versions of the complex are sometimes necessary before a realistic goal is achieved.

9. Promote the financing. The steering committee and all the special interest groups must exert a concerted effort to raise funds and secure backing for the project. (Contact with nearby communities that have recently built aquatic facilities will provide examples of how the community organized itself for the passage of bond issues.)

10. Commission the architect to draw construction plans and working drawings. Arrange for the pool consultant to have access to all the plans and insist that the architect give

serious consideration to the pool consultant's advice.
11. Submit plans for bidding.
12. Administer the construction; that is, make sure that the architect/engineer observes and inspects the project in its various stages of completion. Insist that the pool consultant be aware of proposed construction changes prior to those changes being authorized.

SUPPLEMENTAL LEARNING ACTIVITIES

1. Interview the manager of a local aquatic facility. Report on what the manager considers to be both the good and the poor features of the facility design. What problems have arisen, and how have they been resolved?

2. Obtain the drawings for a typical pool facility. Assume the role of consultant and list all the items you would change, stating the reasons for each change.

3. Use Table 3.2 to examine a local aquatic site and list all items of essential equipment (in your opinion) that are not available.

4. Using any sources available to you, list other books or articles that you feel should be added to the reference list at the end of this chapter.

REFERENCES AND SUGGESTED READINGS

American Camping Association. (1982). Proposed aquatic standards. In R. Clayton (Ed.), *Aquatics now* (pp. 64-75). Indianapolis, IN: Council for National Cooperation in Aquatics.

Costello, M. (1978). Pool design—a look at the future. In B. Empleton (Ed.), *New horizons in aquatics* (pp. 21-25). Indianapolis, IN: Council for National Cooperation in Aquatics.

American Red Cross. (n.d.). *Camp waterfront leadership*. Harrisburg, PA: Author.

Flynn, R. (Ed.). (1985). *Planning facilities for athletics, physical education, and recreation*. Reston, VA: American Alliance for Health, Physical Education, Recreation and Dance.

Gabrielsen, M. (Ed.). (1987). *Swimming pools: A guide to their planning, design, and operation*. Champaign, IL: Human Kinetics.

Hunsaker, D. (Ed.). (1986). *Official swimming pool design compendium* (3rd ed.). Houston: National Swimming Pool Foundation.

Johnson, R., & Pyle, B. (Eds.). (1982). *Aquatic facilities management*. Reston, VA: American Alliance for Health, Physical Education, Recreation and Dance.

Junker, D. (1987, April). *Developing accurate cost projections in planning recreation and aquatic facilities*. Paper presented to the NSPI-NRPA National Swimming Pool and Aquatic Symposium, Indianapolis, IN.

National Recreation and Park Association. (1979). *Small lakes management, manual and survey* (Management Aid Series, Bulletin No. 8); *Public beaches* (Bulletin No. 51); *Marinas* (Bulletin No. 54). Arlington, VA: Author.

Palm, J. (1978). *Alert: Aquatic supervision in action.* Toronto, Ontario, Canada: The Royal Life Saving Society Canada.

van der Smissen, B., & Christiansen, M. (1976). Planning and development guidelines (phase I) and demographic-social characteristics (phase II) for the following activities: boating, canoeing, fishing (boat, shore, stream), ice skating, nonpower boating and sailing, power boating, scuba, surfing, swimming, waterskiing; Activity analysis and land use. Capabilities for beach swimming (phase III), standards related to water-oriented and water-enhanced recreation in watersheds. University Park, PA: Pennsylvania State University, Institute for Research on Land and Water Resources.

Van Dis, J. (1978). Design guidelines for agency aquatic facilities. In B. Empleton (Ed.), *New horizons in aquatics* (pp. 9-21). Indianapolis, IN: Council for National Cooperation in Aquatics.

Webster, S. (1982). Waterfront management: The camp waterfront director. In R. Clayton (Ed.), *Aquatics now* (pp. 55-57). Indianapolis, IN: Council for National Cooperation in Aquatics.

Wong, H. (1982). Humanizing the "multipurpose" pool. In R. Clayton (Ed.), *Aquatics now* (pp. 2-17). Indianapolis, IN: Council for National Cooperation in Aquatics.

Chapter 4

FACILITY OPERATION

Education of the Aquatic Facility Operator
Preparing for the Beginning of a Swimming Season
Swimming Pool Recirculation and Purification Systems
Water Chemistry
Tests of Swimming Pool Water
Pool-Area Sanitation Regulations
Operation Reports for State Health Departments
Sanitation Duties of Employees
Closing the Facility at the End of a Season
Supplemental Learning Activities

The operator of a city water supply system takes in water from the ground or a reservoir, cleans it, puts it into sealed pipes, and pumps it into homes, where it is used for various purposes. There is no chance of the water becoming contaminated between the treatment plant and the end user. Now look at the plight of the swimming pool operator who is given an open tank of water. Leaves fall into it. The wind blows debris into it. People are immersed in it for hours at a time. Yet the job is to maintain "drinking-water quality" at all times. Al-

though the pool operator's job is much more difficult than that of a city water supply operator, the people who come to a beach or pool expect the water and environment to appear inviting and to be harmless to their health.

If aquatic facility employees are to meet this expectation, they must know how to remove physical matter and control bacteria to make swimming water both attractive and safe. This chapter provides the basic knowledge that is needed to meet common water sanitation problems.

EDUCATION OF THE AQUATIC FACILITY OPERATOR

How will the aquatic facility operator or manager gain the knowledge required of his or her position? Education can be divided into two complementary aspects: clinic attendance and printed references.

Pool-operator clinics are conducted by colleges, universities, professional pool associations, health departments, and private companies. In some cases, passing the examination given at the conclusion of such a clinic is required before an individual can be employed as a manager. The National Swimming Pool Foundation offers a course in swimming pool operation and maintains a nationwide register of certified swimming pool operators. Courses on pool operation are also available through the YMCA, the National Recreation and Parks Association, and the Aquatic Council of the American Alliance for Health, Physical Education, Recreation and Dance (AAHPERD).

Study the water sanitation regulations (and handbook, if available) for your state. These regulations and standards relate to water sanitation, swimming pools, and beaches. Facility operators must have access to this material if they are to perform their jobs successfully. In addition, other texts provide detailed procedures for pool operation and water testing as well as solutions to virtually every problem related to water sanitation. This text, or the one by Gabrielsen (1987) or by Van Rossen (1983), should be available at every aquatic facility. Complete publication information for these latter two works is given at the end of this chapter.

PREPARING FOR THE BEGINNING OF A SWIMMING SEASON

Some facilities remain open year-round, whereas others are closed during a portion of the year and are reopened during the warmer months. In the latter case, the facility manager probably will be responsible for preparing the pool or beach prior to its seasonal opening. Perhaps some of the jobs will be delegated to lifeguards and other employees, who must be able to carry out such assignments competently. A checklist for the guidance of whomever is assigned certain tasks is shown in Appendix C.

SWIMMING POOL RECIRCULATION AND PURIFICATION SYSTEMS

Swimming pool water is recirculated for the addition of chemicals and for filtering and heating. The sequence of the recirculation and purification system's components is similar, but not always identical, to that shown in Figures 4.1 and 4.2. For example, alum (if used) is injected into the flow line ahead of the filters, but chlorine and soda ash or acid may be added either ahead of or behind the filters. Also, the pump may be located ahead of the filters for a pressure system or after the filters for a vacuum system. Whichever sequence is used, the facility operator and facility manager (sometimes the same person) must identify the components and their locations in the pool.

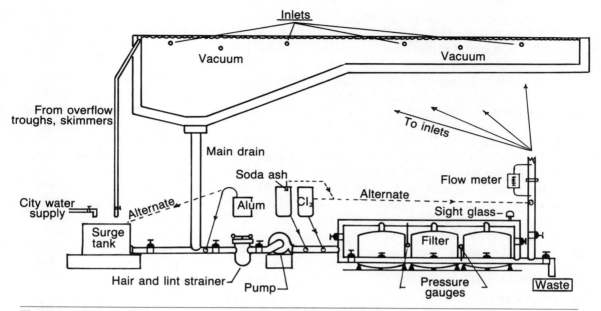

Figure 4.1. Recirculation system: high rate sand and gravel filters.

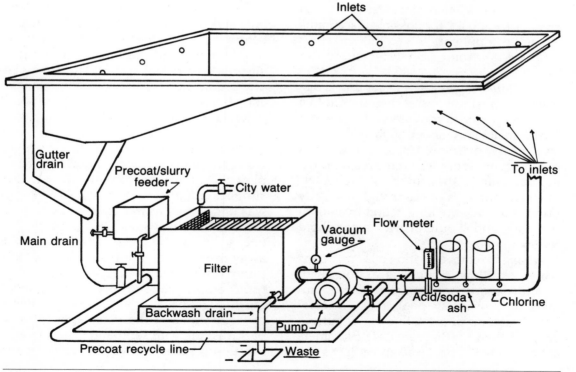

Figure 4.2. Recirculation system: vacuum diatomaceous earth.

Every component of the recirculation and purification system shown in Figures 4.1 and 4.2 plays an important part in maintaining sparkling, hygienic pool water. Each item must be operated according to the details specified by the manufacturer. Because systems made by different manufacturers are not identical, the pertinent instructions may vary. Therefore, it is essential that the instructions for each component of the pool be available. It is recommended that a manual of the complete recirculation and purification system be kept in the filter room and a duplicate kept in the manager's files.

Recirculation System Components

A discussion of the components of a pool recirculation system follows. Refer to Figures 4.1 and 4.2 for possible placements of each component.

Deck drains route drip water and splash to waste.

Overflow troughs catch water that is displaced by swimmers and then send it to a holding tank or to the filters. If the water level is maintained about 1/8 inch above the level of the overflow-trough lip, a skimming action occurs that removes all floating debris from the surface of the water. The configuration of the trough also may provide a wave-quelling action to smooth the water and should provide a handhold for swimmers.

Skimmers remove floating oils and debris when overflow troughs are not used. Health departments usually allow skimmers only on small pools (e.g., in New York State, on pools with a water surface area less than 2,500 square feet). Skimmers are built into the pool wall and adjust automatically to different water levels. They must have a removable basket or screen and be equipped to prevent air locks in the suction line.

Surge tanks (balancing tanks) prevent the loss of heated and treated water due to the rise in water level when swimmers enter the pool. They store water displaced by swimmers until it is returned to the pool when the swimmers leave and also facilitate the addition of make-up water.

The surge tank must have an overflow line to a waste drain. The city water supply line must terminate at least 6 inches above the overflow level of the surge tank so that, in the event of low pressure in the city line, pool water is not siphoned into the city water supply. Chemicals (especially alum) may be added through the surge tank, but chemical feeders are much more efficient.

The *hair-and-lint strainer* removes hair, lint, and coarse materials from the water before it reaches the recirculation pump. It is located in the recirculation line just ahead of the pump and filters. It may be a sealed unit with a noncorrosive, removable strainer or simply a screen at the point where the water enters a vacuum filter tank.

A *recirculation pump* pushes or pulls water through the recirculation line, supplies suction for the vacuum cleaner, and supplies adequate water flow for backwashing. *Backwashing* involves reversing the direction of water flow through the filter so that accumulated material is carried away from the filter surface. Usually, the pump is powered to ensure a 6- or 8-hour turnover. (A 6-hour turnover means pumping through the filters in 6 hours an amount of water equal to the pool capacity). For backwashing with sand-and-gravel filters, the pump should have the capacity for supplying 12 to 15 gallons per minute for each square foot of filter surface. The power of the pump must be matched with the filter size as water forced too rapidly through a filter will cause the filter sand to channel, thus inhibiting the filtering process.

Valves ensure that the flow of water and chemicals is controlled. Valves provide for the release of air from the filters, shut off or redirect circulation to the hair-and-lint strainer to permit cleaning or inspection of the unit, reduce water flow to the pump to create a greater suction for the vacuum cleaner, and reverse the flow of water through the filters for backwashing. Valves may be operated electrically, pneumatically, or manually.

Flow meters indicate the flow of water during normal circulation and the rate of water flow during the backwashing of filters. The flow meter may be located at any point in the recirculation line where there is a straight run of pipe.

Gauges indicate water pressure on influent and effluent filter lines, warn of the loss of head across the filters and of the need for backwashing, and register (temperature gauges) the water temperatures into and out of the water heater.

A *filter* removes particulate matter from the water. There are sand-and-gravel filters, diatomaceous-earth filters, high-rate sand filters, and cartridge filters. If the pool is equipped with a diatomaceous-earth filter, the recirculation line may have a precoat/slurry feed tank for adding diatomite to the system.

Enough material will eventually accumulate in the filter so that the passage of recirculated water will be impaired. At this point, the accumulated materials must be washed away. Sand-and-gravel filters and high-rate sand filters must be backwashed.

Diatomaceous-earth and cartridge filters do not need to be backwashed, but an equivalent process of cleaning is necessary when they become clogged. If the pool is equipped with a diatomaceous-earth filter, the earth must either be dislodged and permitted to recoat the elements or be washed away and diverted to a settling tank or waste drain. Cartridge-filter elements are cleaned by washing and replacing, or new elements are installed. There are four main types of filters:

1. *Diatomaceous-earth filters* are of two types: the *pressure type*, in which water is forced through a sealed unit, and the *vacuum type*, in which water is drawn, by suction, from an open vat. The vacuum type is easier to maintain because the filtering unit is more accessible.

   Diatomaceous earth is composed of the fossilized remains of microscopic water plants called diatoms. The chalklike substance is an effective filtering medium and, unlike some sand filters, does not require the addition of a floc-forming chemical (alum) to complement its filtering action.

   The filtering unit consists of diatomaceous earth that is pressed by water flow against a removable synthetic cloth that covers the filter elements in the form of tubes, plates, or disks. Most filter elements are made of plastic, fiberglass, or corrosion-proof metal. Water passes through tiny openings in the diatomite to the inside of the element and then back into the recirculation system.

   The operation of the filtering unit must be in accordance with the manufacturer's specifications. The flow of water is usually about 1 to 1-1/2 gallons per minute per square foot of filter surface but may be as great as 3 gallons per minute.

2. *Conventional sand-and-gravel filters* remove particulate matter from the water by trapping the small particles on a bed of sand and gravel as the water passes through the filter. Material that is too small to be held by the sand is trapped by a gelatinous alum floc that is added to the surface of the sand. Water is pumped through the filter at a rate not exceeding 3 gallons per minute per square foot of filter surface. The filters should be operated 24 hours per day at commercial and institutional pools.

3. *High-rate sand filters* may consist of sand or of both sand and gravel, but they require higher pressure than do conventional sand-and-gravel filters, and flow rates are increased to about 15 gallons per minute per square foot of filter surface. Alum is rarely used with high-rate sand filters, and, compared to a conventional sand-and-gravel filter, the dirt penetrates deeper into a thicker sand bed.

4. *Cartridge filters* are fiber cartridges (similar to automobile oil and air filters) that are formed into a pleated cylindrical shape and inserted into a filter tank similar to a pressure diatomite filter. The porous fiber elements strain particulate matter from the water. No alum is used with cartridge filters. They have a maximum flow rate of .375 gallons per minute per square foot of filter surface.

A *precoat/slurry feeder* feeds diatomaceous earth into the filter line ahead of the filter to form a layer of earth through which the water is filtered, supplying a continuous addition of earth to keep the filtering layer porous. The slurry feeder may also be a solution tank, into which diatomite is mixed with water before feeding, or it may be a dry feeder, which drops dry diatomite directly into the system.

A *sight glass* permits the operator to see the effluent water from backwashing a filter. The water clarity in the sight glass indicates when a backwash is complete. It is installed on the discharge line of sand-and-gravel filters and sometimes in the tank wall of diatomite filters.

A *water heater* heats the water during circulation.

Inlets return the circulated water to the pool. They are usually located in a position to produce the most efficient circulation of water working in conjunction with overflow troughs, pool drains, and skimmers. They must not be allowed to produce currents that could hamper competitive swimmers.

Vacuum cleaners remove sediment and precipitated material from the pool bottom and sometimes the sides. Cleaners may consist of a portable pump and motor, may be connected to the recirculation pump, or may be self-propelled. When vacuum cleaners are built into the recirculation system, they suck water and dirt off the bottom through a hose attached to sidewall outlets about 8 inches below the water surface. Water flow from the suction cleaner may be routed to a waste drain or to the recirculation line at a point ahead of the hair-and-lint strainer. It may be necessary to reduce the flow from the pool outlets during vacuuming to increase suction.

Self-propelled electric vacuum cleaners have gained widespread acceptance by facility operators. These roll unattended on the pool bottom until they strike a wall; they then turn in a new direction and continue to vacuum sediment from the bottom. Some even climb the vertical wall and fall back to the bottom when they reach the surface. A bag or filter attached to the cleaner collects the dirt. The process continues until a preset timer turns the machine off. They are popular because they can be placed in the pool overnight and save the labor costs of a manually operated cleaner.

Recirculation System Problems and Solutions

Each component of the recirculation system requires careful and constant attention. One malfunctioning component can disrupt the entire process of recirculation and purification. Prevention—the most effective course of action—requires frequent inspection of all parts and diligent performance of all prescribed maintenance tasks.

Even though preventive measures are taken, problems will occasionally arise. Some of these problems are common to all pools, but others are more likely to appear only in certain sections of the country. Because conditions vary geographically, all the maintenance techniques must be those prescribed by the local health department. Furthermore, these techniques must agree with the stipulations of the manufacturers of the individual components.

Unskilled employees can perform the task of observation, but only those employees who have been instructed in the operation and maintenance of each component should assume the more technical tasks. Nevertheless, every employee should have at least a rudimentary knowledge of component maintenance.

Following is a list of potential problems and their solutions.

Pump

Failure to Pump. This could be caused by a lack of priming, the impeller rotating in the wrong direction, or insufficient motor speed.

Reduced Pump Capacity. The causes could be air leaks in the suction lines, clogged or worn impellers, or a clogged filter or hair-and-lint strainer.

Excessive Noise. This could be caused by the misalignment of a shaft, by a bent shaft, or by improper proportioning of the suction and discharge lines.

Filters (Sand-and-Gravel Type)

Air Bind. Open the air-release valve if closed or restore automatic valves to working order.

Mud Balls (Pellets or Chunks of Filter Sand and Dirt Held Together by Accumulated Organic Growth). The solutions are to backwash with increased regularity, to feed an increased amount of chlorine to the water line ahead of the filter, or to apply calcium hypochlorite to the surface of the sand. (Caution: Do not breathe fumes during this operation.)

Clogging of the Filter Surface With Oil and Grease. Stop the pump, drain and open the filter tank, and apply a lye solution (about 1 pound per square foot of filter surface), refill the tank to an inch over the sand surface, and let it stand for several hours. Then thoroughly backwash to a waste drain.

Clogging of the Surface by Encrustation With Calcium Carbonate. Treat the sand as for oil and grease clogging but use sodium bisulfate.

Channeling of the Filter Bed. Look for the cause, which may be an excessive rate of water flow, clogging of the filter surface, or corrosion or clogging in the influent line.

Filters (High-Rate Sand Type)

The problems and solutions are similar to those for sand-and-gravel filters.

Filters (Cartridge Type)

Decreasing Efficiency. If a thorough cleaning does not help, replace the filter elements.

Filters (Diatomaceous-Earth Type)

Clogging by Oil, Grease, or Organic Matter. Recirculate (within the precoat cycle only) a solution of low-sudsing detergent. Use about 1 cup of granular detergent in a filter tank full of water.

Clogging by Minerals (Iron or Calcium Deposits). Remove the elements and scrub them with dilute muriatic acid (about 1/2 cup of acid added to 2 gallons of water). Wear rubber gloves.

Continued Clogging by Minerals. Remove the elements, but do not remove the covers. Scrub the elements with a detergent solution, then with a solution of oxalic acid (about 4 ounces of oxalic acid in a gallon of water), then with muriatic acid (1/2 cup of muriatic acid added to 2 gallons of water). Use rubber gloves. Rinse well and replace. If the problem persists, secure new element covers.

Uneven Filter Coat. Clean the filter elements as just described. If that fails, examine the water-flow pattern during precoat and insert baffles that redirect water so that all elements get an even flow of precoat earth.

Purification System Components

The *alum feeder* introduces alum (aluminum sulfate) into the recirculation line, where it dissolves and forms a gelatinous floc on the top of a sand-and-gravel filter.

A *soda ash feeder* introduces soda ash (sodium carbonate) to the pool water for pH or alkalinity control.

A *bactericide feeder* or *purifying device* introduces chemicals that will kill bacteria. The bactericide may be chlorine, a hypochlorite, a chlorinated cyanurate, bromine, iodine, ozone, a silver salt, or ultraviolet rays. It is common to use a form of chlorine that also kills algae. Bromine is quite common, and ozone is becoming more popular. Chlorine and bromine may be introduced before or after filtering the water.

Purification Equipment Problems and Solutions

Chlorinator

Substandard Performance. Clean the parts of the apparatus with alcohol, detect and correct leaks, and/or install new gaskets.

Leakage. Locate the leak, determine its cause, and take corrective measures. Chlorine is a lethal gas. Any leak in a chlorine system is a serious matter. Never investigate a suspected malfunction without wearing either a gas mask that is specifically approved for use in chlorine gas or a self-contained breathing apparatus. Chlorine may be detected by smell or by putting ammonia on a piece of cotton and then holding the cotton near a suspected leak. A white smokelike vapor indicates the presence of chlorine gas.

Hypochlorinator

Substandard Performance. This usually requires taking the mechanism apart and cleaning all parts with a dilute solution of muriatic acid. Then, after reassembling, pump a dilute acid solution through the hypochlorinator and into the pool for a period of 20 to 30 minutes. Most clogging is caused by deposits of calcium carbonate.

Leakage. This usually requires the replacement of gaskets and the pumping diaphragm. No gas mask is needed, but all hypochlorite should be washed from the skin with plenty of water.

Ozone Generator

Any type of malfunction in the ozone generator requires special knowledge, so specialists should be called on when needed. Ozone can be toxic at higher concentrations.

WATER CHEMISTRY

Sparkling, pure water should be the goal of every pool operator, and attaining it depends on the interaction of pH, total alkalinity, water "hardness," and water purification. The brief overview that follows will emphasize the importance of each of these terms to pool water, but reading this summary is no substitute for attending a water sanitation course or studying the various pool operation books mentioned throughout this text.

pH and Its Importance

The pH of a substance is a measure of its acid or its basic nature. The standard pH scale ranges from 0 to 14, with each unit divided into tenths to give more precise measurements. Pure water, which is neutral (neither acid nor basic), has a pH of 7.0. Values of pH below 7.0 are increasingly acid, and pH values above 7.0 are increasingly basic (see Figure 4.3).

State and local health departments specify the allowable pH range in each locality, usually from 7.2 to 8.2. In this range the water is least irritating to the eyes, chlorine is effective, and flocculation of alum is efficient. Lowering pH is done by adding sodium bisulfate or muriatic acid to the water. It is raised by adding soda ash (sodium carbonate).

Total Alkalinity

Total alkalinity is the total quantity of bicarbonates, carbonates, and hydroxides present in the water. Alkalinity in pool water consists mostly of bicarbonates, with a very small percentage of carbonates. Total alkalinity is related to, but is not the same as, pH. Maintaining the total alkalinity in the range of 80 to 150 parts per million (ppm) will tend to keep the pH more stable and will also prevent extreme fluctuations.

Adding soda ash to the water will raise both pH and total alkalinity, whereas adding sodium bicarbonate (baking soda) will raise the total alkalinity with minimal change in the pH.

Total Hardness

The carbonates and bicarbonates of calcium are part of the total alkalinity of water, but they also are classed with other calcium and magnesium compounds (chlorides and sulfates) that contribute to hardness of water. Some calcium is desirable in pool water as water that lacks sufficient calcium tends to

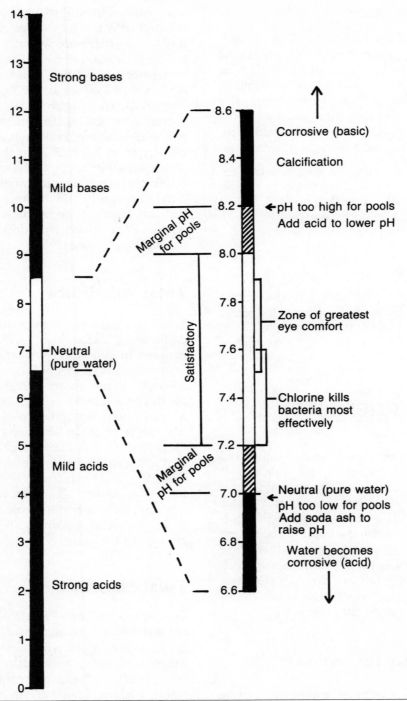

Figure 4.3. pH scale applied to pools.

take calcium from the tile grouting or from the concrete pool lining. Water lacking calcium hardness is said to be ''aggressive.''

Water that contains too much calcium hardness will cause some of the calcium to combine with carbonate alkalinity to produce a precipitate of calcium carbonate. This precipitate will cause ''scaling'' on the pool walls and clogging in pipes.

Pool water must be tested for calcium hardness as well as for total alkalinity. Because calcium hardness represents about 70% of all the hardness in pool water, it is customary to test for total hardness and then estimate the calcium hardness as 70% of the total. However, it is possible to test directly for calcium hardness. Total hardness should be maintained above 180 ppm to prevent aggressiveness but should in most cases be kept under 500 ppm to prevent scaling (precipitation).

Calcium chloride can be added to the water to raise the calcium (and total) hardness. On the other hand, if the total hardness is too high, some water must be drained from the pool and replaced with less-hard water. Trying to soften hard water while it is in the pool may lead to precipitation of the calcium.

Maintaining the delicate balance between pH, alkalinity, and hardness requires knowledge that is best acquired at a water chemistry seminar or from a pool chemistry text.

Water Purification

Although other chemicals (principally bromine) are sometimes used in pools, chlorine is by far the most common water purification chemical employed in U.S. pools. Chlorine performs two basic functions: (a) It kills bacteria and other organisms (disinfection), and (b) it destroys other organic contaminants (dust, algae, body oils) by oxidation. The following definitions will aid in understanding the action of chlorine.

Bactericide

This is any substance introduced to pool water to kill bacteria and includes chlorine, bromine, ozone, silver salts, iodine, and ultraviolet rays.

Residual Chlorine

If chlorine is added to pool water containing bacteria and other organic matter, it will oxidize (burn out or kill) the organic matter. When this process is completed, any remaining (unused) chlorine is called residual chlorine. It remains in the pool and is ready to oxidize any new organic matter brought into the pool. All health departments require a residual bactericide to be present in the pool at all times.

Free Residual Chlorine

If the chlorine remaining in the pool is not attached to any other substance, it is said to be free residual chlorine. It is free to act and is most effective in this form. Free chlorine is highly volatile and dissipates rapidly in sunlight. On hot days it may be difficult to maintain the required free residual in outdoor pools. Most health departments require a free-chlorine residual of 0.6 to 1.0 ppm or a combined residual of 1.5 to 2.5 ppm. The effectiveness of free chlorine decreases somewhat as pH levels increase.

Combined Residual Chlorine

If chlorine is added to the pool in quantities insufficient to oxidize the organic matter completely, the chlorine will combine with organic matter, partially oxidize it, and remain in the pool as a combined residual chlorine. Chlorine usually combines with nitrogen compounds to form chloramines, which are mildly effective in killing bacteria. Because they can kill bacteria very slowly, chloramines are classified as bactericides and are included in measuring the residual bactericide in the pool.

Chloramine is irritating to the eyes and should be kept at minimum levels. Adding greater amounts of free chlorine will burn out the chloramines. Patrons complaining of ''too much chlorine'' in the water are probably suffering from the effects of chloramines, and the remedy is more, not less, chlorine. Patrons will benefit from free-chlorine levels somewhat higher than those required by the health department.

Total Residual Chlorine

This is the free residual chlorine plus the combined residual chlorine in the pool.

Methods of Adding Chlorine

Chlorine may be introduced in its pure (elemental) form or as a compound that releases chlorine when it dissolves. The chemistry of the various compounds used for adding chlorine follows.

Chlorine Gas

Pure chlorine at room temperature is a heavy green gas that is highly toxic. Great care must be taken when handling its containers. Chlorine gas tanks must be chained to a wall to prevent them from tipping and must be stored in a separate room with special ventilation. A breathing system or gas mask approved for use in chlorine gas must be available. When chlorine is under pressure in steel tanks, it is a liquid, but when it is allowed to escape from the pressurized container through a chlorinator, it emerges as a gas.

When chlorine gas enters water, it forms two compounds: hydrochloric acid and hypochlorous acid. Hydrochloric acid is of no use to the pool operator. It causes a sharp drop in the pH of the water and requires the addition of 1 to 1-1/2 pounds of soda ash for every pound of chlorine just to counteract the acid and maintain the pH. Hypochlorous acid (HOCl) is the active compound that kills bacteria very effectively and is measured when the test for free chlorine is performed.

Hypochlorous acid molecules in water tend to break apart (ionize) into electrically charged particles called ions. The hypochlorous acid molecule becomes a positively charged hydrogen ion, H^+, and a negatively charged hypochlorite ion, OCl^-. In this ionized form the two ions are still called free chlorine, but the hypochlorite ion is slower in killing bacteria. The degree to which this ionization takes place is dependent on the pH of the water. At a pH of 7.2, only 34% of the hypochlorous acid is ionized. At a pH of 7.5 about 50% is ionized, and at pH 8.0 about 79% is ionized. Therefore, chlorine is most effective against bacteria at a pH range of 7.2 to 7.5, which is why many health departments require a higher free-chlorine residual in pools that operate at higher pH ranges. For example, New York State requires a free-chlorine residual of 0.6 ppm at a pH of 7.2 to 7.8 but a free residual of 1.5 ppm in pools operating at a pH of 7.8 to 8.2.

A newer method of introducing chlorine into pools is the use of a chlorine generator. Salt is dissolved in the pool water or mixed with water in a container and then is fed through a mechanism that separates the chlorine from the salt mixture by electrolysis. The chlorine thus generated is fed into the recirculation line and into the pool. Because the other product of this method is sodium, which forms sodium hydroxide, the pH is not affected as much as when chlorine gas is added from tanks. This method is safer for operating personnel but is presently more expensive.

Calcium Hypochlorite [Ca(OCl)$_2$]

This compound is a dry granular powder or tablet that contains 65% available chlorine. It should be stored in a clean, dry area. If it comes in contact with water, chlorine gas is released; therefore, handling precautions are important. Calcium hypochlorite is a strong oxidizing agent, and any combustible materials remaining in the container can burst into flames or explode. Do not breathe any dust created when handling it.

When calcium hypochlorite is added to pool water (through a hypochlorinator or directly into the vacant pool), it dissolves to produce hypochlorous acid. A precipitate of calcium carbonate is also formed. There will be a slight rise in pH, and occasionally some acid will be needed to maintain the correct pH.

Sodium Hypochlorite (NaOCl)

This is household bleach but in a more concentrated form. It is a clear, slightly yellow-green liquid containing about 12% available chlorine. It is much safer to handle than the other chlorine sources, but it should be kept away from clothing and should be washed thoroughly from the skin. It deteriorates in sunlight and heat, so it should be stored in a cool, dry area away from sunlight. It should not be stored longer than a month because it will rapidly lose its effectiveness.

Sodium hypochlorite can be added directly to the water when no swimmers are present or can be fed more economically through a hypochlorinator. It does not produce sediments but will cause a rise in pH, which will require the occasional addition of acid to the pool. Sodium hypochlorite is usually diluted with water before being fed through a hypochlorinator and in dilute form (1:5) can be used as a disinfectant and cleaning solution around the pool and bathhouse.

Cyanuric Acid and the Chlorinated Isocyanurates

Chlorine in pool water dissipates rapidly in sunlight. Cyanuric acid in concentrations of 20 to 40 ppm will act as a stabilizing agent that reduces the rate of dissipation in sunlight. Health departments prohibit cyanuric acid in concentrations above 100 ppm. Cyanuric acid can be added directly to the pool regardless of the chlorinating agent used and is called chlorine stabilizer.

Chlorine compounds that already contain some cyanurate can be used to chlorinate the pool. They are the chlorinated isocyanurates and include sodium dichloro-isocyanurate and trichloro-isocyanuric acid. The sodium compound is in powder form and contains about 60% available chlorine. It is soluble and can be added to pool water directly or through a hypochlorinator. The trichloro product is not soluble, so it is added to the pool through an erosion feeder, which erodes it away into the water. Both the dichloro and the trichloro products produce hypochlorous acid, but, because hypochlorous acid is combined with another compound, it has been shown in some tests to be slower acting than the free chlorine produced by the other methods. Some health departments require higher residuals when using a cyanurate stabilizer. The chlorinated isocyanurates have little effect on the pH of water.

Other Methods of Killing Bacteria

Other products are now being used in pools in place of, or in addition to, chlorine.

Bromine

Bromine is in the same chemical family as chlorine. It forms hypobromous acid (HOBr), which is as effective as is chlorine in killing bacteria. The combined form of bromine (bromamine) is just as effective as hypobromous acid, so tests are made for total bromine rather than free bromine. The use of bromine is more expensive than the use of chlorine and is said to be less irritating to the eyes.

Ozone (O_3)

Recently, ozone has gained favor as a bactericide for pools. It does not remain in the water so does not meet health department requirements for a continuous residual. However, when ozone is used in conjunction with a chlorine residual of 0.3 to 0.4 ppm, it is very effective. Because ozone oxidizes most organic matter, very little chlorine is needed to retain a residual.

Although the initial cost for an ozone generator is very high, maintenance costs are low. Start-up costs for ozone may be as much as 10 times greater than those for chlorine alone (Rice, 1987).

Silver Salts, Iodine, and Ultraviolet Treatment

These are three other methods of sanitizing water. They are effective, but technical or economic factors have made their use prohibitive.

Other Chemicals Commonly Used in Pools

Alum (Aluminum Sulfate) [$Al_2(SO_4)_3$]

Alum is used as a filter aid for conventional sand-and-gravel filters. It is added to the recirculation line ahead of the filters immediately after backwashing. Alum reacts with the water's alkalinity to form a hydrous aluminum oxide (a sticky, gelatinous "snowflake" called alum floc). This alum floc settles on top of the filter sand to catch and hold particles that are too small for the sand alone to retain. It is washed to the waste drain at the next backwash. About 2 ounces of alum are used for each square foot of filter surface.

Powdered alum may also be used as a coagulant for heavy turbidity in pools. About 4 ounces of powdered alum per 100 square feet of pool surface is spread over the surface of the water and should be allowed to settle overnight. Powdered alum will clear the water by carrying turbidity to the bottom of the pool, where it can be vacuumed.

Algaecides

Several algaecides are available for pool use. They may be required for stubborn cases, but most algae can be controlled by the proper use of chlorine. The diversity of algaecides makes discussion of them impractical for this text.

Common Water Problems

Most water problems become evident when the appearance of the water changes.

Table 4.1

COMMON POOL WATER PROBLEMS: CAUSES AND SOLUTIONS

Problem: Water clear but emerald green

Cause: Iron in its ferrous state

Solution: Oxidize the iron to its ferric state by superchlorination (i.e., raise the free-chlorine residual quickly to 4.0 ppm and let it drop overnight). The iron will precipitate as rust and can then be filtered from the water.

Problem: Water cloudy green

Cause: Algae

Solution: Superchlorination should kill algae (sometimes an algaecide is necessary). Maintain high free-chlorine residual to prevent algae growth. If these measures do not help, the pool may have to be drained and washed with muriatic acid.

Problem: Water red-brown or coffee color (especially a day after filling)

Cause: Precipitation of iron

Solution: If filters do not clear the precipitation fast enough, stop the pump and sprinkle powdered alum (aluminum sulfate) over the water's surface at the rate of 2 to 4 ounces per 100 square feet. Allow to stand overnight and the next morning vacuum very carefully. Diatomite filters must have a thick precoat before starting again and will require backwashing shortly thereafter.

Problem: Water cloudy but blue

Cause: Alum passing through sand-and-gravel filters or diatomite passing through diatomaceous-earth filters

Solution: For alum, allow it to settle, then vacuum. For diatomite, search for a cracked filter element or a torn element cover.

Problem: Complaints that the hair of blond patrons is turning green.

Cause: Copper in the water

Solution: Copper usually comes from heater tubes and is dissolved when pH is not maintained properly. Drain the pool or drain and add some water each day, thereby diluting the copper. Pay particular attention to maintaining the pH above 7.5. Inspect any copper tubing in recirculation line for damage.

Listed in Table 4.1 are the most common appearance changes, their probable causes, and methods for alleviating the problem.

TESTS OF SWIMMING POOL WATER

Tests must be taken often enough to ensure that the conditions of the water are equal to or above the specified minimum standards. Minor deviations must be discovered before they become major problems, and frequent testing is the only way to guarantee early detection.

Basic Principles of Testing

Because health departments state explicitly that water tests must be performed, a water testing kit is essential. To achieve accurate results, follow these basic principles:

1. Follow the directions for your test kit exactly as they are given.
2. Use the exact amounts stipulated.
3. Avoid contamination of the test sample: Use clean vials to gather the test sample, do not touch the edges of the vials, and do not mix a test sample by placing a finger over the vial top and shaking.
4. When using ortho-tolidine for a free-chlorine test, complete the test within 10 seconds of adding the reagent.
5. Clean the test vials immediately after use.
6. Avoid the interchange of equipment parts (e.g., do not put the dropper from one solution container into another or put the cap from one container on another container).
7. Avoid using the same test vial for different tests.
8. Avoid stirring the solution for one test with the stirring rod used in another test.
9. Store testing equipment where it is not exposed to sunlight or to high or freezing temperatures.
10. Use solutions only from the manufacturer of your test kit and do not keep solutions more than 1 year (6 months for phenol red).

Tests to Be Performed

The aquatic facility manager is responsible for making the following tests, but may assign another employee to make them.

Free-Chlorine Residual

Frequency. Three to four times per day; every 2 hours during peak loads

Desirable Standard. Typically 1.0 to 1.5 ppm (the health department minimum may be less)

Total Chlorine (Free Chlorine Plus Chloramine)

In some states, the health department allows the use of the total chlorine residual as the operating standard. This is not a recommended practice because chloramines are irritating to the eyes, and most pools try to keep the combined (chloramine) residual as low as possible.

Frequency. Three to four times a day, every 2 hours during peak loads

Desirable Standard. Typically 2.5 ppm (set by the local health department)

Comment. If the chloramine residual rises above 0.2 or 0.3 ppm, swimmers may complain of eye irritation.

Superchlorination will remove chloramines. Retaining a free residual of 1.0 to 1.5 ppm will limit the chloramine buildup.

Combined Chlorine (Chloramine)

To determine the amount of chloramine present in the pool, test for free-chlorine residual and then for total chlorine residual. Subtract the free chlorine reading from the total chlorine reading. The result will be the amount of chloramine present.

Frequency. As desired

Desired Residual. Below 0.2 ppm

Bromine
(When Used Instead of Chlorine)

Frequency. Three to four times per day

Desirable Standard. Total bromine should be between 1.5 and 3.0 ppm

Comment. Because bromamines, as bactericides, are equally as effective as bromine, it is necessary to test only for total bromine.

Cyanuric Acid

Frequency. Weekly if cyanurates or chlorine stabilizers are used

Desirable Standard. 30 to 40 ppm (over 100 ppm is toxic)

pH

Frequency. Two to four times per day; every 2 hours if gas chlorine is used

Desirable Standard. pH 7.2 to 7.8

Total Alkalinity

Frequency. Every 2 weeks (more often if using gas chlorine)

Desirable Standard. 80 to 150 ppm

Total Hardness

Frequency. Monthly

Desirable Standard. 180 to 500 ppm, depending on pH. (Consult a pool chemistry text for complete information on balancing pool water.)

Bacteria

Frequency. Weekly, though many pools test only occasionally. The testing of water to determine the number and kind of bacteria is done in a laboratory; generally, a pool or beach employee or an employee of a designated testing laboratory obtains the water sample, which is then delivered to the health department or designated lab for analysis. In some states, the health department inspector will visit the pool and take the samples.

Desirable Standard. 0. Pool operators should strive for a 0 count, though this is virtually impossible. State requirements vary in definitions of total count and in the methods for determining safe water. Check with your local and state health departments.

Temperature and Humidity

Frequency. Temperature twice per day and humidity daily if humidity control is possible

Desirable Standard. The water temperature for recreational use should be about

82 °F; for competition, about 80 °F; for swimming lessons and for children, about 84 °F; and for preschool and handicapped swimmers, about 86 °F to 90 °F. The air temperature should be about 5 °F above the water temperature up to about 85 °F, when it should be the same as water temperature. Low humidity makes the swimmer feel chilled when out of the water; the optimal range is 70% to 80% relative humidity. Read the water temperature while the thermometer bulb is underwater. Measure humidity with a wet bulb thermometer and relative humidity tables. Follow the stated directions.

Iron and Copper

Frequency. When pool is filled and whenever presence of copper is suspected or whenever iron may be causing problems (see Table 4.1)

Desirable Standard. Lowest amount possible

Water Clarity

Frequency. At the beginning, middle, and end of each day

Desirable Standard. A 4-inch-diameter black disk visible in the deepest part of the pool

Automated Tests

Better chemistry control and more economical operation are now being accomplished by the use of electronic metering and control devices that continuously monitor the free-chlorine and pH levels and that automatically adjust the feeders to maintain correct levels. These devices are

highly accurate and, although the initial cost is high, will pay for themselves in reduced chemical use and labor over the long run.

Troubleshooting Operational Problems

When operating problems arise that are beyond the scope of the pool operator, it is sometimes necessary to call in a pool operations consultant. In such cases, much time (and money) will be saved if the information requested in a pool operation form (see Appendix B) is available at the time of the consultant's visit. This information and the pool operating records for the past 2 months often hold the answer to the problem.

POOL-AREA SANITATION REGULATIONS

Most state health departments mention in the printed materials they prepare for pool employees the importance of enforcing sanitation procedures in the pool area. These procedures concern the number and the conduct of patrons as well as the effects of patron action on sanitation.

User Load

Most state health departments establish methods for determining maximum loads. In general, the method is based on the assumption that, at any given time, one of three swimmers (deep-water area) is on the deck and two of four (or three of four) swimmers (shallow-water area) are on the deck. Two pertinent points are that (a) safe loads relate to the rate of pool turnover, the efficiency of the recirculation and purification systems, and the degree to which swimmers comply with regulations; and (b) the health department figures represent maximum limits. Obviously, a smaller figure will mean less congestion and greater swimmer comfort.

Two examples of determining maximum pool-load standards follow.

Standard

One person per 500 gallons of recirculated water per 24 hours.

Formula.

$$\frac{\text{Pump flow rate (gpm)} \times 60 \text{ min} \times 24 \text{ hr}}{500}$$

= daily load

Where the pump flow rate was 250 gallons per minute and the pump was operated 24 hours per day, the maximum daily pool load would be

$$\frac{250 \times 60 \times 24}{500} = 720 \text{ persons per day}$$

Standard

One person per 30 square feet of water surface over 5 feet deep, one person per 15 square feet of water surface less than 5 feet deep, plus 35% more swimmers if the deck area is large.

Formula.

$$\frac{\text{Shallow (sq ft)}}{15} + \frac{\text{Deep (sq ft)}}{30} = N$$

$$N + .35N = \text{load}$$

If the shallow area is 42 feet by 40 feet and the deep water area 42 feet by 35 feet, and if the deck area is large, then

$$\frac{42 \times 40}{15} + \frac{42 \times 35}{30} = 161$$

$$161 \times .35 = 56.35$$

Thus, $161 + 56 = 217$ persons (maximum) should be allowed inside the pool enclosure at one time.

Other Common Regulations

Not all of the following typical regulations are required by every health department. However, the following regulations will contribute to the clean and sanitary operation of the pool.

1. All patrons shall take a hot-water shower and use soap before entering the pool.
2. Urinating, expectorating, or blowing the nose in any swimming pool is prohibited.
3. No person having skin lesions, sore or inflamed eyes or mouth, or nose or ear discharges shall be permitted into the pool.
4. Persons not dressed for swimming shall not be allowed on walks immediately adjacent to pools, and bathers shall not be allowed in places provided for spectators.
5. Persons wearing pins or clips in their hair must wear bathing caps.
6. No person wearing bandages will be permitted in the pool.
7. Animals are not permitted in the pool or the pool area.
8. Bottles, glass containers, food, and drinks are prohibited in the pool and the pool area.

9. Toys of any kind and swimming or learning aids are subject to the approval of the pool manager.

Two regulations deserve special mention. First, although it is almost universal to require swimmers to take soap showers before entering the pool, most swimmers do not, and lifeguards do not enforce the rule. Often the shower water is lukewarm or even cold, so it is understandable why swimmers will not voluntarily take showers.

Second, some outmoded state laws specify that women and girls must wear bathing caps; but this is nonsensical because length of hair is not related to gender. The original intent was to prevent long hair from getting into the filters, where it was thought to cause filtration problems. Experience has shown that this does not occur and that hairpins and clips are more damaging to the pool (causing rust spots on the bottom) than is long hair. Therefore, it is more reasonable to require caps of those who wear pins and clips than it is to require caps for all long-haired patrons.

OPERATION REPORTS FOR STATE HEALTH DEPARTMENTS

All state departments of health require that records of operation be maintained and submitted periodically. The departments will provide forms for this purpose. Some state explicitly which records must be reported. The departments emphasize the responsibility of the facility manager in this process. A sample of a monthly swimming pool report is shown in Figure 4.4.

SANITATION DUTIES OF EMPLOYEES

All employees must demonstrate their commitment to good sanitation. When employees fail to perform their assigned tasks, an environment favorable to contamination is encouraged, and the potential for disease increases. When employees perform their duties diligently, the results are an attractive swimming area and satisfactory tests of water conditions.

Duties Related to the Pool Environment

Ongoing

Enforce regulations pertaining to bottles, food, animals, and so on. Keep the area clean. Keep waste receptacles from overflowing. Keep windbreaks in good repair to limit foreign matter and impurities that can be carried into the water by gusts of wind. Make sure that showers are being used and are operated properly. Inspect swimmers as they enter onto the pool deck. Keep the spectator area clean (mop rather than sweep). Keep dispensers of toilet paper, paper towels, and soap filled. Maintain correct air and water temperatures. Maintain an inventory of the amounts of chemicals on hand. Appraise water clarity (by observation only until it is necessary to apply a specified test).

One or More Times Daily

Estimate and record attendance. Clean and disinfect toilet rooms, shower rooms, and dressing rooms. Clean and disinfect

Swimming pool at _____

Name of pool or owner   City, village, or town

For month of _____19 _____

County

DATE	FILTER WASHED CHECK	POOL CLEANED CHECK	TOTAL NUMBER OF BATHERS	CHLORINE USED LBS/DAY □ GALS/DAY* □	DISINFECTION									ALKALINITY mg/l CaCO₃	pH	POOL DRAIN VISIBLE CHECK	SODA ASH (pounds)	ACID (quarts) □ (pounds) □	OTHER	REMARKS
					RESIDUAL mg/l						Chlorine □ Bromine □									
					1st TEST			2nd TEST			3rd TEST									
					Time	Free	Tot.	Time	Free	Tot.	Time	Free	Tot.							
1																				
2																				
3																				
4																				
5																				
6																				
7																				
8																				
9																				
10																				
11																				
12																				
13																				
14																				
15																				
16																				
17																				
18																				
19																				
20																				
21																				
22																				
23																				
24																				
25																				
26																				
27																				
28																				
29																				
30																				
31																				

Source of water_____ *Pints of___% Chlorine in___Gallons water

Operator's signature_____ Date_____

Figure 4.4. Monthly swimming report. *Note.* Adapted from ''Pool Report Form,'' New York State Department of Health.

benches, seats, and fixtures. Inspect the area and make appropriate requests or recommendations. Clean the pool bottom with a vacuum cleaner. Clean the pool walkways (decks). Clean the toilets, urinals, wash basins, and spit receptacles. Remove visible scum from the water by filling the pool to overflow the troughs or by using a wire frame with a cloth insert to drag across the surface. Perform tests for chlorine, pH, and air and water temperatures on a scheduled basis.

When Necessary

Abide by restrictions on the maximum swimmer load. Forbid swimming when a lifeguard is not present. Post the regulations regarding pool use and keep them up to date. Backwash or clean the filters when pressure gauges dictate. Perform tests on water for cyanurates, alkalinity, and hardness.

Remove hairpins from the bottom (with a magnet on a pole or by swimming underwater with a mask). Clean pool sides with a wall brush. Repair grouting at joints and between tiles. Apply bleach to algae spots on the walkways. Keep gates and doors locked when the facility is not in use. Take water samples for bacteriological analysis in proper containers. Maintain records and fill out report forms. Report detrimental conditions (water color, water cloudiness, algae growth, malfunctions, etc.) to superiors.

Duties Related to the Beach Environment

Ongoing

Keep the area clean. Remove food particles, food and drink containers, and so on. Enforce regulations pertaining to bottles, food, and animals. Keep waste receptacles from overflowing. Keep windbreaks in good repair. See that showers are used and operated properly. Be alert for conditions such as water currents and wind direction that may bring contamination from sewer outfalls, septic tank effluents, refuse disposals, and discharges from boat toilets and bilges.

One or More Times Daily

Estimate and record attendance. Clean and disinfect toilet rooms, shower rooms, and dressing rooms. Clean and disinfect benches, seats, and fixtures. Inspect the area and make appropriate recommendations. Note prevailing weather and water conditions.

When Necessary

Abide by restrictions on maximum beach load. Forbid swimming when a lifeguard is not on duty. Keep gates and doors locked when the facility is not in use. Take water samples for bacteriological analysis in proper containers. Maintain records and fill out report forms. Report detrimental conditions (water cleanliness, algae blooms, malfunctioning equipment, etc.) to superiors.

CLOSING THE FACILITY AT THE END OF A SEASON

When a pool or beach closes at the end of a season, some employees are tempted to leave everything as it is and depart without a backward glance. The major tasks that employees must perform at the end of a season are given in Appendix C.

Some jobs are listed that have no obvious relationship to water sanitation as are some jobs that do not apply in some sections of the United States. Some of the jobs must be performed only by an electrician, an engineer, or an employee skilled in a specific area. Each employee who assists must be instructed to attach an identifying label to each part removed (e.g., pump drain plug, pump switches, and valves) and to see that the part is properly stored or is wired or tied to the item from which it was removed.

SUPPLEMENTAL LEARNING ACTIVITIES

1. Enroll in the Certified Pool Operator course offered by the National Swimming Pool Foundation.

2. Arrange to be present when a local pool is being backwashed. Ask the operator to explain what is happening during each step.

3. Complete the pool information form in Appendix B, using a local pool as the data source. Examine the data and determine potential problem areas.

4. Observe the testing of pool water for residual chlorine, pH, and total alkalinity. At a later time, take such tests yourself and compare your readings with the official records of the pool.

REFERENCES AND SUGGESTED READINGS

Flynn, R. (Ed.). (1985). *Planning facilities for athletics, physical education and recreation.* Reston, VA: American Alliance for Health, Physical Education, Recreation and Dance.

Gabrielsen, M. (Ed.). (1987). *Swimming pools: A guide to their planning, design, and operation.* Champaign, IL: Human Kinetics.

Osinski, A. (1986). Effects of pool water on swimmers' eyes, ears and hair. In L. Priest & A. Crowner (Eds.), *Aquatics: A changing profession* (pp. 124-127). Indianapolis, IN: Council for National Cooperation in Aquatics.

Rice, R. (1987, April). *Chemistry of ozone relative to the treatment of swimming pool and spa waters.* Paper presented to the NSPI-NRPA National Swimming Pool and Aquatic Symposium, Indianapolis, IN.

State of New York. (n.d.). *New York state sanitary code,* Chapter 1, Part 6. Albany, NY: Author.

U.S. Department of Health. (1976). *Swimming pools: Safety and disease control through proper design and operation.* Atlanta: Center for Disease Control.

Van Rossen, D. (Ed.). (1983). *Pool/spa operator's handbook.* San Antonio, TX: National Swimming Pool Foundation.

Chapter 5

AQUATIC SAFETY AND LIABILITY

The Need for an Aquatic Safety Program
Education of the Public
Risk Management
Liability Implications of Aquatic Accidents
Minimizing Personal Risks
Supplemental Learning Activities

Safety has always been a top concern of sponsoring groups and aquatic facility workers. With the tremendous increase in aquatic activities in the past few years, plus the increased tendency of citizens to file lawsuits in cases of injuries and deaths, safety and legal liability issues have become even more crucial to the continued operation of any program. Accidents and lawsuits will occur, but they need not be feared if the program is conducted in accordance with accepted safety principles.

THE NEED FOR AN AQUATIC SAFETY PROGRAM

National Safety Council statistics (1987) show that drowning is the second-leading cause of accidental death in those aged 0 to 45. For children under the age of 5, it is the third-leading cause of accidental death but is the leading cause of death in California, Florida, and Texas, according to the National Swimming Pool Safety Committee (1987). These tragedies occur despite the fact that there has been a 35% reduction in drownings in the decade 1975 to 1985. Although deaths from drownings in the United States have been reduced from 13.5 per 100,000 population (1920s) to 2.4 per 100,000 population in 1985, there are still about 5,700 drownings per year, of which 3,500 (61%) occur during swimming/recreation, while the remainder are work related. Whether at work or play, the victims seldom know aquatic survival techniques, and most are not protected by lifeguards.

Most (90%, or 5,200) of the annual

5,700 drownings occur in open water. Between 50% and 67% of the victims had been drinking, and "many, if not most, are . . . intoxicated, cold-affected younger male non-swimmers who do not intend to enter the water" (Smith, 1982a, p. 140). Of the remaining 500 drownings, the statistics show that about 250 occur in home and apartment pools and about another 150 in hotel and motel pools. Again, these persons lack lifeguard protection. Thus, only about 100 of the 500 pool drownings occur at sites where lifeguards are present. Although these 100 drownings represent only 2% of the entire annual drownings in the United States, the potential number of liability claims is great.

Everyone is aware that drowning is one of the possible hazards of water activities, but fewer people are aware of the deaths or the paralysis caused by diving accidents. According to Zars (personal communication, October 1982), approximately 500 diving-related spinal injuries occur each year. Scott and Evera (1987) report that most of these accidents (81%) occur in privately owned pools or unguarded aquatic sites.

The safety records of certain water parks provide the only bright spot in aquatic safety. While there were 10 water park drownings in 1987, none of these 10 drownings occurred at water parks whose lifeguards were trained by a firm specializing in water park safety. In fact, Ellis & Associates (1987) states that "not one of our clients experienced a major aquatic related accident [for] the third successive year" (p. 2). The water-park safety program will be discussed in chapter 6.

It is our conclusion that (a) there is a need for an aquatic safety program at all sites and (b) if an effective safety system can be implemented at water parks, it also can be done at pools and beaches. The organiza-

tion and management of such a program is the responsibility of all aquatic professionals in the community.

The aquatic safety program consists of four parts: (a) education of the public, (b) implementation of a risk-management program at each facility, (c) an understanding of legal liability, and (d) lifeguarding. (Lifeguarding will be discussed in chapter 6.)

EDUCATION OF THE PUBLIC

Because most drownings and spinal cord injuries occur in the absence of lifeguards, the most effective way to reduce these tragedies is through public education. The responsibility for education is not confined to pool personnel, but operators of marinas, wave pools, scuba shops, and so on all have an equal duty. The teaching of safety skills in classes and special programs will help reduce aquatic fatalities, as will signs posted and audiovisual aids (see list of visual aid sources at the end of this chapter).

The educational efforts that follow are the minimum actions that the aquatic staff must take. Without this education, drowning and diving accidents probably will not be significantly reduced in the near future.

Teaching Safety Skills in Aquatic Classes

Assuming that most persons at one time or another take lessons in swimming, diving, or small-craft operation, it is essential that certain safety techniques and concepts be taught in every class, regardless of the ages of the participants or the location (pool, open water) of the class. The following safety techniques and concepts should be included: (a) the use of personal flotation devices, (b) survival techniques (the heat escape lessening position [HELP], the huddle procedure, survival floating in warm water, clothing inflation for use in warm water, back float while clothed), (c) mouth-to-mouth resuscitation, (d) reaching assists, and (e) safe diving techniques. In addition, the causes and normal patterns of drowning and the relationship between alcohol and aquatic accidents should be taught (allowing for the age of the students). Class members should discuss, see demonstrations and films, and practice the techniques just described. A basic safety unit should be developed and then taught in each class.

The text *Water Wise* (Smith & Smith, 1984) is probably the best source of information related to a comprehensive safety education program. It contains information on drowning, alcohol and aquatics, hypothermia, cold-water survival techniques, personal flotation devices (PFDs), and pool safety and has an extensive reference list.

Teaching Safety Skills Through Special Programs

The local anglers, waterfowl hunters, boat owners, scuba divers, and so on are active members of their special interest groups, and although they need specific techniques to prevent water accidents and to survive when accidents occur, they ordinarily do not seek out aquatic safety classes. However, there are many opportunities to put on demonstrations or show films to such groups. Figure 5.1 illustrates one such occurrence, in which instruction in small

Figure 5.1. Small craft educational program. *Note.* Copyright 1987 by Michael Madrid. Reprinted with permission.

craft safety is given to a group of prospective canoeists.

A universal safety unit can be modified to meet the specific needs of the group. For example, most hunters and fishermen do not know that their clothing can help them float. A special program that gives persons a chance to practice these survival skills is invariably well-attended. Or, to a camping group, the movie *On Drowning* (see the list of visual aids at the end of this chapter) will explode the myth that drowning people yell for help and then go up and down three times before disappearing. The movie *Emergency Care for Cold-Water Near Drowning* (see visual aid list), which emphasizes that persons who have been underwater for long periods of time have been successfully resuscitated and have then lived normal lives, will be valuable to any potential rescuer. Smith (1982a) has outlined effective short courses for these special groups.

Education Through Signs and Posters

Patrons should be reminded of emergency procedures by means of appropriate films, wall posters, signs, and so on placed in strategic locations. Also, signs that alert patrons to the dangerous combination of alcohol and aquatic recreation should be prominently posted. This passive effort, especially at open-water sites, is the minimum that must be done.

Local Resources

At the very least, one or more of the aquatic facilities in a community should have movies on resuscitation and water survival techniques. These should be available to appropriate local groups, perhaps at a rental fee that is adequate to maintain them and to purchase new ones periodically. Also, a list of qualified speakers should be available and publicized; the program chairman of any group will welcome such help. Finally, sources of visual aids (such as those listed at the end of this chapter) should be made known to those who inquire.

RISK MANAGEMENT

Risk management is a term that describes management's responsibility and effort to safeguard the assets of the sponsor—its money and facilities—against possible loss. Gabrielsen and Johnson (1979) point out that aquatic facilities, especially pools, are hazardous environments and that water activity entails risks. They define a hazard as a condition that presents the potential for injury. Risk, on the other hand, is interpreted as the "simple probability of injury in percentages. . . . When a hazard exists, a danger of injury is present. Danger is the unreasonable or unacceptable combination of hazard and risk" (p. 44).

Liability and Losses

"A liability [is] an ever present state of being vulnerable to a peril, force or event capable of causing or contributing to a loss. Existence of a liability generates a risk for the enterprise. . . . This risk, or uncertainty of loss, is what enterprises must learn to manage" (Espeseth, 1985, p. 4).

In aquatics, the loss can be monetary (a drowning causes a lawsuit, which results in a payment being made to the heirs of the deceased) or material (canoes are severely damaged as a result of a storm). In the first case, an insurance company or a self-insured sponsoring group pays the money; hopefully, the payment will not bankrupt the sponsor. (Even if the insurance company pays the entire amount, the cost of insurance the next year may be so great that the facility might have to close.) In the second case, repairing the damage will cost relatively little; it might hamper the program but will not ruin the sponsor.

Master Plan[1]

The facility manager is responsible for developing a risk management master plan which includes four components: (a) iden-

[1]Sources: Espeseth (1985), Johnson (1980), Wagner (1982), and Werts (1985).

tification of the risks, (b) evaluation of their severity and probable occurrence, (c) consideration of various methods to reduce or eliminate risks, and (d) administration of the program. These components and an explanation of the tasks involved in each follow.

Component 1: Identify the Risks

Task 1—Organize. Develop, circulate, and follow an organizational table (or chain of command). This identifies the responsibility and lines of communication of everyone from the board of directors down.

Task 2—Survey. Management and staff should physically inspect the facility and talk to employees to find out which risks are present. Consider all potential accident and emergency situations, beginning with (but not limited to) these examples:

a. Environment—fog, dangerous marine life, tides and currents, lightning, winds, sudden storms, tornadoes
b. Communication—inoperative phone, intercom, radio, or lighting; locked office
c. Lifeguard equipment—empty oxygen tank, broken or missing spine board, inoperative boat, missing oars, locked equipment room
d. Bathers—missing from water or surrounding area
e. Rescue—one victim; more than one victim
f. Evacuation of facility—gas leak, power failure, actual or potential storm damage
g. Crowd control and law enforcement—crowded facility, riot, theft, spectators crowding around victim
h. Medical treatment—spinal cord injury, scuba diver in distress, near drowning, drowning, first aid for nonwater accidents

i. Water craft—capsizing, explosion, sinking, multiple craft incidents
j. After-hours incidents—trespassing, water craft or swimmer in distress, body found in water

Task 3—Understand. Study local and state laws and standards applicable to the facility.

Component 2: Evaluate the Severity and Occurrence of Risks

Task 1—Analyze. Study the records of all past emergencies and accidents, paying special attention to the staff response to the emergency and the results of those actions.

Component 3: Consider Methods to Reduce or Eliminate Risks

Task 1—Educate. Develop appropriate materials and courses to educate the public about safety. Unfortunately, aquatic facility managers often do not take their responsibility for educating the public seriously. It is our observation that a safety unit taught in all classes is seldom done; the common practice is to include safety materials and experiences only if they are required in, for example, the Red Cross or YMCA course being taught.

Task 2—Develop an Action Plan. Describe the step-by-step procedures to be followed when any accident or emergency situation occurs. These plans must lead to "positive, calculated professional actions which become reflexive and instinctive through rehearsal" (Johnson, 1980, p. 19). For each potential incident discovered in the survey (see Component 1, Task 2), a precise listing of each person's assignment and the actions they must take is made. The plan must clearly designate the equipment and facilities to be used and the additional aid to be sought. In short, the action plan must be so complete that it covers every foreseeable circumstance.

The American National Red Cross (1983, pp. 51-52) has developed recommended emergency action plans for a multistaff facility (Figure 5.2) and for a single lifeguard facility (Figure 5.3). These plans should be the basis for any emergency action plan for each potential accident. Although these plans can be adapted slightly to fit each particular situation, the Red Cross plan is still considered the standard to be used in any legal matter.

Task 3—Retain or Transfer Risks. Espeseth (1985) offers other methods whereby enterprises can minimize the identified risks. These methods involve retaining and controlling some risks (i.e., having deductible insurance so that a certain part of the loss is paid for by the sponsor) or transferring the risk (i.e., signing over to an insurance company the entire monetary risk involved if a person should drown). Naturally, there is a payment made to the insurance company beforehand, but the amount (probably thousands of dollars) is considerably less than would be paid (probably hundreds of thousands) in the case of a drowning.

Task 4—Use Qualified Personnel. Reduce or eliminate risks through the employment and in-service training of qualified personnel. It is discouraging to discover, as did Werts (1985), that only 50% of the aquatic facilities surveyed had formal in-service training programs for their lifeguards. Of those facilities that had no programs, most managers felt that "if the lifeguards swam laps and did 'some practice' of the lifesaving skills (mainly releases and escapes), that constituted an in-service program" (p. 14).

Chapter 6 discusses the professional lifeguard, who represents a primary source of defense against injuries and deaths. The employment of certified lifeguards and their continued in-service training are minimum requirements of aquatic facilities.

Task 5—Provide Safe Facilities, Equipment, and Environment. In many cases, the design features of the facility cannot be altered and yet patrons must be provided with a safe environment. However, if managers know the minimum safety standards for their facilities and operations, then adjustments can be made or certain activities curtailed. For example, because diving into water less than 5 feet deep is dangerous, the risk can be reduced by prohibiting diving except in deep water. Admittedly, a "no diving from side" rule is difficult to enforce, especially when diving has been permitted for years in a particular facility. A safety system, however, demands professional judgment and decision making.

Risks can be minimized after a careful analysis of all facilities and equipment—their design, maintenance, and use. Depending on the site, this could include (a) swimming pools, (b) open-water beaches and camp waterfronts, (c) diving boards and slides, (d) first-aid rooms, and (e) security procedures during both hours of operation and closed hours. Safety standards and suggestions for minimal risk operation for these five aspects follow. (Information on safety standards for water parks can be found in the work of Fick, 1986.)

1. *Swimming pool safety standards:* Despite the fact that local authorities must approve plans for the renovation and new construction of facilities, faulty pool design still occurs. (See Appendix D for a summary of desirable safety standards for pools.)
2. *Beach and camp waterfront safety standards:* Beaches present a great safety

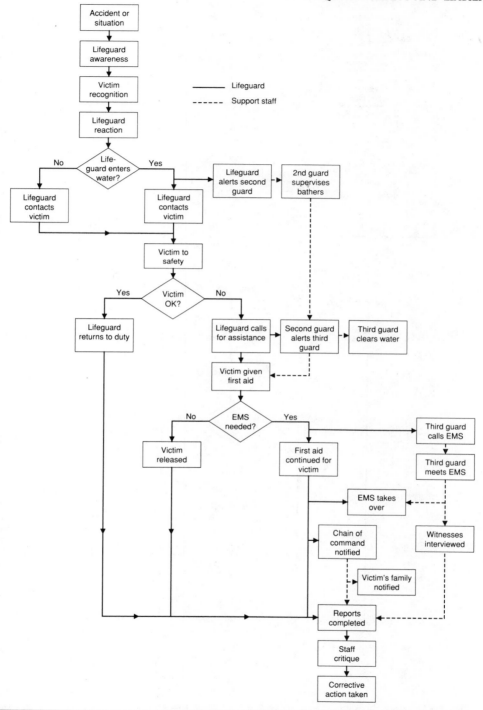

Figure 5.2. Emergency action plan—multistaff facility. *Note.* From *Lifeguard Training* (p. 5.5) by the American Red Cross, 1983, Washington DC: Author. Copyright 1983 by the American Red Cross. Reprinted courtesy of the American Red Cross.

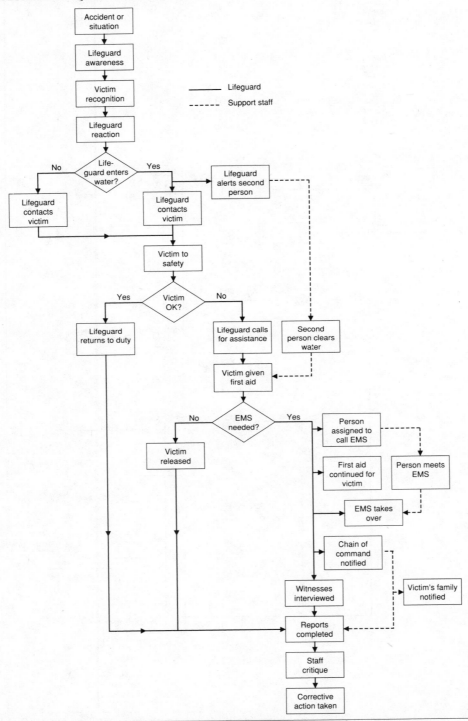

Figure 5.3. Emergency action plan—single lifeguard facility. *Note.* From *Lifeguard Training* (p. 5.8) by the American Red Cross, 1983, Washington DC: Author. Copyright 1983 by the American Red Cross. Reprinted courtesy of the American Red Cross.

problem both in season and in the off-season. "Swim at your own risk" admonitions are not appropriate when a group (e.g., the city park department) is responsible for the safety of an aquatic facility. Safety standards for beaches are given in Appendix D.

3. *Diving and water-slide safety standards:* Diving boards, minitramps, and slides constitute the greatest danger of permanent injury in aquatics. Scott and Evera (1987) examined the extent of spinal cord injuries in the United States and reported that National Spine Injury Control Center statistics show that diving into shallow water (5 feet or less) accounts for 66% of all sports-related spinal cord injuries. Because not all spinal cord injuries are reported, Scott and Evera reported that some researchers are of the opinion that "hundreds more spinal cord injuries are occurring in swimming areas throughout the nation" (p. 3). Finally, they report that, of the persons injured in diving, 92% become quadriplegic.

    In theory, the use of diving boards and slides should be restricted to those who have been properly trained in using them. But, because this is virtually impossible, ensuring that this equipment meets the standards outlined in Appendix D will reduce the risks.

4. *Filter-room, bathhouse, and first-aid-room safety standards:* Any risk management system must also consider facilities other than the pool or open water itself. Because the filter room of the pool and the locker and bathhouse are subject to the rules of, and to inspections by, local and state health authorities, there can be no deviation from the standards established by these groups.

It is the responsibility of both facility managers and lifeguards to ensure that first-aid supplies (listed in Table 5.1) are present and readily accessible to trained personnel. As will be noted in chapter 6, all lifeguards must have current first-aid certification (including that of cardiopulmonary resuscitation [CPR]) from a recognized agency.

5. *Safe pool and beach environments:* Sponsors have two responsibilities concerning the actions of their employees and patrons (see Table 5.2): that employees properly supervise patrons, and that patrons do not damage the facilities (or themselves) at any time. The legal aspects of these responsibilities will be discussed later in this chapter.

A determined effort is essential in preventing the violation of regulations at either the pool or the beach, but the waterfront requires even greater effort because the site is accessible by land and water so that only a constant patrol can be a reasonable guarantee against violations. Conscientious, alert employees must implement security at either site and under all conditions.

Component 4: Administer the Program

Task 1—Recruit. Assign persons specific roles in each particular emergency.

Task 2—Rehearse. Conduct both preservice and in-service training programs at regular intervals and keep records of lesson content and attendance. Involve the public in the in-service exercises.

Table 5.1

ESSENTIAL FIRST-AID SUPPLIES

Applicators: Cotton-tipped sticks, cotton balls, tongue depressors

Approved resuscitation equipment: Manual resusci-bag and mask unit, oxygen supply, airway tubes

Bandages: Various sizes of sterile gauze squares, waterproof sterile strips, gauze roller bandages, triangular bandages, adhesive tape, and burn dressings

Equipment: Safety pins, tweezers, scissors, paper cups, eye cup, sterile needle, blankets, spine board, stretcher, splints, padding

Ointments: Burn medication, petroleum jelly

Solutions: Antiseptic, eye drops

Miscellaneous: Spirits of ammonia, soap, sugar (cubes and solution), ice, plastic bags, disposable surgical gloves

Note. Adapted from Andres (1978), Howes (1973), and Palm (1974).

Task 3—Report Internally.   Develop an accident-reporting system both for present use (insurance, possible liability claims) and for future use (analyzing accidents and their results).

Task 4—Report Externally.   Establish policies and procedures for reporting accidents and emergencies to the police, health department, and media.

Task 5—Evaluate.   Periodically assess the results of emergency responses.

LIABILITY IMPLICATIONS OF AQUATIC ACCIDENTS[2]

Facility personnel have a moral obligation to provide maximum protection to facility users. Unfortunately, accidents and injuries will occur, and injured persons today are quick to file lawsuits for negligence. Risk management and public education are the first two aspects of an aquatic safety system, and an understanding of legal liability is the final aspect. The following terms must be understood before liability implications can be discussed.

Lawsuit.   This is a legal procedure for settling disputes.

Plaintiff.   The plaintiff is the party who complains of injury and seeks aid from the court.

Defendant.   The defendant is the party whom the plaintiff accuses of responsibility for an injury.

Filing.   The plaintiff begins the lawsuit by initiating a court complaint against the defendant.

Complaint.   This is a statement that identifies the defendant, the facts of the inci-

[2]Sources: M. Applewick, personal communication, May 1979; Kaiser (1986a); and van der Smissen (1982).

Table 5.2

SAFE POOL AND BEACH ENVIRONMENTS

During operation

- Cashiers must be certain that swimmers purchase tickets when admission is charged and must deny admission to rowdies and those under the influence of drugs or intoxicants.
- Attendants must control behavior in locker rooms and showers.
- All employees must be vigilant to prevent abuse or misuse of facilities and equipment and should monitor all areas to discourage property defacement and damage.
- Unauthorized persons must be prevented from entering the locker room, which should be considered a private area to those using it.
- Loitering must be discouraged or prohibited.
- Arrangements must be made to check in swimmers' valuables; lockers and baskets must be kept locked.
- At the end of the day, the cashier's receipts should be removed from the premises or stored in a high-quality safe; equipment must be stored.

During nonoperation

- Close and lock all gates, windows, and entrances; try to open them from the inside to make sure they are secure.
- Check storerooms and locker rooms for hidden persons.
- Leave night-lights on inside and outside.
- Post a "pool closed" or "beach closed" sign.
- Provide a nighttime security system. Possibilities include a roving patrol, an alarm system that activates when the water surface is disturbed, and floodlights that are activated by water or door movement.

---

dent, and the injury, and also alleges that the defendant is responsible for the injury and asks the court for a monetary award to compensate the plaintiff for the injury.

Answer. The defendant files a response to the complaint that describes the facts of the incident as the defendant views them, denies any liability, and asks for the dismissal of the case.

Trial. This is a formal court proceeding where witnesses are heard and evidence presented to either a judge or a judge and jury.

Finding of Facts. Because the plaintiff and defendant may disagree on the factual setting, the court (judge) will state what it determines are the facts. This statement is called the "finding of fact."

Conclusions of Law. The pertinent laws are applied to the finding of fact, and the resulting conclusions of law decide the question of liability.

Judgment. This is a statement, based on the conclusions of law, of who wins the case.

Award.   If judgment is given for the plaintiff, the court (judge) will determine the dollar equivalent of the injury the plaintiff has suffered. That amount is the award the defendant must pay the plaintiff. If judgment is given for the defendant, no award is given, and the case is dismissed.

Interpretations of the law have increasingly tended to favor the injured party. Not only have lawsuits to recover for injury become more prevalent, but plaintiffs have won a higher percentage of them, and the awards have been much greater. Charitable organizations, schools, and government organizations that once enjoyed immunity from lawsuits have now lost much of that protection.

As attitudes toward liability continue to broaden, it becomes increasingly important that every aquatic employee be constantly vigilant, taking every precaution to avoid an action that might contribute to the injury of another person.

Civil Liability

Civil liability is determined in an action for tort (Latin for ''twisted'' or ''bent''). The injury is the tort. An action for tort is a lawsuit to recover an award of damages resulting from an injury, the theoretical purpose of which is to make the injured person whole again by giving him or her an amount of money equal to the amount of damage suffered.

In legal use, liability is the conclusion that the defendant was responsible for the injury, which may have resulted from either intentional or unintentional negligent conduct. (A defendant cannot be liable for ''acts of God'' such as earthquakes and tornadoes, which cannot be controlled.) This conduct falls into one of two categories: (a) misfeasance (when a person acts improperly) and (b) nonfeasance (when a person is supposed to act but fails to do so). Both misfeasance and nonfeasance may be negligent conduct, and the difference between them is often unclear.

Before the defendant will be held negligent, the following elements must be proven:

Duty of Care.   The defendant must have owed a duty of care to the injured person. The duty is to conform to a certain standard of conduct and care toward the other person. Generally, the greater the risk of the activity, the higher the standard of care.

Breach of Duty.   This occurs when the defendant's conduct falls below the standard it is expected to meet.

Actual Cause.   The breach of duty must be an actual cause of the injury. That is, if it were not for the breach of duty, the injury would not have happened.

Proximate Cause.   The breach of duty must also proximately cause the injury. If the breach is so remote that no one could have foreseen that injury would result, the breach did not proximately cause the injury.

Damage.   The plaintiff must actually have sustained a physical injury as a result of the defendant's conduct.

Employer, Employee, and Volunteer Liability

The old law of ''master and servant'' carries over into a rule called ''vicarious liability,'' which states that an employer is sometimes responsible for the negligent acts of employees. As a result, both the employer and employees (e.g., the sponsoring group, the facility manager, the head lifeguard, and the lifeguards on duty) are usually named as codefendants in a lawsuit. Kaiser (1986a) points out that supervisors have a legal duty to educate employees, and assuming that the training is correct, municipal supervisors are then not responsible for the actions of employees.

For some governments and municipalities, however, immunity from suits still exists. In many jurisdictions, liability depends on whether the aquatic program is a government function or a proprietary function. Government services are those that the municipality must provide (water, sewer, police, etc.). Proprietary functions are generally optional, profit-making ventures. Not all states make this distinction, and the trend is to decrease immunity and increase liability.

An employee enjoys no immunity from suit regardless of whether or not the governing body can be sued. This point needs to be emphasized to employees who believe that, because they are poor (e.g., working part time or while going to school), no one will sue them. Unfortunately, poverty is no defense.

The sponsor (governmental unit or private) can be held responsible for the misconduct of volunteers, especially if such persons were not trained properly. Volunteers can also be held liable for their own actions.

Negligence

With rare exceptions, the plaintiff must prove negligence on the part of the defendant if the plaintiff is to obtain compensation for an injury. Every employee must avoid negligent action either as misfeasance or nonfeasance. Table 5.3 shows the more common bases for torts and exemplifies some specific bases.

Standard of Care

Under normal circumstances, each person is responsible for showing others reasonable care and avoiding foreseeable harm to those others. A minimum standard of care is required. Van der Smissen (1982) reported that in aquatic safety "There is only one [standard of care]—that based on the activity/participants and NOT on the age, skill, experience, or compensation of the leader" (p. 33). To reiterate, a person hired or volunteering as a lifeguard at a pool or beach must react properly when making a rescue regardless of his or her age, skill, experience, or compensation.

Standards of care are established by experts in a particular field and by the conduct of peers. Expert witnesses (persons who demonstrate expertise in a particular field) will testify in court as to what a trained aquatic worker (who is also a reasonable and prudent person) would do in a similar situation. The opinion of the expert is based on the guidelines and operating procedures of similar facilities and persons. If the defendant fails to measure up to the standards, then negligence might be found.

The duties and standards of care owed to patrons of an aquatic facility are simple. A reasonable and prudent aquatic worker will (a) inspect the facility to uncover hidden dangers, (b) reduce the dangers by appropriate means, and (c) properly supervise the activity of patrons (Kaiser, 1986a).

MINIMIZING PERSONAL RISKS

Aquatic personnel should be reminded that they may be personally liable for their own negligence, which can be defined as the

Table 5.3

LIABILITY SUITS: CATEGORIES AND SOME CAUSES

Misfeasance

A. Improper actions, such as
  - doing more than necessary when giving assistance;
  - giving instruction that is too advanced for a learner's level of ability (e.g., beginning diver attempting an inward dive);
  - giving medication or treatment beyond approved first-aid practices or giving incorrect first-aid treatment;
  - handling an injured person roughly;
  - permitting activities that are dangerous to others (e.g., allowing water polo to be played in a crowded pool); and
  - issuing equipment that is dangerous to the user (e.g., giving scuba equipment to untrained persons).

B. Improper management, such as
  - employing or assigning unqualified personnel (e.g., letting an uncertified person act as a lifeguard; and
  - knowingly permitting dangerous conditions to exist (e.g., failing to correct a dangerous condition that has been reported).

Nonfeasance

A. Lack of action, or failure to
  - comply with the employer's instructions;
  - apply first aid;
  - advise an injured person to obtain follow-up treatment;
  - act promptly in effecting a rescue;
  - restrict swimmers from a diving area or boats from a swimming area;
  - enforce regulations and eject violators;
  - give safety instruction to class members;
  - inspect the facility and equipment periodically;
  - foresee the possibility of an accident; and
  - prohibit the introduction of dangerous objects.

B. Lack of management, or failure to
  - provide safe facilities and equipment (e.g., having steps and handrails that do not comply with governmental codes, no lifesaving equipment ready to use, and slippery decks or docks);
  - supervise properly (e.g., inadequate signs indicating water depth, no warnings pertaining to hazardous facilities or equipment);
  - provide security (e.g., no fence around an outdoor facility); and
  - perform assigned duties properly (e.g., talking to persons while on lifeguard duty, leaving assigned positions, engaging in unapproved activities such as playing on the beach or in the pool instead of lifeguarding).

failure to exercise the care required by law. Persons may be negligent for any action they perform (an act of commission) or any action they neglect to perform (an act of omission). For lifeguards, an act of commission would be to perform resuscitation in a grossly improper manner. An act of omission would be to leave a pool or beach unguarded during a regularly scheduled work period. A lifeguard must realize that he or she is hired to perform a task competently and that if the task is not done correctly and a life is lost or someone is seriously injured, the guard may be subject to a court decision likely to involve a large sum of money.

Personal Liability Insurance

The prudent aquatic facility worker will purchase liability insurance, which is available through membership in professional groups such as the Aquatic Council of AAHPERD or the National Federation Interscholastic Coaches Association, as well as through private insurance companies. In the event of a lawsuit, the insurance company will pay legal fees and, up to the limits of the policy, whatever judgment is awarded. Inasmuch as most negligence lawsuits ask thousands or millions of dollars for damages, we strongly urge aquatic workers to purchase personal liability insurance. Even if the defendant is blameless, it will still cost money to prove it.

Avoiding Lawsuits

The courtroom and the legal process will have a dramatic impact on the professional and personal life of any defendant. Whether the suit is for minor or major matters, court appearances are traumatic. Even if the defendant is found not guilty,

a trial can be psychologically and financially damaging. The best way to avoid this trauma is to prevent accidents; however, if they do occur, make sure that you are not at fault. In particular, facility managers and supervisors should heed the advice of Johnson (n.d.):

Facility: Identify and modify/correct deficiencies in facility design and equipment where possible. Develop and post rules and warnings; make sure that they are enforced by the staff.

Equipment: Conform to state and local laws in regard to availability and working condition of equipment. Use universal/multilingual signs to warn of danger. Identify depth markings in feet (6 Feet) or meters (3 Meters). Maintain proper lighting for the activity.

Water and site sanitation: Follow sanitation rules, which usually indicate specific tests to make and records to keep. Pay special attention to water clarity standards.

Personnel: Ensure that teachers instruct class members in personal and group safety and keep lesson plans and attendance records as proof of these efforts. Control the conduct of beach and pool users.

Have at least two lifeguards on duty at all times, because accident management and simultaneous bather protection are impossible for one lifeguard. Add additional lifeguards as prescribed by the state bathing code. Employ only currently-certified lifeguards, remembering that Advanced Lifesaving and/or WSI certificates are not lifeguard certificates.

Keep records of in-service training for all personnel.

SUPPLEMENTAL LEARNING ACTIVITIES

1. Report on an inspection of an aquatic site, comparing it to the safety standards shown in Appendix D.

2. Report on the safety education program at a local aquatic facility.

3. If possible, interview an aquatic person who has been either a witness or a defendant in a lawsuit and then report on this person's experience.

4. After receiving permission from the facility manager, observe lifeguards on duty at a local site. Report on possible causes for liability suits on the basis of Table 5.3.

REFERENCES AND SUGGESTED READINGS

American National Red Cross. (1983). *Lifeguard training*. Washington, DC: Author.

American Camping Association. (1982). Proposed aquatic standards. In R. Clayton (Ed.), *Aquatics now* (pp. 64-75). Indianapolis IN: Council for National Cooperation in Aquatics.

Andres, F. (1978). New standards for lifeguard training. *Journal of Physical Education and Recreation*, **49**(4), 70-71.

Cerio, P. (1982). Staffing and minimum equipment for a first aid room. In R. Clayton (Ed.), *Aquatics now* (pp. 114-115). Indianapolis, IN: Council for National Cooperation in Aquatics.

Ellis & Associates. (1987). *1986 waterpark safety statistical report*. Houston: Author.

Espeseth, R. (1985). Risk management for recreation enterprises. *National Aquatics Journal* (Fall), **1**, 4-6.

Fick, C. (1986). Waterparks. In L. Priest & A. Crowner (Eds.), *Aquatics: A changing profession* (pp. 100-102). Indianapolis, IN: Council for National Cooperation in Aquatics.

Fick, C. (1987). Designing waterparks for patron safety. *National Aquatics Journal* (Summer), 5.

Gabrielsen, M. (Ed.). (1984). *Diving injuries: A critical insight and recommendations*. Indianapolis, IN: Council for National Cooperation in Aquatics.

Gabrielsen, M.A. (1987). Safety guidelines for pool design and operations. In M. Gabrielsen (Ed.), *Swimming pools: A guide to their planning, design, and operation* (pp. 97-130). Champaign, IL: Human Kinetics.

Gabrielsen, M., & Johnson, R. (1979). Swimming pool safety. *Journal of Health, Physical Education, Recreation and Dance* (June), **(50)**5, 43-45.

Graham, C. (1985). Water park safety: A new challenge. *National Aquatics Journal* (Summer), **1**, 8-10.

Howes, G. (Ed.). (1973). *Lifeguard training: Principles and administration* (2nd ed.). Indianapolis, IN: Council for National Cooperation in Aquatics.

Johnson, R. (1980). Emergency and accident procedures. In L. Priest (Ed.), *Aquatics in the 80s* (pp. 18-19). Indianapolis, IN: Council for National Cooperation in Aquatics.

Johnson, R. (n.d.). *Defenses against aquatic liability*. Mimeographed. Indiana, PA: Indiana University of Pennsylvania.

Kaiser, R. (1986a). Tort reform: Implications for recreation and aquatic managers. In L. Priest & A. Crowner (Eds.), *Aquatics:*

A changing profession (pp. 27-35). Indianapolis, IN: Council for National Cooperation in Aquatics.

Kaiser, R. (1986b). *Liability and law in recreation, parks, and sports.* Englewood Cliffs, NJ: Prentice Hall.

National Safety Council. (1987). *Accident facts* (1986 ed.). Chicago: Author.

National Swimming Pool Safety Committee. (1987). *Operation: Water watch.* Washington, DC: U.S. Consumer Product Safety Commission.

New York State sanitary code. Chapter 1, Part 6. Albany: State of New York.

Palm, J. (1974). *Alert: Aquatic supervision in action.* (Chaps. 2, 5-9). Toronto, Ontario, Canada: The Royal Life Saving Society Canada.

Peterson, J. (1987). *Risk management for park, recreation & leisure services.* Champaign, IL: Management Learning Laboratories.

Pyle, B. (1982). A check list for aquatic equipment management. In R. Clayton (Ed.), *Aquatics now* (pp. 58-63). Indianapolis, IN: Council for National Cooperation in Aquatics.

Scott, K., & Evera, R. (1987). Aquatic spinal cord injury: Impact today, prevention tomorrow. *National Aquatics Journal* (Spring), **3**, 2-6.

Smith, D. (1982a). *Manual on aquatic safety, cold water survival, and hypothermia.* Imperial, MO: Author.

Smith, D. (1982b). Preventing drowning: New and different outlooks through a statistical study. In R. Clayton (Ed.), *Aquatics now* (pp. 140-145). Indianapolis, IN: Council for National Cooperation in Aquatics.

Smith, D., & Smith, S. (1984). *Water wise.* Imperial, MO: Authors.

Stern & Hendy. (1977). *Swimming pools and the law.* Milwaukee, WI: Author.

U.S. Department of Health, Education and Welfare. Public Health Service. Center for Disease Control. (1976). *Swimming pools: Safety and disease control through proper design and operation.* Washington, DC: Author.

U.S. Lifesaving Association. (1981). *Lifesaving and marine safety* (pp. 147-173). Piscataway, NJ: New Century.

van der Smissen, B. (1982). Legal liability and risk management. In R. Clayton (Ed.), *Aquatics now* (pp. 32-37). Indianapolis, IN: Council for National Cooperation in Aquatics.

Wagner, A. (1982). Emergency procedures for aquatic facilities. In R. Clayton (Ed.), *Aquatics now* (pp. 116-121). Indianapolis, IN: Council for National Cooperation in Aquatics.

Webster, S. (1982). Waterfront management: The camp waterfront director. In R. Clayton (Ed.), *Aquatics now* (pp. 55-57). Indianapolis, IN: Council for National Cooperation in Aquatics.

Werts, T. (1985). Emergency and risk management. *National Aquatics Journal* (Summer), **1**, 14-15.

RESOURCES

Visual Aids

AFW Company of North America, Suite 311, Bank of New York Bldg., 201 N. Union St., Olean, NY 14760 (diving caution poster)

Concept Systems Inc., 2619 Canton Ct., Fort Collins, CO 80525 (slides and tapes)

Council for National Cooperation in Aquatics, 901 W. New York St., Indianapolis, IN 46223 (diving caution poster)

National Swimming Pool Foundation,

10803 Gulfdale, Suite 300, San Antonio, TX 78216 (pamphlets)

Recreonics Corporation, 7696 Zionsville Rd., Indianapolis, IN 46268 (wall charts)

Water Safety Films, 3 Boulder Brae La., Larchmont, NY 10538 (films, wall charts)

Safety Information

American Camping Association, Bradford Woods, Martinsville, IN 46151

Boat Owner's Association of the United States, 880 S. Pickett St., Alexandria, VA 22304

National Marine Manufacturer's Association, 353 Lexington Ave., New York, NY 10016

National Safety Council, 444 N. Michigan Ave., Chicago, IL 60601

U.S. Coast Guard, 2100 2nd St. SW, Washington, DC 20593

Sources of Personal Liability Insurance to Members

American Alliance for Health, Physical Education, Recreation and Dance, 1900 Association Dr., Reston, VA 22091

National Federation Interscholastic Coaches Association, Box 20626, Kansas City, MO 64195

LIFEGUARDING

Current Lifeguard Preparation
A New Standard for Lifeguards
Lifeguard Certification Programs
Lifeguarding Principles
Characteristics of Competent Lifeguards
Primary Faults of Lifeguards
Lifeguard Selection
In-Service Training of Lifeguards
Evaluation of the Lifeguard System
Supplemental Learning Activities

Lifeguarding is the application of the skills and techniques necessary to control and prevent aquatic accidents. It is dangerous, monotonous, and tiring, and not nearly as glamorous as is portrayed in television commercials for suntan lotions.

The purpose of this chapter is to discuss lifeguards—those concepts and characteristics that superior guards possess—and to offer advice on the selection and training of such persons.

CURRENT LIFEGUARD PREPARATION

Most states have adopted regulations for lifeguards. For example,

Lifeguards shall have a current lifesaving certificate, be in good physical condition, and competent in artificial resuscitation techniques. Current training as a lifesaver or water safety instructor by the American Red Cross, YMCA, or equivalent will satisfy this requirement. (State of Illinois, n.d., p. 102)

Because of similar wording in the regulations of other states, the Advanced Lifesaving or WSI certification has become the de facto standard for lifeguards. However, the Red Cross never claimed that its Advanced Lifesaving course prepared lifeguards. Furthermore, the WSI has nothing to do with a lifeguarding course; holders of it "have not achieved a higher level of lifesaving ability or certification; they have only earned the privilege of teaching lifesaving and other Red Cross swimming courses" (Clayton, Gabrielsen, & Johnson, 1987, p. 41).

The inadequate preparation of swimming pool lifeguards can be estimated by con-

sidering the data of Berry (1987), who studied the qualifications of pool lifeguards in 113 colleges nationwide and 17 city recreation departments and YMCAs in the middle Eastern Seaboard states. Although separate lifeguarding courses have been available since 1974 (YMCA) and 1983 (American National Red Cross [ARC]), Berry found that only 41% (recreation departments) and 34% (colleges) of the guards had lifeguard certification. All required guards to have lifesaving (either ARC or YMCA). Only 50% of the colleges and 58% of the recreation groups tested their guards in either fitness or skills. In emergency treatment preparation, 94% of the recreation guards had CPR certificates (compared to only 67% of the college guards), and 65% had first-aid certificates (compared to 49% of the college group). Figure 6.1 presents these data.

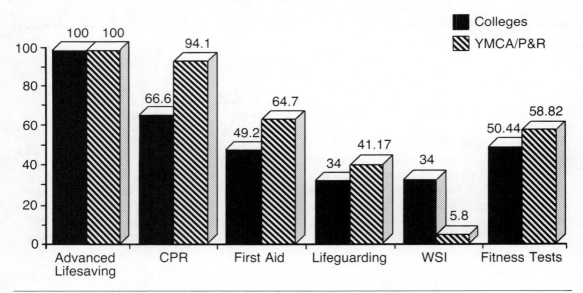

Figure 6.1. Preparation of swimming pool lifeguards—comparison between colleges and regional recreation departments. *Note.* From "An Analysis of Lifeguarding Qualifications in Aquatic Facilities" by D. Berry, 1987. Paper presented at the convention of the American Alliance for Health, Physical Education, Recreation and Dance, Las Vegas. Used by permission.

Contrast this preparation with that established for certain water-park lifeguards. According to Graham (1985, p. 9), "pro-lifeguard" programs of water parks are meant to instill a feeling of pride, professionalism, and even superiority over other lifeguards at other facilities. The objectives are to be physically fit, highly competent, and professional in appearance and to score at or above the 90th percentile (in comparison with pool lifeguards) in lifesaving skills. These objectives are met through preemployment testing, orientation to the particular facility, and regular in-service training throughout the season.

It is the contention of Pia (1982) that lifeguards are professional members of an emergency service unit rather than a segment of a beach patrol or a recreation staff. We agree, and add that lifeguards should be skilled far beyond the competence of advanced lifesavers. When a drowning or serious injury occurs, the performance of lifeguards becomes the issue. Did the lifeguard promptly take the correct action? If there is any question at all or if the plaintiff is looking for legal grounds for a lawsuit, the certification of the guard is examined. Unfortunately most pool and beach lifeguards in the United States are certified as "lifesavers" and not lifeguards.

A NEW STANDARD FOR LIFEGUARDS

Why do college and recreation department administrators employ persons who are not certified as lifeguards? The answer is twofold: First, outdated state regulations, such as those found in the Illinois statutes, permit uncertified persons to act as lifeguards. Second, administrators often do not realize

that the standard of care expected of lifeguards (see chapter 5) is unknown to lifesavers. Werts (1987, p. 10), formerly the national director of water safety activities for the American Red Cross, has clearly stated the difference between lifesavers and lifeguards. It is foolhardy (from a liability standpoint) for an administrator to hire a person who is not certified as a lifeguard. Those in authority should understand that trained professional lifeguards are a necessity and not a luxury.

Since the advent of separate lifeguard courses, it has become possible to require appropriate standards for lifeguards. New Jersey has changed its regulations for open-water lifeguards and now requires potential lifeguards to meet the standards of the United States Lifesaving Association. In many facilities, a pool lifeguard must have a certificate earned in the Red Cross Lifeguard Training course or the equivalent YMCA course; it is our observation that those facilities with competent professional leadership already have such a requirement. We believe that the pressure of insurance companies, attorneys for plaintiffs, and safety experts will soon cause states to adopt regulations that reflect this much higher standard.

LIFEGUARD CERTIFICATION PROGRAMS

The following organizations offer programs that lead to lifeguard certification:

- *American National Red Cross:* General lifeguarding course
- *Boy Scouts of America:* General lifeguarding course

- *Ellis and Associates:* Pool and water park courses
- *Royal Life Saving Society Canada:* Core lifeguarding course, plus options in pool, waterfront, or surf beaches
- *United States Lifesaving Association:* Surf lifeguarding course
- *YMCA:* Separate courses for pool, lake/river, and surf lifeguards

Only an instructor approved by the appropriate group can offer certificates. If such a person is unavailable, a local lifeguard course based on the recommendations of the Council for National Cooperation in Aquatics is the only other choice available. However, this course does not provide certification. Outlines for both surf lifeguarding and pool lifeguarding courses can be found in the Council for National Cooperation in Aquatics (CNCA) publication *Lifeguard Training: Principles and Administration* (Howes, 1973).

LIFEGUARDING PRINCIPLES[1]

The basic concept of lifeguarding is that preventing accidents is more desirable than performing successful rescues. Therefore, lifeguards should keep people from being in dangerous situations. Knowledge of and adherence to the following principles is an indication that the lifeguard accepts responsibility for the safety of the facility's patrons.

1. *Danger areas of aquatic sites should be continuously and closely observed:* At least one specified guarding position

(tower, dock, chairs, etc.) must be occupied at all times. A quick communication system between or among guards is essential. Lifeguards should anticipate problems by watching potential victims or trouble areas. Danger areas are as follows:

- Pool: Slippery decks, the areas in front of diving boards and around ladders, and the semideep (chin-level) water found at the breakpoint between shallow and deep water
- Beach: Underneath the dock, underneath the far side of rafts, semideep water (same as for pools), known drop-offs, slippery dock surfaces, water adjacent to lifelines marking the swimming area, and known undertow areas

2. *Essential rules should be enforced tactfully:* Rules vary, but the universal ones are to swim only when a guard is present, to obey signs and guards, and to talk to lifeguards only about safety at the facility. Additional rules that apply to specific sites follow:

- Pool: No running on deck; take a thorough shower before swimming.
- Beach: Swim only within marked areas; swim close to a partner; be aware of changing (daily, seasonal) waters; parents should watch young children.

3. *Lifeguards should be seen and be heard:* Wearing a distinctive uniform and carrying a whistle are universally required of lifeguards. A bright-colored uniform will help patrons spot the lifeguard quickly. Guards should realize that a quick response is expected when the situation warrants. For example, wearing laced shoes or

---

[1]Sources: Andres (1978, 1979, 1980), Palm (1974), and Pia (1978).

a sweatshirt would certainly hamper a rescuer in an emergency swimming situation—and would lead to sharp questioning by the plaintiff's lawyer.

Being seen also entails being in a location known to all patrons. Figure 6.2 shows the recommended positions for lifeguard stands for different pool configurations. In our view, at least one stand must always be occupied even if only one swimmer is in the water. It is preferable that the "main" lifeguard stand remain the same at all times, but environmental conditions (e.g., glare on the water or rain) may force a change.

The whistle and the public address system should be used selectively. Sometimes it is wise to call everyone's attention to a rule violation or potential danger, but if facility patrons assume that the lifeguard is making another "don't swim under the board" announcement, they probably will not listen. Using the public address system or a whistle is the quickest, surest, and easiest method to get patrons' undivided attention.

CHARACTERISTICS OF COMPETENT LIFEGUARDS

Lifeguarding is a serious, responsible, and demanding job. At least one season of experience is required for a person to become a competent guard, as some things cannot be learned from a book or from limited practical experience. A good lifeguard is characterized both by attitudes and by actions.

Attitudes of Competent Lifeguards

Emotional Maturity

Because lifeguards assume an enormous responsibility, they must demonstrate emotional maturity. Regardless of age, they must be able to hold a responsible and potentially dangerous position. Of course, a person can develop emotional maturity, but he or she must do so before becoming a competent lifeguard.

Dependability

Suffice it to say that an undependable guard (one who is habitually late, does not remain at the assigned post, and is inattentive, etc.) is unacceptable. From a legal standpoint, the continued employment of such a person may have devastating effects on the career and pocketbook of the supervisor.

Judgment and Tact

The enforcement of rules demands more than just a loud voice. Younger guards tend to be dogmatic; if a rule is broken, the swimmer is "kicked out" for a time. Experience teaches that, because each case is different, it is sometimes better to have flexible punishments for rule violations. Tact is gained with experience, and experience leads to maturity. Veteran guards usually have few problems and seldom force a swimmer to leave the facility. This does not imply that they do not enforce regulations, but it does demonstrate that they temper enforcement with judgment and tact.

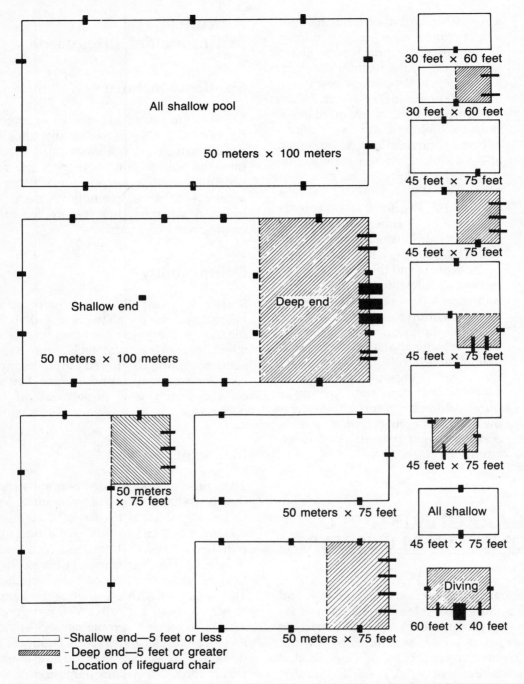

Figure 6.2.   Recommended locations of lifeguard stands. *Note.* From *Swimming Pools: A Guide to Their Planning, Design and Operation* (p. 114) by M. Alexander Gabrielsen (Ed.), 1987, Champaign, IL: Human Kinetics. Copyright 1987 by the Council for National Cooperation in Aquatics. Reprinted by permission.

Actions of Competent Lifeguards

Maintenance of Physical Strength

The importance of maintaining physical strength after being hired as a lifeguard is not overlooked by competent guards or managers. Considering the consequences of attempting to rescue a much stronger person, the lifeguarding certificate could become a death certificate. Even though a water rescue is carried out as a last resort, adequate physical strength must be maintained by competent lifeguards.

Periodic Review of Technical Skill

Good lifeguards know that a prompt and correct response to danger comes only after repeated practice. This response can be expected only of lifeguards who do what doctors, nurses, firefighters, and law officers do—review their skills on a regular basis. Competent lifeguards accept in-service training sessions as a necessary part of their preparedness (see the section on in-service training in this chapter).

Constant Alertness

The ability to react quickly and correctly is an obvious criterion for competent lifeguarding and can be expected only of lifeguards who are vigilant, as described in the following techniques.

One technique that lifeguards must master is the habit of visually scanning the entire surface of the water constantly. Too many guards devote most of their attention to the deep water or to one or two swimmers. Ideally, the guard's head should not be still for more than 10 seconds. When guards realize that accidents can happen to swimmers of all ages, in all depths of water, and to both sexes, they readily learn to practice this radarlike searching action. The "10/20 rule" (recognize a problem in 10 seconds and effect a rescue in the next 20 seconds) is an objective measure of a guard's efficiency. Being able to recognize a problem in 10 seconds is appropriate for all guards at any site; however, completing the rescue in the next 20 seconds may not be possible in some open-water situations.

A second technique that lifeguards must master is "selective listening," or the ability to distinguish between shouts of joy and shouts for help. In most aquatic sites, the word "help" is heard several times a day, but seldom does it mean that a guard should react. Swimmers (especially younger ones) pay little attention to the words they use. A guard whose eyes have been scanning the assigned area is able to discern which noise demands a response.

Some guards cannot seem to talk to swimmers without taking their eyes off the water. Although it is considered rude not to look at a person during a social conversation, it is negligent to do so while guarding.

In poorly supervised facilities, lifeguards are sometimes seen listening to radios with earphones. This is not appropriate behavior, and it would be viewed in court as evidence that the complete attention of the guard was not on his or her job. Background music played over the public address system is perhaps permissible if it is at a low volume and is not distracting.

Education of the Public

Because most drownings occur when lifeguards are not present (see chapter 5), aquatic personnel must interject safety education at every opportunity. It is important that the lifeguard and the swimming teacher (often the same person) explain why certain actions (such as boating without wearing a lifejacket) are dangerous and why other actions (dive only in water deeper than 5 feet) are desirable.

Prompt and Accurate Reporting of Accidents

The competent lifeguard completes an accident report (similar to that in Table 6.1) as soon as possible after an accident has occurred. No attempt should be made to conceal facts that may appear harmful to the facility or to the lifeguard. To ensure this, an accurate listing of the witnesses and a report of their accounts are imperative. The accuracy and completeness of the report prevents legal decisions that are unjustified by the facts.

Careful Maintenance of Equipment

First-aid kits are often short of supplies, lifelines become twisted and unusable, and resuscitators disappear or fail to work properly. Employers—and the courts—expect that equipment be available and in good working order.

PRIMARY FAULTS OF LIFEGUARDS

The faults of lifeguards can be summarized in four main categories:

1. *Inattention to all swimmers:* Nothing creates greater ill will among the parents of swimmers than their belief that lifeguards are not watching everyone in all areas. Spectators are quick to note any action that takes the attention of the guards away from the swimmers. The sight of a guard eating while on duty is especially disturbing. Although the occurrence of stomach cramps may be grossly overestimated, a guard who eats on duty immediately loses the public's confidence.

2. *Overattention to certain swimmers:* Although a certain amount of interest in individuals is acceptable, it should be demonstrated outside of working hours. The guard's primary duty is to all the patrons and not merely to a particular person or group.

3. *Deterioration of rescue skills, physical condition, and/or certification:* Considering the potential hazards that a lifeguard faces, the maintenance of skills and certification is essential. Many guards and administrators do not realize that certificates expire and that to an opposing lawyer the presence of a guard with an expired certificate is a clear indication of negligence. Even worse than a guard with an expired certificate is one who, when an emergency arises, does not respond properly.

4. *Poor role models:* Lifeguards should serve as examples to swimmers. For example, some guards require pool patrons to shower before swimming yet themselves enter the water without showering. They walk on the pool deck in street shoes, eat or smoke in the swimming enclosure, or push people in the water. They do all these things but do not tolerate such behavior from swimmers. Both swimmers and guards should follow the same set of rules. A guard who does not do so will find it difficult to enforce those rules among swimmers.

LIFEGUARD SELECTION

Because of legal liability, lifeguard selection must be a process that ensures that com-

Table 6.1

A SAMPLE FORM FOR REPORTING ACCIDENTS

Complete three copies of this report. (Two are sent to the headquarters or employers; one is kept with the pool records.) Every injury, no matter how trivial, must be noted. Forms must be completed immediately after an accident.

1. Victim's name _____ Age _____

2. Address _____ Phone _____

3. Place where accident occurred _____

4. Date of accident _____ Day of week _____ Hour _____

5. Describe the accident. _____

   _____

   _____

6. Was the injured disobeying any rule or regulation in force at the time of the accident?

   _____ If yes, explain. _____

7. Supervisor in charge of the activity _____

8. Probable nature of the injury _____

9. Who determined the nature of injury? _____

10. Total number of persons present at the time of accident _____

11. Names and addresses of those who saw the accident:

    1) _____ 2) _____

    3) _____ 4) _____

12. What was done for the injured? _____

    _____

13. Was the family notified? _____ Remarks _____

Report submitted by _____
                     Name   Title

Report received by _____
                    Name   Date

Note. From *Lifeguard Training: Principles and Administration* (p. 223) by G. Howes (Ed.), 1973, Indianapolis: Council for National Cooperation in Aquatics. Copyright 1973 by Council for National Cooperation in Aquatics. Adapted by permission.

petent people are hired. The steps involved in hiring—job description and prerequisites, written screening exam, practical screening exam, and preservice training—all serve to narrow the number of applicants to those who are qualified to be employed. (Chapter 8 discusses the usual process of hiring staff.) A discussion of these steps follows.

Job Description and Prerequisites

The first step, making a job description, is based on the qualifications desired and the actions and duties expected of a lifeguard (see Table 6.2).

Once the job description is formulated, prerequisites must be considered. There are

---

Table 6.2

QUALIFICATIONS AND DUTIES OF LIFEGUARDS

Qualifications

Maturity and experience: At least 17 years old; at least 1 year of experience as lifeguard aide, junior lifeguard, etc.

Education: Certified as a lifeguard by ARC, BSA, RLSSC, USLA; certified in first aid and CPR by a recognized group

Physical attributes: Possession of adequate size, strength, endurance, plus correct rescue techniques

Attitude: Successful experience as a lifeguard or aide

Duties (Example #1)

Exercises sound judgment and actions
Practices preventive lifeguarding
Administers first aid as needed
Rescues all persons regardless of their size, strength, and actions
Continues in-service training on a regular, periodic basis
Supervises and maintains a safe environment in an assigned area
Closes and secures facility at proper time

Duties (Example #2)

A job announcement from the City of San Clemente describes the duties as follows:

Watches a designated section of the beach and water from an assigned station, warns bathers of water hazards, enforces beach regulations on safety and conduct, responds to emergency and rescue situations, performs resuscitation as needed, uses auxiliary equipment such as rescue boards, rescue buoys, and swim fins, answers questions of beach visitors, takes charge of lost children, administers first aid, maintains beach safety and rescue equipment, keeps activity reports, and operates a motor vehicle on the beach (City of San Clemente, n.d.).

Note. Adapted from Albuquerque Parks and Recreation Department (1987), Andres (1979), and City of San Clemente (n.d.).

differing thoughts on this topic. One view is that possessing certain certifications (usually Advanced Lifesaving, Lifeguarding, CPR, or first aid) is adequate evidence of competence. This implies that all certificate holders have a certain level of skill and/or knowledge. Our experience is to the contrary, as we have encountered many persons who could not successfully demonstrate skill or knowledge despite having a current certificate.

A second view is that only general requirements should be set (e.g., for open-water guards, having a high school diploma, being age 16, and having a driver's license, or being mentally alert and in excellent physical condition and having 20/50 vision correctable to 20/20 and a Social Security card). In this case the sponsor must accept anyone meeting these prerequisites and then offer specialized training (e.g., a certified lifeguard course plus the additional skills needed for that facility).

The third view, which we support, is to list the general job requirements and then administer a job-related test (or tests) to the applicants. For example, the United States Lifesaving Association (1981, p. 5) advocates that surf lifeguard candidates be age 17 and have normal hearing, uncorrected 20/20 vision, normal heart and lungs and reflexes, and no disabling deformities or conditions and that they demonstrate the ability to handle all situations indigenous to the area of responsibility. In addition, surf lifeguards should demonstrate physical skills by swimming 1,000 meters in 16 minutes or 500 meters in 7.5 minutes and/or successfully complete a 1,200-meter run-swim-run.

Receiving Applications

The use of a standard application, to be received by a certain date, will ensure that each candidate provides the needed information: name, phone, experience, certifications held, and so on. In most cases, more applications will be received than there are jobs, but a review of the applications will locate those who appear qualified.

Written Screening Exam

At this point, and especially in cases with large numbers of applicants, some sponsors require a written test. If a written test is given, a study guide should have been previously given to the candidates. The purpose of this test is to confirm that they know certain material, not to see what they do not know. Those who do poorly are not given further consideration.

Practical Screening Test

The candidates who remain after the initial inspection of applications and after the written test are then called in to take a practical screening test. Each item in Table 6.3 has been recommended by someone or some group as an action a guard must perform. It is not logical to administer every test item shown in the table. However, we recommend that all applicants be evaluated by some of the items in each of the four categories: swimming skill and endurance, lifesaving skills, knowledge, and current certification.

After the screening process the candidates are grouped into two categories: (a) prospects and (b) those who need further preparation. This grouping is based on scores attained in the screening test(s). It is logical to weight the items according to their importance at a particular site. For example, the time attained on a 500-meter open-water swim by a beach lifeguard is

Table 6.3
POSSIBLE CRITERIA FOR LIFEGUARD SCREENING TESTS

(All Items Pass/Fail)

Swimming skill and endurance
Pool guards
- Swim 50-yd freestyle under 40 sec
- Swim 200-yd freestyle under 3 min 45 sec
- Swim 500-yd freestyle under 10 min

Calm-water guards
- Any preceding item
- Run 100 yd, enter water, swim 100 yd, remove victim from water with appropriate carry

Surf guards
- Any preceding item
- Swim 600 yd (pool) under 10 min
- Run 1.5 mi under 12 min
- Swim 400 yd with rescue tube
- Swim underwater 125 ft, surfacing four times, taking only one breath at each surface, and not touching any wall

Lifesaving skills
Pool guards
- Swim 25 yd, cross-chest carrying a victim of same size
- Swim 50-yd sidestroke, carrying a 10-lb brick, under 1 min 10 sec
- Swim 50-yd elementary backstroke, carrying a 10-lb brick, under 1 min 20 sec
- Tread water for 2 min, supporting a 10-lb brick with both hands
- Front surface approach 25 yd, place victim of equal size in cross-chest carry, carry victim 25 yd
- Correctly perform front and back releases on victim
- Surface dive in 12 ft of water to recover 10-lb brick

Calm-water guards
- Any preceding item
- Correctly use paddleboard or rowboat
- With paddleboard or rowboat, travel 100 yd to victim and correctly position victim for CPR

Surf guards
- Any preceding item
- Shallow dive, swim 50 yd to victim of equal size, tow victim with cross-chest carry for 50 yd, emerge, carry victim 50 ft, position victim for CPR, all under 4 min
- Escape from front head hold, rear head hold, and double grip on one wrist

(Cont.)

Table 6.3 (Cont.)

Knowledge

Lifeguards (all sites)
- Pass (90%) an open-book exam on a nationally published lifeguarding text
- Pass (90%) a first-aid examination
- Pass (correct explanation) a CPR examination
- Pass (90%) a written test on water safety and basic life-support principles and procedures

Certification

Lifeguards (all sites)
- Display current appropriate certificates (lifeguarding, CPR, and first aid) from a national agency

Experience

Surf Lifeguards
- One year's successful experience as a pool or calm-water lifeguard (verify with letter of recommendation)
- One season's experience as junior lifeguard in the same site

Note. Adapted from Albuquerque Parks and Recreation Department (1987), Andres (1979), City of San Clemente (n.d.), Nassau County (1979), and U.S. Department of the Interior (1979).

more important than the time scored by a pool lifeguard candidate. Likewise, describing an escape from a front head hold on a written test might be less important than actually demonstrating that ability.

Those who need further preparation should be told what their deficiencies are and encouraged to try again when they have improved.

Preservice Training

Preservice training is held before any candidate is hired and includes those who have continued seeking the position. Preservice training (a) provides certification/recertification in first aid, CPR, and lifeguarding; (b) teaches the particular skills and knowledge applicable to the specific facility; (c) familiarizes the candidates with the standard procedures and rules of the facility; and (d) permits instructors (usually regularly employed supervisors) to evaluate the candidates periodically. Eventually, each student is given a ranking within the group.

The scheduling of preservice training is relatively easy in a seasonal operation, where a large number of applicants are competing at the same time. The usual procedure is to have Saturday/Sunday sessions for two or three consecutive weekends. In other situations, preservice training sessions are scheduled on a monthly, bimonthly, or quarterly basis, depending on the needs of the facility. In both cases, attendance by the candidate is required to still be considered for the position.

Hiring

Positions are offered to the top members of the preservice training sessions. Because it is not unusual for persons to take the preservice training, rank high, and then refuse a job offer, all candidates should be ranked so that the person next in line can be offered the job.

IN-SERVICE TRAINING OF LIFEGUARDS

It is difficult for swimming pool lifeguards to maintain their rescue skills simply because situations in which the skills are needed occur so infrequently. For example, Ellis (1987) reported that no public pool surveyed by him had more than 10 rescues in one season, with the majority ranging from 1 to 4 per year. Conversely, a minority of lifeguards (found at open-water sites, and water parks) make the majority of the rescues. D. D'Arnall (personal communication, March 1987) reported that around 250 rescues are made on certain days at a California ocean beach, while Ellis (1987) observed that the average water park makes up to 700 rescues per year. This difference in number of rescues reflects the degree of environmental danger as well as the disparity between the number of patrons among the various aquatic sites.

Lifeguard skills must be maintained regardless of how frequently they are used. Berry (1987), in his study of 113 colleges and 17 city recreation departments, found that 73% of the colleges and 94% of the recreation departments offered in-service training for their guards, usually on a quarterly or semiannual basis. Unfortunately, only 31% of the colleges and 50% of the rec-

reation departments included a local Emergency Medical Service in their program.

Mention was made earlier of the exemplary safety record of most water parks (up to 750 rescues per season with few drownings). In part, this is due to rigorous in-service training that includes both physical and mental tests. If a guard does not score above 70% on the in-service physical test, he or she is put on probation and is dismissed if a retest does not meet the 70% minimum. More important, lifeguards are evaluated by supervisors during actual rescues.

A record should be kept of in-service training. This not only will remind administrators of the legal and practical necessity of the procedure but will prove valuable in defending any alleged incompetence of lifeguards.

A regularly scheduled (at least bimonthly) training program must be planned to include the following items:

1. *Rehearsal of emergency plans:* See chapter 5.
2. *Practice of technical skills:* These skills are summarized in Table 6.4. Over a 6-month period all the items should be covered.
3. *Physical conditioning:* According to Andres (1980), a lifeguard should maintain the physical attributes of respiratory endurance, muscular strength, local muscular endurance, flexibility, and speed. He suggests that conditioning can be accomplished in the following ways:
   - *Swimming:* Swim a long distance at a slow speed; swim a short distance at a fast speed, then slow; swim a short sprint followed by a short rest; tow a partner for a specified distance.

Table 6.4

TECHNICAL SKILLS NEEDED BY LIFEGUARDS

Reaching assists

1. Towel, pole, arm, and so on. Be prepared with an alternative skill because a distressed or drowning victim is apt to ignore these items.

Rescue with equipment

2. Rescue board (paddleboard). Useful for giving artificial respiration while in deep water. Avoid injuring swimmers while passing through them on the way to the victim.
3. Boat. Most useful outside the swimming area or surf.
4. Ring buoy. Seldom used because they are difficult to throw accurately, and drowning victims are so preoccupied with up-and-down arm movements they cannot grasp the buoy. However, as long as state regulations require this equipment, it must be part of in-service training.
5. Rescue tube. An essential piece of equipment, useful in a reaching assist or as a flotation device.

Swimming assist without equipment

6. Push to safety. The most desirable technique because it limits contact with the victim.
7. Supporting the victim. Useful for a distressed victim, but technique must prevent being grabbed or held.

Swimming rescue: passive victim*

8. Approaches (front, rear, submerged). Rear approach is most desirable. According to Pia (1978) front approach is used only when the victim is submerged.
9. Carries (cross chest, armpit). Used only when push to safety or assists are not feasible. Variation of cross-chest carry (rescuer's arm under the arm of the victim instead of over the shoulder) is preferred by many professional lifeguards.

Swimming rescue: active victim*

10. Approaches and carries (see under "passive victim").
11. Defenses and releases (block, block and carry, block and turn, front and rear headholds). All are dangerous because the victim may not react as "pseudovictims" do in practice.
12. Wrist releases (single, double). Sometimes are not done if the victim can be towed safely.

Multiple victim rescue*

13. Separate victims, control and then carry. Need to practice with a partner.

(Cont.)

Table 6.4 (Cont.)

Removal of victim from water

14. Arm assist. Despite any protests, victims should be walked to shore and placed in resting position.
15. Spine board. An essential item at every site.
16. Lifts (pool, two- and three-person). Performed only in the absence of spine board or when no neck or back injury is possible.

First aid

17. Resuscitation, CPR, placing direct pressure on wound, treating head or spinal injury, shock, cramps, comas, seizures, hypothermia, etc.—everything that could occur at the site. Follow latest techniques advocated by the Red Cross, American Heart Association, or other recognized agencies.

Accidents (dock, pier, surf, scuba, boating, pool deck)

18. Techniques specific to the site must be practiced.

Note. Adapted from Albuquerque Parks and Recreation Department (1987), Andres (1979), Pia (1978), and United States Lifesaving Association (1981).

*All swimming rescues should culminate in the use of a rescue tube.

- *Running:* Run a short distance at a fast speed, then a longer distance at a slower speed.
- *Circuit training (running and swimming):* Complete a timed route including such activities as a sprint to beach, a swim for distance, a surface dive, positioning a partner for resuscitation, towing a partner to shore, and so on. Items included in the preemployment test (see Table 6.3) are appropriate. All guards should run this circuit once or twice per week and keep track of the times.
- *Water games:* These can include water polo, underwater tag, novelty swims, paddleboard races, water wrestling, underwater hockey, and so on.

4. *Guarding techniques:* Classroom sessions followed by on-site practice should be used to improve and maintain guarding techniques. For example, showing videotapes of actual incidents at the facility would be ideal, but this is seldom possible. An effective alternative would be to use a videocamera to reenact a past or potential emergency. This calls for cooperative patrons or guards to act the role of the victim while the other staff members respond appropriately.

At the very least, lifeguards should observe patrons in actual emergency situations by viewing the film *On Drowning* (see the resource list at the end of this chapter), which shows actual situations at an open-water facility. Specific drills on such basic practices as scanning and observation of patrons, disciplining, educating, and communicating are described by Palm (1982).

Remember that rescue techniques vary because victims react differently, depending on the situation and their aquatic backgrounds. For example, distress victims, because they have positive or neutral buoyancy, can often reach safety by themselves with only limited physical support by the lifeguard. Drowning victims, whose usual actions include no kicking, no calling for help, and continual up-and-down underwater arm movements, must be first supported by the lifeguard and then towed to safety.

Table 6.5 presents an example of

Table 6.5

IN-SERVICE AQUATIC STAFF TRAINING PROGRAMS
(CITY RECREATION DEPARTMENT)

Staff selection
Screening of applicants:
January 23, 12 noon to 3:00 p.m.   January 30, 8:00 a.m. to 11:00 a.m.
Selection:
January 23, 3:00 p.m. to 4:00 p.m.   January 30, 11:00 a.m. to 12 noon

Safety training (must attend one)
January 27, 6:00 p.m.   February 22, 6:00 p.m.   March 25, 6:00 p.m.

Lifeguard training (must attend one at each facility)
City pool   *EPIC pool*
January 27, 7:00 p.m. to 9:00 p.m.   January 28, 5:00 p.m. to 7:00 p.m.
February 1, 5:00 p.m. to 7:00 p.m.   February 2, 7:00 p.m. to 9:00 p.m.

Water relaxation (must attend one)
January 30, 5:00 p.m. to 7:00 p.m.   February 10, 7:00 p.m. to 9:00 p.m.

Water polo and other games (must attend one)
February 14, 5:30 p.m. to 8:30 p.m.   February 20, 5:30 p.m. to 8:30 p.m.

Teen night and water games (must attend one)
February 5, 7:00 p.m. to 9:00 p.m.   February 12, 7:00 p.m. to 9:00 p.m.

Fitness instructor, swim instructor, and adapted aquatics instructor training
To be announced.

First-aid course (choose one for certification)
February 20, 8:00 a.m. to 4:00 p.m.   February 27, 8:00 a.m. to 4:00 p.m.

CPR (for recertification, practice on your own and choose one time to test; for initial certification, attend all sessions)
February 16, 6:00 p.m. to 9:00 p.m.   February 17, 6:00 p.m. to 9:00 p.m.
February 18, 6:00 p.m. to 9:00 p.m.

Note. Adapted from Fort Collins (CO) Parks and Recreation Department (1988).

an in-service training schedule for lifeguards of a city recreation department with two pools.

EVALUATION OF THE LIFEGUARD SYSTEM

From the standpoint of drowning, guarded swimming pools are about 10 times more dangerous than are water parks. Guarded pools have one drowning per 280,000 visits, whereas water parks (which have many more opportunities for accidents because of their numerous activities) have one drowning per 3.7 million visits (Ellis, 1987). Actually, there were no drownings among the 13,000,000 who attended water parks in 1984 (White, 1984).

Perhaps the safety record of pools would improve if they adopted the use of water safety audits as water parks have done. As reported by Ellis (1987), unannounced visits are made by an outside evaluator. After observing safety practices at various points, a simulated emergency is then conducted: A person acts as a victim, or a mannequin or colored ball is thrown into a specific activity area. Evaluation is based on the 10/20 rule. The penalties for failing the test are stringent. A written report is immediately given to the park manager, and deficiencies are noted. Another water safety audit is conducted by a different evaluator within a week. If the water park fails the second test, the insurance is immediately canceled and the facility will have to close.

Similar procedures are used by competent facility managers at beaches and pools except that the facility does not have to close if the test is not passed. However, supervisors and lifeguards might pay more attention to in-service training if they are faced with suspension or dismissal because

of their failure to pass a similar unannounced test.

SUPPLEMENTAL LEARNING ACTIVITIES

1. After receiving permission from the manager, observe a recreational swim period at an aquatic site. Report on the performance of the lifeguards in these areas: (a) judgment and tact in enforcing rules; (b) observation of danger sites; (c) use of whistle or public address system; (d) vigilance; (e) proper conduct; and (f) education of the public.

2. Talk to experienced guards about (a) whether they have lifeguard certificates (not lifesaver certificates); (b) their years of experience; (c) number of rescues they have made and which rescue techniques were used; (d) when they last practiced lifeguarding skills by actually being in the water; and (e) the probability of their successfully rescuing a 200-pound person from a pool, lake, or surf beach.

3. Prepare a report on your actions if any of the following situations arose while you were guarding: (a) two people are in serious trouble simultaneously in widely separated areas; (b) a canoe has tipped over outside the swimming area, and the occupants are clearly in trouble; (c) a person is missing from the beach as the sun begins to set; (d) a power failure shuts off pool lights during a crowded family swim period; and

(e) a 200-pound ex-boxer encourages his son to take the family dog for a swim in your pool.

REFERENCES AND SUGGESTED READINGS

Albuquerque Parks and Recreation Department. (1987). *1987 lifeguard practical test.* Unpublished manuscript.

Andres, F. (1978). New standards for lifeguard training. *Journal of Physical Education and Recreation, 49*(4), 70-71.

Andres, F. (1979). Swimming pool lifeguarding. *Journal of Physical Education and Recreation, 50*(5), 42-43.

Andres, F. (1980). *Lifeguarding: A syllabus for the aquatic council courses "teacher and master teacher of lifeguarding".* Reston, VA: American Alliance of Health, Physical Education, Recreation and Dance.

Berry, D. (1987, April). *An analysis of lifeguarding qualifications in aquatic facilities.* Paper presented at the convention of the American Alliance for Health, Physical Education, Recreation and Dance, Las Vegas, NV.

City of San Clemente. (n.d.). *Seasonal ocean lifeguard.* Mimeographed. San Clemente, CA: Author.

Clayton, R., Gabrielsen, M., & Johnson, R. (1987). A new standard for lifeguards. *Trial, 23*(4), 41-42.

Ellis, J. (1987). Testing through emergency situations—Waterparks. *National Aquatics Journal* (Spring), 3(2), 16.

Fort Collins (CO) Parks and Recreation Department. (1988, January). Unpublished manuscript.

Freeman, M. (1982). YMCA lifeguard training programs for summer camps. In R. Clayton (Ed.), *Aquatics now* (pp. 48-49).

Indianapolis, IN: Council for National Cooperation in Aquatics.

Gabrielsen, M. (Ed.). (1987). *Swimming pools: A guide to their planning, design, and operation.* Champaign, IL: Human Kinetics.

Graham, C. (1985). Water park safety: A new challenge. *National Aquatics Journal* (Summer), 1(2), 8-9.

Howes, G. (Ed.). (1973). *Lifeguard training: Principles and administration.* Indianapolis, IN: Council for National Cooperation in Aquatics.

King, E. (1986). Does your rescue technique spell failure? In L. Priest & A. Crowner (Eds.), *Aquatics: A changing profession* (pp. 55-57). Indianapolis, IN: Council for National Cooperation in Aquatics.

Langridge, J. (1982). Boy scout lifeguard training. In R. Clayton (Ed.), *Aquatics now* (pp. 48-49). Indianapolis, IN: Council for National Cooperation in Aquatics.

Palm, J. (1974). *Alert: Aquatic supervision in action.* Toronto, Ontario, Canada: The Royal Life Saving Society Canada.

Palm, J. (1982). Training aquatic staff re lifeguarding. In R. Clayton (Ed.), *Aquatics now* (pp. 111-114). Indianapolis, IN: Council for National Cooperation in Aquatics.

Pia, F. (1978). Observations on the drowning of non-swimmers. *Journal of Physical Education* (July/August), 44, 163-166.

Pia, F. (1982). Applying organizational systems theory to lifeguarding. In R. Clayton (Ed.), *Aquatics now* (pp. 103-107). Indianapolis, IN: Council for National Cooperation in Aquatics.

State of Illinois. Department of Public Health. (n.d.). *Rules and regulations governing public swimming pools and bathing beaches* (Circular No. 4: p. 102). Springfield, IL: Author.

United States Lifesaving Association.

(1981). *Lifesaving and marine safety*. Piscataway, NJ: New Century.

Werts, T. (1987). Lifesaving and lifeguarding programs of the American Red Cross. *National Aquatics Journal* (Spring), **3**(2), 10-11.

White, B. (1984). Water park safety. In L. Priest & A. Crowner (Eds.), *Opportunities in aquatics* (pp. 8-9). Indianapolis, IN: Council for National Cooperation in Aquatics.

RESOURCES

Lifeguard Certification Courses

American National Red Cross (general lifeguard training course). Contact the local Red Cross chapter.

Boy Scouts of America (general lifeguarding course), 1325 Walnut Hill La., Irving, TX 75261.

National Pool and Waterpark Lifeguard Training (a commercial program of specialized lifeguard training for swimming pool and water-park lifeguards).

Contact Ellis & Associates, 15 Greenway Plaza #18C, Houston, TX 77081.

Royal Life Saving Society Canada, The (core course plus options in pool, waterfront, or surf beaches), 64 Charles St. E., Toronto, Ontario, Canada M4Y 1T1.

United States Lifesaving Association (surf lifeguarding course), P.O. Box 366, Huntington Beach, CA 92648.

YMCA (pool, lake/river, surf courses), 110 N. Wacker Dr., Chicago, IL 60606.

Training Aids

Mannequin for lifeguard training and testing. Suspended Aquatic Mentor, Box 364 Homecrest Station, Brooklyn, NY 11229.

Rescue products developed by professional lifeguards. Marine Rescue Products Inc., Box 3484, Newport, RI 02840.

Visual aids: *On Drowning* (movie); *Drowning Facts and Myths* (movie); *Why People Drown* (videocassette); *Universal Drowning* (poster). Water Safety Films Inc., 3 Boulder Brae La., Larchmont, NY 10538.

Chapter 7

BUDGETING

Preparing the Budget
Income Sources
Expenses
Budget Reduction
Supplemental Learning Activities

Sponsoring groups must develop and follow realistic financial plans. Income must be maximized, expenses minimized, and adjustments made in line with the group's goals. Nonprofit programs ordinarily are designed to be self-sufficient; if the deficit becomes too great, the program may be dropped.

Although one consolidated budget should be presented to the sponsoring group, each facility of the program (pool, lake, beach, marina, etc.) should be budgeted separately.

PREPARING THE BUDGET

No two aquatic programs are the same, but the budget preparation processes for all are similar. In an ongoing program, the process begins with an analysis of the past year's actual figures. For a new program, educated guesses (based on similar programs at other facilities) may have to suffice. Table 7.1 lists appropriate income-expense categories (an explanation of some items will follow). Obviously, certain categories will not be needed in every program. Be aware that it is common to be overly optimistic on income and seriously deficient on the estimates for expenses. The contingency fund (normally 10% of income) is almost always used by the end of the fiscal year.

INCOME SOURCES

Depending on the facility, the primary sources of income are participation fees, rental of facilities and equipment, and concessions.

Table 7.1

CATEGORIES AND ITEMS IN AN AQUATIC BUDGET

Income
1. *Fees*
    1.1. Admission (recreational use)
    1.2. Lessons (swimming, scuba, sailing, etc.)
    1.3. Memberships (teams, clubs)
    1.4. Supplies and equipment sales (goggles, life jackets, gasoline for power boats, etc.)
2. *Rental and Sales*
    2.1. Facilities (pools, picnic/swim areas)
    2.2. Equipment (surfboards, masks, canoes, etc.)
3. *Concessions*
    3.1. Vending machines
    3.2. Concession stands
4. *Fund raising* (swimming, swimming lengths, selling goggles, etc.)
5. *Donations* (parents clubs, civic groups, etc.)
6. *Miscellaneous*

(Note: Skip several numbers here in case new categories are added.)

Expenses
11. *Wages*
    11.1. Fixed salaries (manager, head guard, water sanitations specialist, etc.)
    11.2. Hourly (instructors, guards, maintenance persons)
    11.3. Commissions (private teachers, coaches, supervisors)
12. *Taxes*
    12.1. Payroll (FICA, income, unemployment, disability)
    12.2. Property (facilities, equipment)
13. *Utilities* (gas, electricity, oil, water)
14. *Insurance* (liability, property)
15. *Fringe benefits* (health insurance, etc.)
16. *Supplies*
    16.1. Facility (chemicals, etc.)
    16.2. Office
    16.3. First aid
    16.4. Cleaning
17. *Promotions* (advertising)
18. *Equipment*
    18.1. Maintenance

(Cont.)

Table 7.1 (Cont.)

    18.2. Repair
    18.3. Purchase
  19. *Debt retirement*
  20. *Contingency*

Note. Adapted from Donohoe (1978) and Gabrielsen (1987).

Fees

Fees represent by far the greatest income in most programs. They are generated either from lessons or from recreational use of the facility. Today, programs are seldom entirely free, although that is the ideal in a tax-supported program.

Determining fees for a specific course is not easy because too high a fee will eliminate some patrons whereas too low a fee might result in a money-losing endeavor. The hidden overhead of a facility (taxes, insurance, debt retirement, equipment maintenance and repair, etc.) refers to costs that cannot be directly charged to a specific program or course, yet these costs must be covered. For this reason, we believe that all courses and activities (with the possible exception of those for the disabled) should generate a small profit.

The basic formula for establishing recreational fees is

$$\frac{\text{(Expenses)}}{\text{(Hours of operation)}} = \frac{\text{Cost per hour}}{\text{of operation}}$$

$$\frac{\text{(Cost per hour of operation)}}{\text{(Number of patrons per hour)}}$$

$$+ \text{ Profit for overhead} = \text{Fee}$$

Table 7.2 indicates how fees might be set in keeping with this concept.

Given that fees are necessary, it is important that all patrons either pay or show a pass. When the admissions system is so loose that some do not pay, a small but significant loss of income will follow. Likewise, the system should be set up so that the manager can swiftly and accurately account for all monies; to do less is to invite theft.

Fees for recreational use are normally set up on a one-time admission charge. A sliding scale (e.g., $1.50 for adults, $1.00 for children ages 13 through 18, $.75 for ages 3 through 12) is common. However, the amounts charged vary greatly among different parts of the country and among different facilities. The goal is to achieve maximal income (i.e., large attendance) from minimal fees. The fees established should be based on costs incurred, which are hard to predict without access to past records.

The possibility of providing a reduced-admission pass (e.g., 10, 15, or 20 admissions) should be explored. These passes are greatly appreciated by patrons, and they can be money-makers for the facility. The money is received in a lump sum, and in some cases the pass is not completely used. Passes should be transferable because in the long run the greater variety of patrons will generate more interest in the program.

Rental and Sales

Facility rental and equipment sales are major sources of income at most aquatic

Table 7.2

ESTABLISHING FEES FOR AQUATIC CLASSES

Explanation	Example
Assumption: Each class should show a 10% profit to cover hidden overhead.	
1. Establish the minimum number of students enrolled to maintain a class	10
2. Instructor's salary (including benefits) × length of one session (hour) × number of sessions	$8.25 × 1 × 10 = $ 85.00
3. Add administrative fee (record keeping, clerical help, etc.) × minimum students	$3.00 × 10 = $ 30.00
4. Add expendable supplies (paper, postage)	= $ 20.00
5. Add profit (10% of costs thus far)	$135 × .10 = $ 13.50
	$148.50
6. Divide expenses by minimum students to set course fee	$148.50/10 = $ 14.85 per student

Note. Because this formula guarantees a small profit for each class on minimum enrollment, additional students would mean a much greater profit. If only a break-even point is desired, change the "minimum number of students" to the actual number (estimate, or based on past history of the same class) and eliminate the 10% profit. However, the hidden overhead costs will, at the end of the fiscal year, result in a deficit budget. Adapted from Beaulieu (1986).

sites. For many swimming pools, it is common to rent facilities to organized groups such as swim teams, scuba shops, kayak clubs in the winter, and so on. In most cases, it is preferable for the sponsoring group to set the fees, which should be based on hourly operating costs. Fee negotiations between the manager and the group are often less than satisfactory to both parties.

In some cases (e.g., canoes at a lake) the rental of equipment is almost essential. However, it should be permissible to use safe personal equipment, especially at a tax-supported or nonprofit facility. Oftentimes,

a private facility will not permit this because equipment rental is a significant income factor.

The rental of lockers and/or locks is an overlooked source of income. Persons who have paid large sums of money for equipment (e.g., a bike ridden to the lake or a watch that should not be left in an unlocked locker) are quite willing to pay a small sum for the added protection of lockers and locks.

Public facilities are beginning to sell equipment (goggles, shampoo, visors, sunglasses, etc.) to tap all sources of revenue. Bulk purchasing from direct-mail "swim-shops'' may seem cost-effective; however, in the long run, little money is saved. The cost of postage and the inability to get instant returns on or replacement of defective merchandise negate whatever lower initial price was quoted, to say nothing of antagonizing local merchants. The best solution is to seek bids from local sources and, if prices are within reason, to buy from these sources.

Aquatic facilities should make available for purchase at least one durable, high-quality, and fairly priced safety device for the activities they sponsor. For example, personal flotation devices (Types I, II, and III) for adults and tots should be sold at pools and lakes, and flotation jackets for sportspersons should be available at marinas. The purpose is not to make a profit but to provide the public with proper advice and a quality product. An alternative to selling the equipment is to display the recommended equipment and then indicate where it can be obtained (preferably locally).

Concession Sales of Foods

Food sales are a major source of income at all facilities. The two main ways to provide food are through a service counter and through vending machines. The first is more costly (the cost of the food and the labor to cook and serve it and the cost of food being eaten by employees or spoiled in preparation). On the other hand, prepared food provides a great potential for income. Vending machines have great appeal to the facility manager. They are inexpensive (either provided free or leased from a vending company), labor free (the vending company stocks them), available at all times the facility is open, and provide consistent income.

Although most Americans seem partial to junk food, most parents would rather have their children consume more nutritional food such as fruits and juices. Patrons may complain about the selection, but they will buy what is available.

Other Sources of Income

Fund-raising is more often a disappointment than a success, and swimathons, candy selling, and so on can be overdone. Youth nights (when the pool is open for an all-night swim that shows aquatic-theme movies and serves food) can be successful (chapter 9 will discuss activities like this in more detail).

Many private facilities (e.g., the YMCA, Boys Clubs, etc.) depend on contributions from civic groups or the United Fund for a portion of their income. To ensure this continued support, attendance records are vital when trying to convince the group that its contribution helps many people.

EXPENSES

The facility manager should know the facility's cost of operation at all times so that income can be adjusted immediately or expenses reduced to a proper level. Wages, utilities, insurance, and debt retirement are the greatest expense items for all aquatic facilities. These and all other expenses determine the cost per hour of operation (total costs per year divided by the total yearly hours of operation). The resulting figure is used to prepare the budget for the coming year as well as to make current adjustments.

Wages

Normally, wages and related costs are the major expense items. Salaries fluctuate with supply and demand, prevailing economic conditions, and wage standards. If the facility manager's salary is 100%, the other positions would earn proportionately less:

1. Assistant manager, head lifeguard: 85%
2. Instructors, lifeguards: 65% to 70%
3. Water-sanitation specialist: 65% to 95% (depends on employment status, as some are full-time employees)
4. Office manager, bookkeeper: 40% to 60% or minimum hourly wage
5. Maintenance, locker room persons: 35% to 60% or minimum hourly wage

It might seem more economical to employ private teachers on a commission basis, as the savings in payroll taxes and fringe benefits are considerable. Both Sevelle (1984) and Cranch (1984) considered the possibility of employing independent contractors for various jobs in and around the facility. Private companies can be contracted to clean the pool, maintain the building, teach, lifeguard, do the programming, and so on. Essentially, the pool owner would be leasing the building to a private contractor.

This landlord-contractor relationship can be seen in private profit-making sport facilities. The concept might be favored by cities as a means of balancing budgets while still providing aquatic services to citizens. However, in our view, independent contractors, especially teachers and lifeguards, see themselves not as employees of the sponsor but as employees of their independent companies. This independence could cause problems, depending on the professionalism of the employees.

Utilities

Observation of daily operations can often suggest ways to reduce utility bills. For example, one sign of waste is when the water in the showers is so hot that patrons must use cold water when showering. Patrons as well as employees can be careless about leaving lights on, turning up heat needlessly, leaving doors open, and so on; no one really believes that utilities are a great expense. However, when employees and patrons are reminded through memos, notes, signs, and verbal admonitions, they can significantly reduce the amount of the utility bills.

Insurance

Private profit-making facilities often discover that insurance is their single greatest expense. Conversely, a new city pool or lakefront is often covered by an already existing policy. Regardless, insurance is something that is essential to protect the enterprise against monetary loss.

Liability insurance covers the acts of employees (see chapter 5). However, because the cost of insurance keeps rising each year, many cities now cooperate with others to develop joint insurance coverage. In some instances, cities are self-insuring, that is, placing the amount normally paid in premiums into a fund that hopefully will cover the cost of any liability. The main way to control the cost of insurance is to develop and administer an effective risk-management program and by hiring only qualified employees.

Debt Retirement

Debt retirement is a significant cost for private profit-making facilities, but in many city operations it is not charged as a budget item. In theory, the absence of debt repayment means that municipal programs should cost less than private ones, but this is not always the case.

Promotions/Advertising

A private profit-making facility usually allots 2% to 5% of its budget to promotion and advertising, whereas the average public facility usually spends very little. Effective promotion (see chapter 9) will pay for itself in increased revenue and is the reason why some private programs are less expensive than their public counterparts.

Supplies and Equipment

Although supplies and equipment do not represent the major items in a budget, their effect on final expenses is significant. Certain supplies and equipment must be replaced periodically; however, adherence to the following principles of purchasing and issuance almost always results in noticeable savings.

1. *Buy early and according to need:* Early buying means that an item that is not satisfactory can be returned to the dealer for replacement. Purchasing an oversupply of certain items creates a storage problem and ties up a portion of the available money in the budget. An up-to-date inventory will prove invaluable.
2. *Buy official, standard, and quality equipment:* Rules of the governing orga-nizations (FINA, USS, etc.) specify the requirements for items used in competition. Buying inexpensive, low-quality equipment is a false economy.
3. *Buy cautiously:* To avoid choosing inferior products, inspect and (if possible) test samples. Obtain correct measurements before ordering.
4. *Buy according to the policies of the sponsor:* Obtain proper authorization for purchases, purchase only with written orders, inspect all deliveries for correct number and compliance with specifications, and keep a codified record of all purchases. Computer systems can simplify this procedure.
5. *Identify equipment items:* Reduce losses by marking and numbering each item that belongs to the organization.
6. *Assign responsibility for issue:* Make a trustworthy person responsible for issuing equipment.

BUDGET REDUCTION

Sevelle (1984) points out that the budget may call for "no-frills programming" in the future and that there are certain nonfrills (lifeguards, minimum water temperature, slides, etc.) that must be maintained or else there will be no patrons. But there are hidden frills that can be cut (e.g., guard suits, office supplies, and high water temperature). And, if things really become bad, a bare-bones program can be conducted on these guidelines: reduce staff by one third and at the same time increase the number of volunteers, adopt a lower water temperature, reduce administrative supplies, do not replace play equipment unless it is damaged or has become unsafe, postpone a major renovation of the facility, and have repairs and maintenance performed correctly the first time.

SUPPLEMENTAL LEARNING ACTIVITIES

1. If possible, secure an actual budget from an aquatic facility. Compute its hourly cost of operation.

2. Develop a logical budget for an outdoor pool that will be open during the 3-month summer season, offers 2 hours of swim classes per day and 6 hours of recreational swimming per day, and has an average attendance of 75 per hour.

REFERENCES AND SUGGESTED READINGS

Bartling, M. (1985). *Contracting recreation and park services*. Champaign, IL: Management Learning Laboratories.

Bartling, M. (1986a). *Controlling park and recreation costs*. Champaign, IL: Management Learning Laboratories.

Bartling, M. (1986b). *Cost-cutting strategies for the park and recreation agency*. Champaign, IL: Management Learning Laboratories.

Beaulieu, C. (1986). Cost recovery in aquatic programs. *National Aquatics Journal* (Winter), **2**(1), 10-13.

Cranch, B. (1984). Programming for profit. In J. Bangay (Ed.), *Aquatic programming: Reaching today's market* (pp. 23-24). Toronto, Ontario, Canada: The Royal Life Saving Society Canada.

Donohoe, M. (1978). Pool management and financing. In B. Empleton (Ed.), *New horizons in aquatics* (pp. 83-90). Indianapolis, IN: Council for National Cooperation in Aquatics.

Gabrielsen, M. (Ed.). (1987). *Swimming pools: A guide to their planning, design, and operation* (pp. 11-14). Champaign, IL: Human Kinetics.

Harden, J. (1986). *Revenue management*. Champaign, IL: Management Learning Laboratories.

Kelsey, C., & Gray, H. (1986). *Budget process*. Champaign, IL: Management Learning Laboratories.

Sevelle, T. (1984). No-frills programming. In J. Bangay (Ed.), *Aquatic programming: Reaching today's market* (pp. 25-26). Toronto, Ontario, Canada: The Royal Life Saving Society Canada.

Chapter 8

STAFFING AND MANAGING

Hiring Employees
Job Performance
Firing Employees
Management Concepts and Strategies
Management Styles
Effective Management Techniques
Record Keeping
Supplemental Learning Activities

Staffing, budgeting, and programing are three interdependent components of a successful aquatic operation. The staff must offer the programs to entice patrons to pay for services, and the income must be adequate to hire a staff. The budget establishes financial limitations, especially those related to labor. The job titles of essential workers begin to emerge as the budget becomes firm, but the exact number of employees cannot be predetermined and even then is subject to change once the program is under way.

The goal is to hire persons who are both qualified (at least minimally) and enthusiastic toward the overall program. Obviously, the technical competence that is gained through specialized training and experience is expected of employees. Ideally, they should be capable not only of performing

their jobs at a high level but also of teaching others to do the same.

In a superior program, all employees complement one another and work together harmoniously. The degree of harmony attained depends not only on the competence of the administrator but also on the employees' understanding of the activities offered and on their willingness to assume responsibility for improving the program. Each employee must appreciate the objectives of the program and be dedicated to accomplishing those objectives.

Each employee will be responsible for specific assigned duties, but all staff members must share responsibility in at least three major areas: safety, public relations, and maintenance. Specifically, each employee should be continually aware of the need for

1. safety and security while trying to avoid negligent actions;
2. public relations, that is, working to create a favorable impression when dealing with the clientele, especially when controlling the behavior of those who use the facility; and
3. maintenance and protection of facilities and equipment, which is accomplished by actively aiding in improving the maintenance of services and the general appearance of the premises.

HIRING EMPLOYEES

Hiring practices of public agencies must conform to certain legal requirements—job descriptions, adequate recruitment periods, nondiscrimination policies—that vary according to the job. Those involved in hiring should be aware of the current legal requirements concerning the advertising of positions, the selection of applicants to be interviewed, the interview itself, and the employment process in general.

Job Description

The hiring process begins with a job description, or a listing of the qualifications expected in the employee. The roles of the facility manager and the aquatic staff members differ in both scope and responsibility. All personnel should be qualified by education, experience, and personality to develop and conduct sound programs, but the wide-ranging duties of the manager demand a higher level of expertise in a variety of areas.

Almost always, the facility manager once held an aquatic specialist position. The manager, in addition to being a specialist in one or more aquatic areas, must now be knowledgeable about all aspects of the program (recreation, instruction, needs of special groups, and competition) and fully understand equipment, safety systems, lifeguarding, and water sanitation. Equally important is the ability to manage people, which is both an art and a science. Table 8.1 presents a job description for the facility manager (normally the first person hired).

The Hiring Process

The hiring process includes the following eight steps:

1. *Advertise the position:* Send the job description to persons on the employment list, put ads in papers, contact other aquatic agencies or colleges with aquatic specialist programs, and so on.
2. *Construct an application form:* Obtain personal information, aquatic certifications and experience, and names and phone numbers of references.
3. *Interview selected applicants:* Designate a committee of supervisors and representative employers. Only those questions related to the job in question may be asked in the interview. The basic criteria are ''Is this information really important to job performance? Is it necessary to ask questions in this area?'' Marital status, religion, spouse's occupation, membership in social organizations, birthplace, and height and weight are commonly asked, but it is illegal to do so. Richardson (1987) presents helpful information in this regard.
4. *Administer tests if necessary:* For example, water performance tests are essential for lifeguard candidates.

Table 8.1
QUALIFICATIONS AND DUTIES OF THE FACILITY MANAGER

Qualifications

Maturity and experience: Must be at least 21 years old, or have 2 years experience as assistant manager. Must be recognized as a facility manager by the Aquatic Council of AAHPERD and/or have appropriate certification of other recognized professional aquatic organizations.

Current certifications: Must be certified in lifeguarding (which includes CPR, and first-aid) and pool operation or appropriate course for an open water facility. Other certifications (e.g., scuba, adapted aquatics, coaching, etc.) are desirable.

Duties

Administration: Makes decisions regarding program organization/administration, facility and equipment operation, risk-management implementation, lifeguarding.

Supervision: Actively supervises (or assigns assistant to supervise) lifeguarding, first-aid treatment, and instruction.

Management skills

Personnel: Hires and trains staff, hears grievances, establishes work schedules, and evaluates job performance.

Safety: Establishes emergency procedures and educates staff concerning liability and negligence.

Financial: Develops and follows a realistic budget.

Program: Organizes a total program and monitors progress toward attainment of program objectives.

Maintenance: Oversees facility and water sanitation operations, equipment repair, and preventive maintenance.

Public relations: Creates and maintains good public relations and deals tactfully with complaints and problems.

Observation of prospective teachers in actual teaching situations is desirable though seldom feasible.

5. *Select successful applicant(s):* Evaluate each applicant on the basis of the information gained from the application form, the interview, test scores, and comments from references. Pay special attention to the comments by former employers or teachers, as the superior candidate will receive superlative comments and the average one more neutral remarks.

6. *Rank the candidates in order of hiring preference:* In the event the top person declines the offer, the next person can quickly be contacted without the necessity of holding another committee meeting.

7. *Contact the successful applicant and complete hiring details (when to report, where, etc.).*

8. *Notify all applicants:* After filing the applications of the unsuccessful applicants, notify these people that the job has been filled. In any written or oral discussion with any of the unsuccessful applicants, emphasize the superior qualifications of the person selected as opposed to any possible deficiencies in those not selected.

Once the facility manager is hired, he or she usually directs the search for subsequent employees. In a seasonal facility, maintenance and water sanitation jobs are often combined with the guard-instructor-office positions.

Volunteer Workers

Many aquatic facilities seek the service of volunteers primarily as instructors for various swimming and diving classes. In most cases, this is beneficial both to the facility (which gets competent instructors at no additional cost) and to the volunteer (who can maintain teaching skills and certification). Skillful managers are able to attract many qualified volunteers because they understand the reasons why such persons participate: "People volunteer essentially for accomplishment, recognition, interest and challenge, responsibility and socialization. They quit for lack of time, a loss of interest in the job or project, or because of family responsibilities" (Kent, 1987, p. 27).

Ideally, volunteers should receive the same preservice and in-service training as do regular employees. Requiring such a time commitment might reduce the number of volunteers interested in working for the facility, but responsible positions (i.e., instructors, lifeguards, etc.) must be filled with only qualified persons.

Volunteers expect to receive no remuneration, but wise managers make sure that some benefits are available. Such "perks" as reduced costs for lessons or free passes to the facility for the immediate family cost very little, and the loss of income is far less than paying for more instructors.

JOB PERFORMANCE

Successful programs are not necessarily found in excellent facilities. Or, to put it another way, people are more important than their surroundings. Competent managers use both in-service training and evaluation as ongoing practices to develop superior programs.

Orientation

An orientation program is customary for new employees because certain procedures and customs must be followed. Because these procedures and customs affect all the programs and personnel, it is essential that new employees receive this information.

In-Service Training

Because of the danger inherent in aquatic programs (especially drownings and paralyzing accidents), minimal in-service training must include the periodic rehearsal of emergency procedures. As described in chapter 6, this normally includes lifeguard rescue skills, first aid, crowd control, and response procedures related to notifying the rescue squad.

Ideally, in-service training programs not only should include safety procedures but should also touch on every aspect of the program, especially the teaching function. It is logical to schedule sessions on different teaching methods, on the use of new equipment, and the maintenance of equipment at the site.

Because of legal liability, it is essential that records be kept of the in-service sessions. The date, the participants, and the exact material covered should be recorded and kept by the facility manager.

Employee Review

Employees should be given periodic feedback on their job performance. Unless a review is officially scheduled, it can be easily overlooked. A review of job performance should be done for new employees during the fourth and eighth weeks of their employment and at least every 6 months thereafter.

A job performance form should be constructed that includes a listing of the qualitative factors vital to the job (e.g., attitude, knowledge, work habits, and relations with patrons and other employees). In some cases, quantitative factors are reviewed (e.g., the number of students who return for the next class). A rating scale (1-10) is recommended as is additional space for written comments.

The immediate supervisor (e.g., head lifeguard) should meet with each employee (lifeguard) under his or her control. Before the meeting, one copy of the review form should be filled out by the supervisor and another by the employee. Both discuss the items, and at the conclusion of the meeting a summary paper is signed by both to indicate that the material was discussed. The report, which is confidential, is then placed in the employee's files. Killian (1982)

points out that the rating should be for the overall job performance and not be unduly influenced by one or two relatively minor incidents.

Employee Evaluation

Evaluation means setting performance standards, measuring the results, and then comparing the difference between the two. An evaluation should be done for all employees at least annually.

Employee evaluation, if not planned beforehand, can be an unpleasant task. At the beginning of the season, the manager and employee need to develop a list of performance standards (e.g., percentage of students passing beginning swimming classes, a certain increase in the membership of the USS team, the average number of persons who complete each sailing course, the water quality ratings, etc.). This form and records of periodic reviews are the basis on which job performance is judged.

Successful managers prepare for the evaluation by inspecting reviews already completed and by making informal comments and observations throughout the year. The final evaluation report should contain no surprises; mediocre employees will have been alerted to their deficiencies by several tactics, for example, changes in duty assignment, forced attendance at extra in-service training programs, more frequent job reviews, and so on.

FIRING EMPLOYEES

It is the duty of the immediate supervisor to recommend the discharge of an employee if a situation warrants. The key phrase is "if the situation warrants." It is preferred that, when a problem is noted, a written record be made and the specific problem discussed with the employee. Suggestions (or orders) are given so that the situation does not happen again. If it does or is so serious (e.g., a lifeguard not being at his or her assigned post) that a second chance is not appropriate, then firing is necessary. Firing an employee must be for a just cause and not because of a personal bias held by the superior. Especially in public agencies, firing procedures must be followed precisely to prevent a lawsuit. A confidential written record of the entire situation, including minutes of any meetings, should be kept by the facility manager.

MANAGEMENT CONCEPTS AND STRATEGIES

The manager's role is easily defined: to use all human and material resources effectively to meet the goals of the organization. Decisions concerning material resources (what to order, how much to pay, etc.) are relatively easy to make, whereas decisions about staff are more difficult because of the emotional involvement of both parties.

A harmonious relationship among the staff is developed, not foreordained. In a typical aquatic operation, many regular employees have responsibilities that involve directing others (being the head lifeguard from whom other guards take direction, being a teacher assisted by aides, or being the full-time maintenance person working with part-time help). In short, each regular employee is, in a sense, a manager. In the end, however, it is the facility manager who is responsible for the overall operation and who establishes the management style followed by the group. Because an aquatic program involves people (employees and patrons), there often are no absolute rules of management that hold true in every instance. The discussion that follows contains guidelines rather than rules.

A basic concept of management is that someone is in charge! This implies that a chain of command is established and that employees are familiar with it. A diagram (Figure 8.1) is an effective way to ensure that employees understand who has the responsibility and authority to make decisions at various levels.

To achieve the desired goals, successful managers should adhere to the following strategies:

1. *Delegate tasks and responsibilities:* When the workload is evenly distributed, everyone in the group feels better because no one is doing someone else's job. The supervisor is freed from less important tasks. The identity and importance of the subordinate is thus enhanced.
2. *Communicate with subordinates:* The subordinate knows what is expected, feels free to ask questions without fear or embarrassment, can suggest alternatives, and can disagree or complain within reason.
3. *Motivate staff members:* Each subordinate must be inspired to put forth maximum effort and to take pride in total staff achievement. Motivation occurs in various ways, and, contrary to popular opinion, more money will not necessarily motivate employees.
4. *Praise in public, criticize in private:* The quality of a subordinate's work

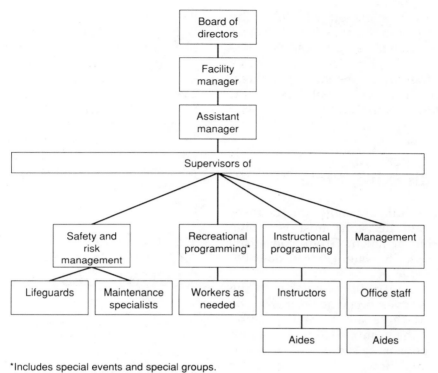

*Includes special events and special groups.

Figure 8.1.   Typical chain of command in an aquatic facility.

is often in direct proportion to the praise and acknowledgment received; however, being embarrassed before one's peers can lead to humiliation and resentment.

5. *Be sensitive to the reactions of each subordinate:* Pleasant surroundings and satisfying working conditions result in greater effort; demonstrating interest in the problems and aspirations of subordinates will foster loyalty and admiration.

MANAGEMENT STYLES

Management styles are a reflection of the basic personality of the top administrator.

Whatever style (or combinations thereof) is employed, it must suit the manager. Many aquatic managers use a combination of the three styles described by Killian (1985).

The Directive Style

In this style, decisions are made by the manager or superior, and input from subordinates is not encouraged or even welcome. In aquatics, the directive manager "runs a tight ship" and is recognized for the efficient, organized manner in which the organization functions. Classes start exactly on time, lifeguards are always at their assigned station, and preventive maintenance is done on schedule. The manager tends to remain somewhat aloof and distant from the employees. He or she is regarded as very competent by superiors but as unfriendly by the staff. The directive manager wins respect but does not win friends with the staff.

The Democratic, or Nondirective, Style

Here there is little direction from the manager, so group decisions must determine the action to be taken. Group consensus is not necessarily sought, but it does become the mode of action. In aquatics, the democratic manager is popular with the staff because everyone who desires can be a leader. If there are several "natural leaders" in the group, each in a different area of responsibility, a great deal of teamwork results. However, because of the numerous programs and persons involved, the democratic system sometimes results in chaos, as no one wants to make an unpopular decision.

The Interactive Style

In this style, management fosters involvement with all employees and seeks input on matters that affect the organization. Routine matters are standardized. Although group consensus is deliberately sought, management retains the responsibility of making the final decisions.

Preferred Style

Inasmuch as the aquatic program should employ competent and motivated workers, it stands to reason that the interactive style is preferred. This style involves all employees (or at least a representative group), with the result that decisions from managers are more accepted by employees. Even though all employees should be motivated toward achieving the objectives of the group, "it should be remembered that individuals have the option of how much effort they put forth and how much support will be given to management's proposals" (Killian, 1985, p. 23).

EFFECTIVE MANAGEMENT TECHNIQUES

By definition, management involves the effective use of both human and material resources, and successful managers can use at least four strategies to achieve this. One has been discussed—the necessity for developing flexible yet effective guidelines for the review and evaluation of employees. A second strategy involves planning for every detail that can be standardized (e.g., standard operating procedures). A third strategy calls for involving employees in solving problems, and a fourth provides for the resolution of conflicts among both employees and patrons.

Standard Operating Procedures

Standard procedures for every possible situation are written in an operations manual, which is found in every superior facility. Without such a manual, supervisors or managers must try to remember the information. Although they may accomplish tasks on time, they sometimes merely react to situations rather than prevent them.

The operations manual is divided into sections, each dealing with a separate aspect (e.g., water maintenance, small-craft repair, equipment purchase, etc.). Depending on the item, employees might have some flexibility, but basically the manual should be followed as written. Certain procedures (e.g., those related to safety regulations, emergency action plans, water sanitation, etc.) must be followed exactly.

The manual (or at least sections of it) should be available to employees and in some cases a copy of the entire manual given to each. Periodic reviews and revisions are done with primary input from those employees most closely related to the area under review or revision.

Advisory Groups

One effective way to accomplish the interactive (also called participatory) style of management is to organize advisory groups. (Currently, this technique is called "Quality Circles" after the Japanese techniques of improving quality in auto production by involving groups of workers to consider and then solve quality problems.) In an aquatic setting, the intent is to have the group consider or identify a problem connected with the organization (e.g., how to keep the locker room clean, how to get patrons to return PFDs to the proper rack after a canoeing session, or how to improve the facility's accessibility to handicapped persons). Topics for discussion can be suggested by either management or the group. An unstructured approach permits the group to use various techniques (brainstorming, committees, general discussion) to examine the problem and recommend solutions. Because the group is small (3 to 10 members), there may be several such groups in one facility. It is best if the group meets on a regular basis and for no more than 1 hour per session. Both full- and part-time employees should be paid for attending; the few dollars expended will be repaid by the problems solved and the improved zeal of the workers.

Advisory groups are great aids to managers, especially in facilities that sponsor many different activities. Group thought about ongoing or new programs and solutions to recurring problems can lead to a much better organization.

If an advisory committee is not used, one staff member should be designated as the liaison between the facility and each special interest aquatic group (e.g., scuba club, USS age-group team, etc.). This role of liaison should be a part of their job description and not a task that is added to their already crowded list of duties.

Conflict Resolution

In any organization, there are bound to be disagreements between employees, management and employees, and employees and patrons. Some conflicts are real, whereas others can be perceived by the individual but not by the rest of the group.

If the disagreement is related to standard operating procedures or organizational policy, the directives of management must be followed. This is not to say that policies are never changed or even discussed but only that, until the policy is changed (preferably by the interactive management style), a previously decided issue should be dealt with in a certain way. For example, if the policy is that all canoeists must wear life jackets, then each employee must enforce that rule, irrespective of personal feelings.

Conflict resolution between persons is a more difficult matter. Steps include (a) awareness of the difficulty, usually noticed by observation or by complaints brought by employees or patrons (in some cases, job performance deteriorates so dramatically that the conflict is apparent); (b) getting the facts and then talking directly to the person; and (c) taking action, as failure to do so could leave the impression that the superior is weak in enforcing directives.

Most conflicts can be prevented by good communication, by being fair, and by everyone knowing what is expected of them. However, conflict resolution must be a process that is planned and periodically evaluated.

Sometimes conflicts simply cannot be resolved at a particular level. Provisions for the subordinate to "go over the head" of the supervisor should be available. Subordinates should clearly understand that the responsibility for final decisions rests with persons occupying appropriate management positions. If there is still disagreement after a final decision is made, resignation or dismissal of the subordinate may be the only solution. A disgruntled employee is the "bad apple" that spoils the situation for all concerned.

RECORD KEEPING

It is imperative that records of all aspects of the operation (income and expenses, accidents, class details, personnel records, etc.) be kept in an organized and secure manner. Rarely should the facility manager or the aquatic specialists do the filing of records, make copies of class rosters, and personally supervise every detail of the office. But managers are bound by duty to the sponsoring group to see that records are accurately prepared and maintained.

SUPPLEMENTAL LEARNING ACTIVITIES

1. Secure an application for employment at a local aquatic facility and complete it. Would you be qualified for a position?

2. Talk to an employee of a facility. What are the best features of his or her job? How is he or she motivated to do a better job?

3. Interview a facility manager. Did he or she lack any managerial skills when they were employed? If so, how was this deficiency overcome? What are the greatest problems this facility manager faces?

REFERENCES AND SUGGESTED READINGS

Achieving quality. (1986, September). *The Press*, p. 26.

Bellenger, D. (1985, February). Employee evaluation: A how-to guide. *Sports Merchandiser*, p. 6.

Kent, J. (1987). Volunteer management. In C. Wilson (Ed.), *The world of lifesaving* (pp. 27-28). Toronto, Ontario, Canada: The Royal Life Saving Society Canada.

Killian, R. (1982, August). How to review. *Sporting Goods Dealer*, p. 23.

Killian, R. (1985, July). Managing inter-activity. *Sporting Goods Dealer*, p. 23.

Killian, R. (1987, May). Resolving conflicts. *Sporting Goods Dealer*, pp. 16-17.

Richardson, D. (1987, May). Test your knowledge of interviewing. *The Press*, p. 11.

Chapter 9

PROGRAM DEVELOPMENT AND PROMOTION

Responsibilities for Program Development
Activity Selection
Aquatic Program Promotion
Corporate Sponsorship
Program Evaluation
Supplemental Learning Activities

In aquatics, the programming process refers to the selection, promotion, and evaluation of all aquatic experiences offered at a facility. The programming process is a continual one, with activities being periodically monitored to see whether they still meet the needs of patrons. Likewise, new activities are introduced as the result of this ongoing process.

This chapter deals with the programming process, whereas chapters 10, 11, and 12 discuss in greater detail the organizational elements of the recreational, instructional, and special group categories of aquatics.

RESPONSIBILITIES FOR PROGRAM DEVELOPMENT

Sponsors of aquatic programs have different emphases regarding the use of their facility for recreation, instruction, competition, and special groups. Figure 9.1 illustrates the approximate time devoted to each.

Although the sponsoring group may have some basic ideas about appropriate

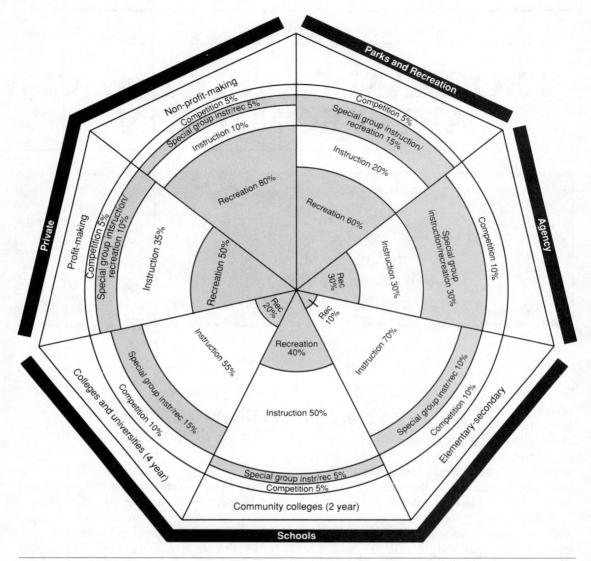

Figure 9.1. Sponsoring groups and approximate time devoted to their program facets. *Note.* Adapted from M. A. Orphan, personal communication, 1980. Used by permission.

aquatic activities that meet its overall goals, the aquatic manager and his or her staff do the actual program development. The task is easier if the facilities are first-rate, but the efforts of the staff are far more important than are the facilities. The assistant man-

ager and the appropriate aquatic specialists (lifeguards, instructors, etc.) are often assigned the primary responsibility for developing a particular program. Once it is developed, the program can be monitored on a daily and budgetary basis by an aquatic specialist, but the ultimate responsibility remains with the manager and his or her assistant.

ACTIVITY SELECTION

Two basic issues must be resolved before activity selection can begin: (a) What are the goals of the sponsor? (b) Will the total aquatic program be self-supporting, or profit making, or allowed to operate at a deficit? These two issues cannot be separated, as each directly influences the other. For the purposes of this text, we will assume that the sponsoring group has determined that (a) the overall goal is to use each part of the facility for as many activities as can be safely accommodated and that (b) the budget for the total program (not necessarily each activity) must be balanced annually.

Research

The selection of activities is preceded by research and market awareness (Moore, 1984). Research data, beginning with information gleaned from the population base of those who will use the particular facility, are usually gathered through questionnaires and personal interviews. Basic information to seek includes the ages and number of potential patrons, income levels, family composition, location and types of living sites, and available transportation to and from the facility. Equally important are the desires of the potential patrons: Exactly what kinds of activities do they want?

At the same time, the patrons (if any) of the present facility need to be queried. Why do they come to the facility? How often do they come? What activities should be added? What is good and what is bad about the present programs? This aspect of research should be ongoing, with suggestion boxes and activity evaluations being constantly monitored.

Another source of data is knowing the aquatic activities and experiences offered at other facilities, especially if the situations are similar. Visitation, talking with colleagues at professional meetings, and attendance at seminars and conferences will almost always suggest useful enrichment activities or ideas for promotion.

Although the main purpose of this research is for immediate aid in developing programs, it also helps plan for the future. This is especially true when capital expenditures are involved. For example, adding a wading pool or slides, constructing a sailboat facility, and providing access for the handicapped all have to be planned well in advance. A programming plan for the next 1 to 3 years will prove beneficial.

Market Awareness

The proliferation of fitness clubs and private sports facilities is an indication that the public is favorably disposed toward certain activities and will quite often pay substantial sums of money to belong to a facility that caters to their needs and desires. For example, in the past only the wealthy were members of athletic or yacht clubs; today, persons of various income levels will stretch their budgets to become members of sporting groups that have pools, sailboats, waterskiing facilities, and so on. These groups attract the paying public because they offer, for example, open use of facilities (e.g., lap lanes at all hours), miniclasses in popular subjects (e.g., scuba and snorkeling), extended hours of operation, social gatherings, and food and drink services.

To succeed, an aquatic facility needs to attract patrons, often at the expense of its competitors. Doing this requires an awareness of the features of other local facilities.

The Selection Process

Following the research and market awareness aspects, the staff begins to select activities. Each segment of the facility (open-water area, diving well, wading pool, picnic area, etc.) should be examined, preferably in a brainstorming session that involves the whole staff. Brainstorming (hearing suggestions without any initial judgments as to their feasibility) will prove invaluable. Persons in the brainstorming session should be cognizant of the research and market awareness data that have been gathered. Likewise, they should realize that adults make up the greatest segment of the population and that the declining birthrate indicates that persons over 18 years of age will be the majority of patrons in the foreseeable future (Cranch, 1984).

To provide an example of program development, Blaicher and Stansbury (1984) reported that a waterfront staff developed four major program components: (a) water-based activities such as public swimming, lessons in swimming and lifeguarding, small craft (sailboard, water ski, scuba, etc.), and special events such as canoe races, across-lake swims, and lifeguard competitions; (b) beach-based activities, which encompassed facilities for volleyball, tetherball, and building sand castles; (c) land-based activities, exemplified by antique boat shows, arts/crafts exhibits, concerts, and cookouts; and (d) such winter activities as ice-skating, ice fishing, and snowmobiling.

If the staff thinks beyond the traditional program of recreational swimming, swim-team practice and meets, and swimming lessons, this kind of program development can take place in a pool setting.

AQUATIC PROGRAM PROMOTION

Aquatic program promotion implies the development of strategies for getting the public to take part in at least one aspect of the total program. The rise of private profit-making fitness and sport clubs attests to the fact that persons are willing to pay for programs that meet their needs. However, unless the program is known to the public, they will not attend. Effective promotional techniques try to make programs known to the public. The amount of time, money, and effort spent on marketing is not necessarily the same for each segment of the program. Nevertheless, a planned approach is the ultimate factor in determining which segments of the program will prosper most.

Usual Promotion Efforts

Except for the private profit-making clubs, promotion has traditionally been neglected in aquatic programming. The usual approach has been to rely on public announcements and word-of-mouth publicity to entice participation. News releases containing the hours and admissions charges for various activities are sent to the local newspaper, the radio and television stations, and sometimes the schools. Occasionally, a feature story on a special event (a regatta or a synchronized-swimming show) is written by someone involved in the event. Once or twice a year, brochures or flyers are distributed. But because it takes skill to compose these stories, the effort is infrequently made.

Even today, few aquatic persons (including managers) have expertise in promoting aquatics, nor do they think it is important. Instead, they depend on popular activities and good facilities to draw patrons or use the excuse that their older facility just cannot compete with the newer ones. Because the sponsor provides the facilities and pays the salaries, managers (especially those at public facilities) think that attendance and/or income is of little concern. But today, nothing could be further from the truth.

Responsibility for Promotions

As with programming, the ultimate responsibility for promotions rests with the facility manager. Because many managers have limited experience in this area, they assign the duties to their assistant or to other staff members, and often the results are not exemplary. Better solutions are to hire a part-time consultant to provide guidelines for the overall promotion efforts or for a particular project. In either case, the consultant will have two responsibilities: (a) to complete the specific assignment and (b) to educate the manager and other key staff about the principles of effective promotion.

Communication and Motivation

The basic strategy in promotion is to communicate with the public and through that process to motivate them to participate in a specific program. In aquatics, communication with the public takes three forms: interpretation, publicity, and public relations. Although these are discussed separately in this section, the distinction between them is often unclear.

Interpretation

The purpose of interpretation is to explain one or more aspects of the program. Examples of interpretation would be periodic written or oral reports to the sponsor, articles for the local media, and brochures explaining all facets of the program. Often, a demonstration or exhibition at the facility will adequately accomplish this purpose.

Publicity

Publicity is used to generate and sustain public interest in specific events and, ultimately, to persuade the public to use the facility.

Ongoing publicity is a task that should be accepted by a qualified person, either the manager or another full-time staff member. This person is responsible for writing and submitting stories on a regular basis to the local media. There should be a written schedule that indicates exactly when each activity of the program (swim instruction, recreational canoeing, scuba club instruction) should be publicized. Each activity should be publicized at least annually in either an interpretive or a publicity mode.

Newspapers and radio are the most common publicity outlets. However, because reporters often are primarily interested only in the unusual (programs or persons), any publicity for regular program or "common" events (swim meets, programs for adults, etc.) must be prepared by the group involved. The publicity must then be submitted in a polished written form because in most cases it will be read on the air or printed exactly the way it was submitted.

Public Relations

The purpose of public relations is to earn and keep the goodwill of current and potential patrons. The goal is to create a favorable image so that the particular facility or program achieves a good reputation. "A satisfied customer is the best advertisement" may be considered the unofficial slogan of successful programs. Public relations is not so much a listing of specific procedures as it is treating patrons as welcome guests. Good programs, effective promotions, superior and motivated employees, and cleanliness and proper maintenance of the facility will, in the long run, develop the desired reputation.

A Successful Promotion

Beaulieu (1986) cited a promotion in a metropolitan recreation pool that shows how careful planning and thoughtful publicity can result in a good public relations effort. A "dive-in movie" was held, the purpose of which was to get people into the facility, not necessarily to make a great amount of money. Underwater lighting was used with adequate deck light and minimal bleacher light. Several speakers, instead of the main public address system, made the sound more audible. A regular projector showed the movie across the pool's width, focusing on a screen made of white sheets that were sewn together. Safety was paramount: more lifeguards were employed (some were underwater in

scuba gear), parents were asked to be in the water with their children, and staff members were clearly identifiable by wearing special arm bands and hats. Life rafts and PFDs were available. Publicity included press releases, advertisements in class brochures, paid radio ads featuring theme music, and newspaper listings in the special events section. Needless to say, the evening was a great success.

Dive-in movies, using such films as *Jaws*, *The Sinking of the Titanic*, and *Yellow Submarine*, have proven very popular. Before you undertake the project for the first time, however, we advise either consulting those who have done one or referring to articles such as that by Beaulieu (1986).

CORPORATE SPONSORSHIP

There are specialized consulting and educational companies that can aid sport administrators in developing strategies to raise money and assistance for their organizations. The basic idea is that "you have to give to get"; that is, you must offer potential benefactors something in return for their help (Wilkinson, 1987).

Some events are so important or large that outside help must be sought to ensure their success. For example, to attempt a massive learn-to-swim campaign, a regatta, or a local "Olympics" with the present staff and facilities might be impossible. In these cases corporate sponsorship is essential.

Staunton (1987) pointed out that preplanning is essential before approaching a potential sponsor. Statements must be formulated that indicate why support is needed, exactly what is to be done, and why it cannot be done with present resources. It is also helpful to know a potential sponsor's needs (e.g., an increase in the sales of a particular product, improvement in the sponsor's public image, or enhancement of the quality of life in the community).

The staff develops a list of the benefits to a sponsoring group and identifies or creates marketing elements (products or events) that can be sold to sponsors in return for their support. Examples of such elements include sponsorships of all or part of the event, logos and licensing of products that can be sold, television commercials, souvenir programs, and concessions.

When the presentation is made to each potential sponsor, the benefits to both parties should be stated clearly. Then specific requests for assistance are made, whether for money, labor (executive, clerical, or technical), the use of a computer, the dissemination of literature, the purchase of specific equipment, and so on. An agreement is then reached as to what each party will do. Examples of corporate sponsorship for various aquatic programs follow.

Example 1: Large City, Various Aquatic Programs

An aquatic operations specialist for a large metropolitan recreation district in the United States obtained help from a soft-drink company, radio and television stations, and an oil company to sponsor learn-to-swim programs, ditch safety, and competitive swimming teams and meets (see Waters, 1987). Beginning months before any program was to start, he identified potential sponsors such as local agencies with national programs, local small organizations with consumer products, and banks and other financial institutions. In his presentation to various potential sponsors, he listed the benefits of sponsorship.

1. *Exposure:* The sponsor's names would appear on all printed materials, thus assuring constant product exposure and promotion.
2. *Sales:* The participants, primarily youth, have considerable discretionary spending money.
3. *Repeated exposure:* The sponsor's names will be prominently displayed at the pools.
4. *Public service image:* Sponsors will receive recognition for money and services donated, thus enhancing their public image.

Depending on the particular company, each sponsor was asked to provide money, services, and/or goods that could be used to obtain publicity and exposure that the aquatic program could not get on its own. As a result, the program benefited from billboards on the streets, prizes for special events, printed award records, printed flyers, bus billboards, and radio and television coverage.

Example 2: Regional Aquatic Festival

Baley (1987) reported on the success of one group that followed the marketing advice of Wilkinson (1987). After identifying the needs (objectives) for a local "Aquarama" (annual beach festival), specific goals were created (see Table 9.1). Following the "give to get" principle, eight specific marketing elements were chosen (see Table 9.2). An action plan for each of these was developed and implemented (see Table 9.3).

Table 9.1

OBJECTIVES FOR AQUARAMA BEACH FESTIVAL— "FUND-RAISING AND FUN IN THE SUN"

1. To profile the RLSSC at peak of aquatic season.
2. To offer the "Life Saving Challenge" to public on a populated beach.
3. To offer Beach Festival Activities to attract people.
4. To generate revenue for the RLSSC Water Rescue Services.
5. To further develop volunteers' leadership skills.

Note. From *The World of Lifesaving* (p. 20) published by The Royal Life Saving Society Canada. Reprinted with the permission of the publisher.

Table 9.2

MARKETING ELEMENTS FOR AQUARAMA BEACH FESTIVAL

Sponsorship	Beach volleyball
	Hawaii raffle
	Fashion show
	Heritage 85
	Pledged lake swim
Public relations	Sport marketing production
	Celebrities
	Television
	Radio
	Weekly newspaper
Promotions	Beach festival activities
Fund-raising	Heritage 85
	Hawaii raffle
	Pledged lake swim
Gambling	Hawaii raffle
Souvenir programs	Life saving challenge
	Pledged lake swim

(Cont.)

Table 9.2 (Cont.)

Direct mail	Invitation to target groups
Effective presentations	Corporate sponsors Regina Beach town council

Note. From *The World of Lifesaving* (p. 20) published by The Royal Life Saving Society Canada. Reprinted with the permission of the publisher.

Table 9.3

AQUARAMA: MARKETING ELEMENT—PRESENTATIONS

Products and activities	How	Where	When	Who
Before				
RLSSC AGM	Marketing presentation	Saskatoon	March	Fundraising
RLSSC national conference	Event presentation	NS	May	Pub & Prom
Reps workshop	Marketing presentation	Camp	May	Fundraising
Town council meeting	Event approval	RB	May	Aquarama Ch
Sport conference	Marketing illustration	Reg	June	Aquarama
Corporate sponsors	Proposals/meetings	Office	June	Fundraising
During				
After				

Note. From The World of Lifesaving (p. 20) published by The Royal Life Saving Society Canada. Reprinted with the permission of the publisher.

Table 9.4

POSSIBLE OBJECTIVES FOR AQUATIC PROGRAMS

Recreational swimming
1. Lap swimming will be possible at least 80% of the total time the facility is open.
2. Attendance at the swimming beach will be increased 5% because of the five special events to be scheduled.
3. Reserved space for parent-tot play in the wading pool will be available at least 3 hours per week, to include morning, afternoon, and early evening hours. An average attendance of five parent-tots is expected.

Springboard diving
1. At least one board of each height will be available for public use during open recreation hours.
2. If the diving club has 25 members (or more), it will have the option of renting the diving well for up to 6 hours per week.

Instruction
1. At least 675 beginners (all ages) will earn certificates this year.
2. One lifeguarding class will be held every 3 months.

Snorkeling/scuba
1. A supervised snorkeling area, complete with underwater objects, will be open for 2 hours per day during the summer season.
2. Supervised time for individual scuba practice in the diving well will be available at least 2 hours per week.

Small craft
1. A year-round boat launching site at the lake, maintained at taxpayer expense, will be operational by June 1.

Swim team
1. By August 1, the swim team membership (age group 8 to 10) will increase by 10% over the total of last August 1.
2. At least 90% of the regular (4 hours per week) swimmers will record personal best times in at least one event by May 31.

PROGRAM EVALUATION

The organization of the aquatic program begins with the formulation of goals and objectives and concludes with their periodic evaluation. Evaluation should begin at the lowest level; that is, specialists should submit an annual report to their immediate supervisors that comments on the personnel and programs in relation to the written objectives. The supervisors then evaluate the specialists, and the sponsoring group evaluates the manager for progress toward the goals.

Many facility managers believe that evaluation relates only to pass/fail judgments of students in classes, but this is not so. Program evaluation (judgments based on measurable objectives) is the logical concluding process of program development, leading to the retention, revision, elimination, or inauguration of new activities. Without objectives, a program has neither direction nor a way to evaluate its worth.

Objectives should be stated in such a way that they can be measured easily; this means that the objectives should state clearly what must be done, under what conditions it is to be done, and how well it must be done (for examples of appropriate objectives, see Table 9.4).

SUPPLEMENTAL LEARNING ACTIVITIES

1. Interview a facility manager. How does he or she justify each activity offered—on the basis of attendance, income, public relations, tradition, or what?

2. Compare the activities offered by a local private facility (e.g., health club, home owner's pool, marina, etc.) with a similar public facility. Are there differences in the number of activities offered, in the types of activities offered, and in the cost for the patrons?

3. What kinds of promotion activities are done at a local public pool or beach? Compare these with promotions done by a private facility.

4. If possible, interview someone who has secured services or funds from an outside sponsor. How was it done? What did the benefactor receive in return?

REFERENCES AND SUGGESTED READINGS

Baley, R.R. (1987). Marketing for money: An aquatic illustration. In C. Wilson (Ed.), *The world of lifesaving* (pp. 19-22). Toronto, Ontario, Canada: The Royal Life Saving Society Canada.

Beaulieu, C. (1986). Cost recovery in aquatic programs. *National Aquatics Journal* (Winter), **2**(1), 10-11.

Blaicher, J., & Stansbury, J. (1984). Waterfronts—your fun in the sun. In J. Bangay (Ed.), *Aquatic programming: Reaching today's market* (pp. 32-35). Toronto, Ontario, Canada: The Royal Life Saving Society Canada.

Cranch, B. (1984). Programming for profit. In J. Bangay (Ed.), *Aquatic programming: Reaching today's market* (pp. 23-24). Toronto, Ontario, Canada: The Royal Life Saving Society Canada.

Hewitt, M. (1984). Programming ideas for adults. In J. Bangay (Ed.), *Aquatic programming: Reaching today's market* (pp. 12-13). Toronto, Ontario, Canada: The Royal Life Saving Society Canada.

Moore, P. (1984). The programming game. In J. Bangay (Ed.), *Aquatic programming: Reaching today's market* (pp. 20-21). Toronto, Ontario, Canada: The Royal Life Saving Society Canada.

Palent, S. (1986). *Fundraising for park,*

recreation and conservation agencies. Champaign, IL: Management Learning Laboratories.

Sevelle, T. (1984). No-frills programming. In J. Bangay (Ed.), *Aquatic programming: Reaching today's market* (pp. 25-26). Toronto, Ontario, Canada: The Royal Life Saving Society Canada.

Staunton, G. (1987). Corporate sponsorship. In C. Wilson (Ed.), *The world of lifesaving* (p. 25). Toronto, Ontario, Canada: The Royal Life Saving Society Canada.

Waters, L. (1987, April). *Promotions and programs*. Paper presented at the convention of the American Alliance for Health, Physical Education, Recreation and Dance, Las Vegas, NV.

Wilkinson, D. (1987). Marketing for money: Principles. In C. Wilson (Ed.), *The world of lifesaving* (p. 19). Toronto, Ontario, Canada: The Royal Life Saving Society Canada.

Chapter 10

RECREATIONAL PROGRAMS

Content
Management Suggestions
Program Evaluation
Record Keeping
Supplemental Learning Activities

As described in chapter 1, there are numerous aquatic recreational opportunities in every community, including activities enjoyed by individuals either alone or with a group. Those activities sponsored by a formally organized group (e.g., swim team or scuba club) are discussed in chapter 12. This chapter will discuss the content of aquatic recreation programs and offer suggestions relative to the management of such programs.

CONTENT

Theoretically, the following recreational activities can be done:

- *Pool:* Swimming, diving, synchronized swimming, scuba, kayaking, snorkeling, parent-tot programs, fly and bait casting, lap swimming, team practice,

beginning sailboarding, and games such as underwater hockey
- *Lake, river, gulf, or ocean beach:* Diving, sailing, canoeing, windsurfing, waterskiing, rowing, fishing, hunting, spearfishing, kayaking, rafting, tubing, ice-skating, and outboard and inboard boating

Provisions for spectators and for semi-active participants should also be made. Consider the number of people who go to the beach on a nice day. They take one brief plunge and then lie in the sun for a long period of time. Their real purpose is the sunning, and the water is useful only to cool off. Likewise, facilities with saunas or hot tubs attract patrons who seldom swim more than the width of the pool. Picnics in connection with sailing or snorkeling trips are another example of out-of-water recreation that should be considered by the aquatic staff.

It is obvious that unless an activity can be done with safety it should not be offered at the facility. Provisions must be made for a sufficient number of lifeguards wherever swimming is permitted; water marshals and vehicles for emergency aid must be on duty where open water is under a sponsor's control. Emergency equipment manned by trained personnel must be ready for instant use. Finally, unless an individual can perform the activity safely, he or she should not be permitted to try it.

MANAGEMENT SUGGESTIONS

Although no two situations are alike, suggestions for the planning, scheduling, and fee structure for recreational aspects of the aquatic program follow.

Planning

Variety in Activities

A basic goal in planning is to have recreational opportunities for each age and interest group available throughout the day, paying special attention to adults. Restricting usage to one group (e.g., adult lap swimming only from 11:30 a.m. to 1:00 p.m. each day) will not please those adults who have children with them. Conversely, if there are no lap lanes available during recreational swim hours, some exercise swimmers will be shut out. Special events for the various age and interest groups should likewise be planned.

An excellent example of variety in indoor aquatic activities is shown in Figure 10.1.

The two pools in this city of 90,000 offer many different classes and special events as well as sessions for special interest aquatic groups.

Space Restrictions

In some cases, activities need to be restricted in space. For example, diving from the board during open-swim hours may have to be curtailed or sailing or water-skiing on a small lake may require some type of regulation. Because boating and swimming are often done at the same lake facility, care must be taken to keep each group separated. Power-boat operators are resented by fishermen, waders, scuba divers, and canoeists. For the safety of all these groups, specific areas must be designated and restrictions regarding their use enforced. On the other hand, some groups (e.g., parent-tot and divers) can sometimes share the same facility for recreation. Or, scuba persons can be in the deep end of the pool while water exercise classes can meet in the shallow and mid-depth areas.

Safe Equipment

Sufficient funds must be available to ensure that equipment used by patrons is safe, adequate in number, and maintained. For example, PFDs must be issued to all passengers in rental boats, and boats must be in good repair and inspected daily. Sometimes, patrons bring unsafe equipment to pools or lakes. It is desirable to make suitable equipment (tubes, kick boards, canoes, air mattresses) available. Ideally, the admission fee should be adequate to purchase and maintain such equipment. Where this is not feasible, safe equipment should be available for rental (Figure 10.2).

SWIMMING

FORT COLLINS COMMUNITY POOL (FCCP)

This indoor facility is open year-round for educational and recreational swimming. It is used jointly by the City of Fort Collins and Poudre R-1 School District and is located at 424 S. Sherwood. Phone 221-6659.

The facility features a 25-yard by 25-meter U-shaped pool with two 1-meter diving boards and a wading pool. Water temperature is held between 82 and 84 degrees constantly; air temperature is approximately 86 degrees.

Spectator seating is provided. Vending area and classroom space are available.

SWIM SCHEDULE: (effective September 7-December 31)

Recreational Swim*:	7:00-10:00 PM, Monday, Wednesday & Friday
	8:00-10:00 PM, Tuesday & Thursday
	1:00-4:00 PM, Saturday & Sunday
	6:00-9:00 PM, Saturday
Adult Lap Swim:	7:00-8:00 AM, Monday through Friday
(18+ years only)	Noon-1:00 PM, Daily
Older Adult Lap Swim:	8:00-9:00 AM, Monday through Friday
(50+ years only)	
Spa:	7:00 AM-10:00 PM, Monday through Friday
	Noon-9:00 PM, Saturday
	Noon-4:00 PM Sunday

NOTE: Tuesday — Half-price Night — all persons admitted for half the regular price
Friday — Family Night — family groups admitted for a 10% discount
Saturday — Scuba Night — the deep end made available to persons with scuba/snorkel gear only
* During recreational swim, two or more lanes are made available for adult lap swimming.

HOLIDAY & SCHOOL BREAK SCHEDULE: (effective September 7, November 27 and December 21 through January 1)

Recreational Swim:	1:00-4:00 PM, 6:00-10:00 PM
Adult Lap Swim:	11:30 AM-1:00 PM
Older Adult Lap Swim:	8:00-9:00 AM

HOLIDAY CLOSURES:

All day	— Thanksgiving, November 26
	— Christmas, December 25
	— New Year's Day, January 1
At 4 PM	— Christmas Eve, December 24
	— New Year's Eve, December 31

EDORA POOL ICE CENTER (EPIC)

This new addition to the Fort Collins Parks and Recreation Department is located at 1801 Riverside. EPIC is open year-round for recreational activities. Phone 221-6679.

Included in the facility is a 50-meter by 25-yard pool with two 3-meter and two 1-meter diving boards, ten racing lanes, and two movable bulkheads that create three separate swimming areas to accommodate different programs. A separate warm water therapeutic pool and a wading pool are available.

SWIM SCHEDULE: (effective September 7-December 31)

Recreational Swim:	9:00-11:00 AM, Monday through Friday
	1:00-5:00 PM, Monday through Friday
	7:00-10:00 PM, Monday through Thursday; Saturday
	1:00-5:00 PM, Saturday & Sunday
	5:30-8:30 PM, Sunday
NOTE: Thursday — Family Night — family groups admitted for a 10% discount	
Sunday — Water Sports Night — water polo, water basketball, volleyball, gutterball, and drop-in water polo (5:30-8:30) — instruction and critique of water polo skills	
Teen Night:	7:30-10:00 PM, Friday (special fee; see information below)
Adult Lap Swim:	6:30 AM-10:00 PM, Monday through Thursday
(18+ years only)	6:30 AM-7:00 PM, Friday
	10:00 AM-10:00 PM, Saturday
	Noon-8:30 PM, Sunday
Therapeutic Pool:	6:30 AM-10:00 PM, Monday through Thursday
	6:30 AM-7:00 PM, Friday
	10:00 AM-10:00 PM, Saturday
	Noon-8:30 PM, Sunday
Wading Pool:	9:00-11:00 AM, Monday through Friday
	1:00-5:00 PM, Daily
	7:00-10:00 PM, Monday through Thursday; Saturday
	5:30-8:30 PM, Sunday

NOTE: At times, space available to the public in the wading pool and therapeutic pool is limited due to scheduled classes. Therapeutic pool available to persons 17 years and younger during recreational swim hours only. Please see posted rules for use.

HOLIDAY HOURS:

1:00-5:00 PM — Thanksgiving, November 26
— Christmas, December 25
— New Year's Day, January 1

EPIC POOL CLOSURES:

Saturday, September 26 — Colorado Invitational for Girls
Saturday, November 7 — Colorado State Girls' Swim Meet
Saturday, December 19 — Colorado Invitational for Boys
Thursday, December 24 at 5:00 PM — Christmas Eve
Thursday, December 31 at 5:00 PM — New Year's Eve

DROP-IN SWIM FEES — BOTH POOLS:

	Single Admission	30-Admission Pass
Youth (17 & under)	$1.00	$22.50
Adult (18+)	$1.50	$33.75
Older Adult (50+)	$1.25	$25.00
Under 24 mo.; over 85	FREE	
Teen Night (EPIC only)	$2.50	
Other: Towel Rental	$.25	

NOTE: Admission is free to those who assist the disabled. If disability is not obvious, proof must be shown with medical evaluation. Low-income fee available upon request and qualification.

Group Fees

These reduced admission fees are for groups only and are available to non-profit and community organizations. A group must consist of at least 10 participants, and pre-registration is required.

Youth (17 & under)	$ .75
Adult (18+)	$1.25
Older Adult (50+)	$1.00

(Cont.)

Figure 10.1. Example of a varied aquatic program. *Note.* From *Recreator*, Fall 1987, pp. 39-41. Copyright 1987 by the City of Fort Collins Parks and Recreation Department. Reprinted by permission.

CLASS INSTRUCTION

GENERAL INFORMATION

The instruction program offers aquatic classes for young and old alike. All classes are taught by certified Red Cross Water Safety Instructors and certificates will be issued to participants upon completion of the requirements on the last day of the session.

Descriptions for all classes are available in the swimming schedule which is available at the Fort Collins Community Pool, Edora Pool Ice Center, the Recreation office, and other city facilities.

Prior to registration, we encourage you to have your child tested for proper placement. Testing will be done at the FCCP or EPIC free of charge during recreation swim hours.

The format for **Toddler** and **Beginner** lessons includes 3 stages of advancement within each level. If you are registering a child for one of these levels, you may sign up for one session only. It is necessary for you to find out from the instructor on the **7th day of instruction** whether or not the child is ready to advance to the next stage before registering for a subsequent session.

If the class you wish to register for is filled, please place your name on our waiting list. We make every attempt to accommodate the demand for swim instruction.

NOTE Only swim students are allowed on the pool deck except for the last day of class.

FALL CLASSES

The following classes are available this fall:

Learn to Swim	ONGOING SERVICES
Swim Parent	**Advanced Swim Instruction**
	Basic Rescue and Water Safety
Toddler:	
Polliwog	Water Safety Aid
Sunfish	
Starfish	Advanced Lifesaving
Beginner:	Lifeguard Training
Minnow	
Stingray	**Special Interest**
Shark	Scuba Lessons
	Snorkeling/Skin Diving
Advanced:	Pre-competitive Stroke Clinic
Advanced Beginner	
Intermediate	Kayak
Swimmer	
Advanced Swimmer	Springboard Diving
	Synchronized Swiming
Teen Beginner	**Adapted Aquatics**
	Youth Mentally Disabled
Adult Beginner	Youth Physically Disabled
Adult Stroke Improvement	Adult Mentally Disabled
Adult Conditioning	Adult Physically Disabled
	Multiple Sclerosis
Fitness	Muscular Dystrophy
Twinges in the Hinges	
Senior Aquarobics	Aquathenics
Aquarobics	Youth Aquaphobia
Prenatal Water Exercise	Adult Aquaphobia

> The Fort Collns Area Swim Team (18 years & younger) competes year-round. Call Don Donahoo at 484-9233 for more information.

ONGOING SERVICES

Call the appropriate facility for further information.

FCCP — 221-6657
EPIC — 221-6679

SWIM & STAY FIT: ADULT LAP SWIM (FCCP & EPIC)

Set fitness goals for yourself and work at your own speed. Monitor your progress by joining the American Red Cross "Swim & Stay Fit" program. Achievement awards available for 10, 20, 30, 40 and 50 miles.

OVERNIGHT PARTIES (FCCP & EPIC)

Fully-supervised overnight parties for groups, birthdays, or any occasion are available. Twelve-hour parties are highlighted with swimming and skating at midnight, hot tub, pizza, and a poolside breakfast. Call now for reservations (only one booking per week).

MOONLIGHT FITNESS (FCCP)

Shift workers, unite! Do you ever wish there was a place for you and your co-workers to go after work to release tension, unwind, and relax? The Fort Collins Community Pool can be made available to groups for lap swimming, exercise programs and spa use between the hours of 11:00 PM and 5:00 AM. Reservations must be made in advance. Minimum of 10.

FUND RAISERS (FCCP & EPIC)

Sponsor a swim party and raise money for your school or organization. We offer reduced admission for all members of your group with games and activities — all fully supervised.

Great for family, teen and social groups.

YOUTH WATER SAFETY (EPIC)

Attention, youth service volunteers! Bring your scout troops and other youth groups to either pool to complete badges, learn and experience water safety; or just for fun. Arrangements must be made 5 days in advance and prices vary according to group size and activity.
TIME: 5:00-7:00 PM, Saturday

LAP SWIMMERS CHILD CARE CO-OP (EPIC)

Want to swim laps, but you don't have someone to watch your pre-school children (including infants)? Join the co-op.
TIME: 9:00-11:00 AM, Tuesday & Thursday
       7:30-9:30 AM, Monday, Wednesday & Friday

BIRTHDAY PARTIES (FCCP & EPIC)

A swimming or skating party can be scheduled during recreational hours. Party hosts will supervise water activities as well as other games. Fees include decorations, paper products, treat bags, punch, and supervision. Pick up a birthday party flier at any recreation facility or call for specific information.
NOTE: Parties are also scheduled at The Farm at Lee Martinez Park. Call 221-6640 for information.

POOL RENTAL (FCCP & EPIC)

The pools are available for rent for private use. Social and corporate events, baptisms, and athletic events are a few of the many activities available.

PRO SHOP (FCCP & EPIC)

The pro shops at the Fort Collins Community Pool and Edora Pool Ice Center can handle your basic swimming and skating needs from swimming caps to nose plugs and hockey sticks to skate laces. Special t-shirts, sunglasses, mouthguards, and much more are available.

Figure 10.1 (Cont.)

SPECIAL PROGRAMS

SPLISH 'N' SPLASH (EPIC)

The program provides child care for lap swimmers and includes fun in the water as well as stories, games and other activities. Children should wear swim suits and bring towels.
AGE: 2-6 years
TIME: 11:00 AM-1:00 PM, daily
FEE: $1.00 daily, $9.00 monthly
NOTE: Pay the daily fee or register monthly at EPIC.

UNDERWATER PHOTO PROGRAM (FCCP & EPIC)

Underwater photos of your children or family are great gifts or special mementos for children and adults alike. Pre-registration and a $5.00 deposit is required for each photo session. No photo fee is charged if you choose not to purchase, but a $2.00 administrative fee will be held from the deposit.
FEE: $12.00 for the first photo; $20.00 for two; $25.00 for three
FCCP
TIME: 4:00-6:00 PM, second Saturday of each month
EPIC
TIME: 6:00-8:00 PM, second Thursday of each month

RELAXATION (EPIC)

Water wellness takes many forms. If you have trouble sleeping, if the stress of daily life has taken its toll, or if you just need some time for yourself, try water relaxation. Calm — quiet — soft music — warm water — flotation devices allowed.
TIME: 8:30-9:30 PM, Sunday
FEE: $1.50 per visit
AGE: 18 and older

DISCOVER SCUBA (FCCP)

Films, slides, and discussions will start the evening. This is your opportunity to experience scuba diving. Let a certified P.A.D.I. instructor show you how to breathe underwater with scuba equipment. No registration required.
DATES: Thursdays, September 24, October 15,
November 19 and December 17
TIME: 7:00-9:00 PM (ongoing, each half hour)
AGE: 12 and older

DAYCARE SWIM & SKATE INSTRUCTION (FCCP & EPIC)

Specially-arranged swim instruction for groups such as daycare organizations and private schools is available at both the Fort Collins Community Pool and the Edora Pool Ice Center.
For information, call 221-6657 or 221-6679.

SPOOK SPLASH (EPIC)

It's the time of year when all ghosts, pumpkins and weird creatures stalk the town. The wind whistles through the hollow trees, spreading the news of the annual Spook Splash!
All good goblins, can swim, ice skate, play games, compete for prizes, and have a great time before the "bewitching hour".
DATE: Saturday, October 31
TIME: 1:00-5:00 PM
FEE: Regular fees apply
AGE: Any

SANTA'S HELPER SWIM (FCCP)

Hey, Mom & Dad! Let us be your "Santa's Helper". Leave your children at the pool while you finish Christmas shopping.
Movies, swimming, a visit from Santa, and refreshments will be provided. Let us help you during the holiday season.
DATE: Saturday, December 19
TIME: 1:00-4:00 PM
FEE: Regular fees apply
AGE: Any

OPEN KAYAK SESSIONS (FCCP)

Water sportsmen, be prepared for the spring whitewater by practicing your skills. The pool is open for kayak each Sunday morning from 10:00 AM-Noon. Participants should bring their own equipment. Some crafts will be made available by Wildwater Discovery, Inc.
Sessions are supervised by Robert Breckenridge who has over 10 years of kayak experience as well as having taught for 4 years. Call 224-3379 for more information.
FEE: $1.50 per session; $33.75 for a 30-admission pass
BEGINS: September 13

PARKS & RECREATION BOARD & SENIOR ADVISORY BOARD

These two boards advise the City Council regarding matters affecting the Parks and Recreation program of the City of Fort Collins. Members serve four-year terms & they serve without compensation.

The Parks and Recreation Board meets on the fourth Wednesday of each month at 6:30 PM at the Parks and Recreation Administration Office, 145 E. Mountain Avenue.

Current board members and their term expiration dates are as follows:

Cathy Mulcahy, President	July 1, 1990
Karen Schubert, Vice President	July 1, 1988
Robert Aukerman, Secretary	July 1, 1990
Mike ImMasche	July 1, 1989
Bill Loy	July 1, 1988
John Rabun	July 1, 1988
Richard Ramirez	July 1, 1989
Ricki Slack	July 1, 1989
Ann Schroeder	July 1, 1989

Loren Maxey is the City Council representative to the board.
Ron McClary is an ex-officio member representing the Poudre R-1 School District.
H.R. Phillips, Director of Cultural, Library and Recreational Services serves as city staff representative to the board.

The **Senior Advisory Board** meets the second Wednesday of each month at 1:30 PM (location announced one month in advance).

Current members and their term expiration dates are as follows:

Roxanne Smock	July 1, 1991
Phillip Simon	July 1, 1988
Arlene Simon	July 1, 1988
Dwight M. Saunders	July 1, 1988
Ruby Lynch	July 1, 1988
Clark M. Long	July 1, 1989
Mildred Arnold	July 1, 1989
Joseph F. Campanella	July 1, 1990
Yetta Rollin	July 1, 1990
Ellen Connelly (Alternate)	July 1, 1989
Sam Rosenthal (Alternate)	July 1, 1988
Nancy Luttropp (City staff support)	

Larry Estrada is the City Council representative to the board.

Figure 10.1 (Cont.)

Figure 10.2. Aquatic activity sponsored by a city recreation department. *Note.* Reprinted courtesy of the Albuquerque Parks and Recreation Department.

Scheduling

Time Allotment

It is obvious that not all activities can be done at the same time. Planning for such variety is done by listing both the hours available in each facility area and the chosen activities. Activities are normally scheduled according to their popularity. For example, 75% of the time might be available for open swimming/diving, whereas only 5% of the time is set aside for scuba diving/snorkeling. Although certain activities such as springboard diving occupy a large space for relatively few participants, having minimal space (e.g., one diving board) available at all times will slowly but surely encourage more to participate in that activity.

Lap Swimming

Because many adults are interested in lap swimming, at least one lane should be available at all times. Many adults prefer early-morning and late-evening sessions because these hours fit into their work schedules. More important to some adults, the early and late hours mean that the facility is not overrun by young children who are apt to swim wherever they please.

Crowding

A maximum of five swimmers per lap lane is usual; should this be inadequate, scheduling more lap time is desirable. It is also possible to take reservations for half-hour segments in an assigned lane.

Fee Structure

The budget should anticipate maximum costs (lifeguards and other staff) and realistic attendance. The fees, based on budget expectations, may be adjusted at periodic intervals, usually annually (for further elaboration on this point, see chapter 7).

Spectators

Spectators should not be charged admission, although this is a source of income at some facilities. Many parents will bring their young children to the pool or beach, but not all parents wish to swim. Spectators can become swimmers quickly, especially at a beach. In that case, everyone (or no one) should pay.

Passes

Seasonal or multiadmission passes are highly desirable. Passes should be transferable because it is difficult to prevent passes from being used by others and the larger the number of people using the pass, the more potential participants there will be.

Lockers

If a separate fee is charged for checking clothes or equipment, some patrons will leave their personal belongings on the locker room benches or near their cars on the beach. This leads to messy facility areas as well as to poor public relations when items are stolen. Locker rental fees should be included in the admission charge. Lockers with built-in key locks are desirable. For identification, rubber bracelets with key attached work well.

Deposits

The rental of certain items of equipment (e.g., canoes) requires a deposit large enough to discourage equipment being stolen. Positive identification (a picture ID) must be recorded. One solution is to keep the driver's license until the equipment is returned.

PROGRAM EVALUATION

Recreational programs should be evaluated on three bases: total attendance, how much money was gained or lost, and the accident ratio (serious accidents:attendance). Accurate records need to be kept and reviewed periodically. One season's records become the basis for the next season's budget.

RECORD KEEPING

It is essential to keep complete records of both water and facility sanitation and maintenance as well as a complete description of first-aid treatment given for each accident. The sanitation records are required by law, and all records are essential because accurate testimony is required in a court action.

In addition, the daily labor cost (i.e., the number of guards and support staff) and the weather (for outdoor facilities, especially) should be noted. Budget preparation for the next season is greatly aided when these latter items are available.

SUPPLEMENTAL LEARNING ACTIVITIES

1. Interview a facility manager or another knowledgeable person concerning a specific program. How many different activities are scheduled? Who does the scheduling? How is scheduling done? How are fees determined?

2. Observe a recreational period at a facility. What safety practices do you note?

Chapter 11

INSTRUCTIONAL PROGRAMS

Safety
Management Suggestions
Models for Instructional Programs
Aquatic Programs for Preschool Children
Program Evaluation
Record Keeping
Supplemental Learning Activities

Although the recreational use of water involves more people than does the instructional use, aquatic facilities often are developed to provide instructional programs of all kinds. This chapter will cover safety considerations, management suggestions, and content for traditional instructional programs including preschool swimming.

SAFETY

In addition to the suggestions on safety given in chapter 5, it is important that an instructor be competent, as judged by (a) earning a certificate from an officially recognized agency and (b) maintaining that certification. The first step in hiring instructors is to list their qualifications and duties (see Table 11.1). This description should be modified for the particular position and should specify the precise certification needed. In view of the responsibility involved in the instructor position, a jury might find it negligent if instructors without the minimum certifications were hired.

Once hired, instructors are sometimes careless about maintaining their certifications. One constant problem is the need to remain current in first aid and CPR. A solution is to schedule these courses in sequence, so that instructors can take the needed segment of the course before the expiration date. To ensure that this happens, the supervisor needs an up-to-date

Table 11.1

QUALIFICATIONS AND DUTIES OF THE AQUATIC INSTRUCTOR

Qualifications

Maturity and experience: At least 17 years old; at least 1 year of experience as an aquatic aide

Education: Certified instructor (Aquatic Council of AAHPERD, Red Cross, YMCA, etc.) in the specialty advertised

Knowledge: Class organization, teaching strategies, safety procedures

Duties

Exercises sound judgment based on education

Teaches any level of class needed in the specialty

Organizes classes (prepares course objectives, plans lessons, selects appropriate drills, and evaluates students and course)

Teaches competently (presents proper demonstrations, explains the why and how, analyzes and corrects performance, minimizes fear, and uses appropriate teaching devices)

Is safety conscious (properly classifies students, maintains a safe instructional environment, and teaches safety procedures)

---

list of the certifications held by each instructor (the computer is invaluable for this purpose).

MANAGEMENT SUGGESTIONS

Although each program is different, certain suggestions concerning planning, scheduling, and enrollment of students are valid for most classes.

Planning

Teaching Ratio

The ideal teacher-pupil ratio is 1:5 for beginning classes and somewhat larger for more advanced classes. To help in reaching this ratio, the use of teacher aides is recommended. They must be trained and preferably must have earned a certificate. Aides (who may even be nonswimmers) can record test results, gather equipment, and so on.

Class Control

Insist that classes be organized and under control. Pupils must not be permitted to engage in horseplay, nor should they be neglected or allowed to become separated from the group.

Teaching Methods

Permit each instructor to use the teaching methods that he or she has found to be effective. Insist, however, that all instructors emphasize and require the same standards for evaluating strokes and techniques.

Intensity

Place sensible limits on the intensity of learner activity. The younger the student, the less intense (i.e., the more fun) the instruction should be.

Spectators

Although spectators may be a distraction, the motivational benefits gained by permitting parents and friends to observe the sessions will outweigh the disadvantages.

Awards

Present each learner with some card or certificate of accomplishment. The use of YMCA, Red Cross, or park department cards is recommended.

Scheduling

Variety

Plan an instructional program that includes, insofar as possible, a variety of classes and skill levels. This will be appreciated by parents who bring children to more than one level of class. Having classes of different ability levels will also better utilize water space (e.g., beginning swimmers in shallow water, intermediate swimmers at mid-pool, and advanced swimmers or personal rescue students in deep water).

Seasonal Classes

Schedule fewer classes during the fall, winter, and spring than during the summer months (perhaps vice versa for indoor pools in certain locations). People are more swim oriented during the summer and are likely to have fewer conflicting interests.

Number of Classes

Schedule more beginning classes than advanced ones and more basic water rescue classes than lifeguard classes.

Teaching Stations

Because diving is a noisy activity, do not schedule diving instruction concurrently with swimming classes. Recreational swimming and team practice should not be permitted when swimming instruction is being given in the same area.

Number of Lessons

Total class sessions constituting a complete series of lessons may range from 8 to 20 (most commonly 10).

Makeup Lessons

Arrange for one or two makeup sessions for each series of lessons. These can also be used for extra practice for those who need it.

Classes per Week

Classes that meet daily will show the most student progress, but it is difficult for all but retired persons and students on vacation to take them. Classes that meet once or twice a week are better for most patrons.

Holidays

Check the calendar to avoid scheduling classes on holidays or school vacations.

Play Periods

Plan for a free play period of 5 to 15 minutes between classes to be used by both the coming and the going class members. The learners will be less inclined to play during class time, and the instructor may have an opportunity to relax briefly. During this time, the teaching aides (if qualified) can assist the lifeguards by watching the swimmers.

Review of Schedule

After planning the schedule, let other staff members review it. They may be aware of problems that have been overlooked in the past.

Student Enrollment

Preregistration

Establish a preregistration enrollment plan, which makes it easier to control the enrollment and will permit the scheduling of additional classes if the demand warrants.

Registration Priority

Decide whether preference will be given to those previously enrolled in classes or to those who register first. First come, first served is preferable, with these exceptions: (a) Give preferred enrollment status to members of the sponsoring organization, and (b) give preference to any volunteer.

Age Limits

Enforce age prerequisites firmly for those classes that have them.

Height Limit

As a minimum height requirement, the student should be able to stand in the water with his or her head above the surface. A minimum of 36 inches from the floor to the learner's shoulders is recommended for children without parents in the water. The use of ''Tot Docks'' (see resource list at the end of this chapter) is a safe way of temporarily making the pool shallower.

Class Size

Both the number of teachers' aides and the ability level of the students affect class size. For a beginner class, a limit of 5 is ideal, 10 is acceptable, and 15 is acceptable only if there are competent aides. Because expert swimmers require less individual attention, a larger number may be enrolled in advanced classes.

Qualifications

Establish acceptance qualifications at each level of instruction and confirm student competence by a short screening test. Many Red Cross and YMCA courses have prerequisites; follow these exactly.

Fees

Amount

If a fee is charged for instruction, establish one that is reasonable and realistic (see chapter 7). The fee for a series of 10 lessons may vary from none or little (in a neighborhood pool or tax-supported program) to $5 to $10 in a program supported by public subscription and membership (YMCA) to

$25 or more in a program that must be self-sustaining and/or profit making.

Prepayment

Usually, persons who pay in advance plan to attend all sessions. Prepayment enables the teacher or manager to know precisely what the dollar income that is earned from a series of lessons will be.

Refunds

If fees are charged, establish a no-refunds policy. It is difficult to ascertain which excuse justifies a refund and which does not. A preferred procedure is to schedule make-up sessions or to permit free enrollment at a later time.

MODELS FOR INSTRUCTIONAL PROGRAMS

There are at least seven categories of aquatic instructional programs: (a) swimming (preschool through advanced; (b) springboard diving; (c) personal safety/survival swimming (formerly lifesaving); (d) lifeguarding; (e) specialized group instruction (scuba, synchronized swimming, adapted aquatics); (f) small craft; and (g) instructor classes for each of the above.

In the United States and Canada, well-developed aquatic courses at all levels have been established by the Red Cross, the YMCA, and the Royal Lifesaving Society Canada. If at all possible, one or more of these programs should be followed. Their courses, which move logically from level to level, are expertly designed and universally accepted. Each organization offers both numerous publications pertaining to its courses and standardized instructor courses.

For various reasons (in some cases political), certain local groups develop their own aquatic courses. In almost all cases these are combinations of Red Cross and YMCA items plus some individual preference skills. The content and conduct of such courses is often excellent, and, under the guidance of a competent aquatic professional, students can receive a superior education. However, in view of the mobility of the population, students might be better served if they receive a national certificate, which can be used and is accepted in other locations.

Because a quality program exists in part on the broad knowledge of the instructors, each facility should have its own library. Instructors should be encouraged to read and use the material. The number of texts will increase rapidly if (a) one staff member is given the responsibility (and budget) to develop the library and (b) individual instructors are encouraged to purchase books for the library (and then of course are reimbursed).

An annotated bibliography of useful texts for various aquatic courses is given at the end of this chapter.

AQUATIC PROGRAMS FOR PRESCHOOL CHILDREN

Teaching school-age children to swim has always been of paramount importance to parents, instructors, teachers, and agencies. Not until the early 1960s was there enthusiasm for enrolling very young children (6 months to 1 year old) in classes as it was previously felt that these children were "too young" to learn. However, agency and private pool operators quickly found that these children could learn to enjoy the water and that parents were quite willing to pay for this instruction. Now, nearly every agency, public pool, city recreation program, and private instructor conducts a preschool learn-to-swim program. To ascertain the extent of such programs, Hicks-Hughes and Langendorfer (1986) surveyed 250 aquatic facilities in the United States. A response of 56% (139 agencies) found the following.

Scope.   The authors estimated that over 5,000,000 young children are annually enrolled in preschool aquatic programs, with the beginning age ranging from 3 to 9 months.

Agency Type.   Most (75%) of the responses in the sample were from YMCAs, but YWCAs, colleges, local recreation departments, and Red Cross programs were also represented.

Enrollment.   Programs averaged 710 children per year (range of 6 to 5,100); most (67%) of the children enrolled were ages 3 to 6; 23% of the programs enrolled children at ages 3 to 6 months, and another 59% began admitting children at ages 6 to 9 months.

Safety.   Some type of reportable water emergency was noted by 47% of the respondents; 17% had near drownings, and 5% (4 cases) reported a drowning.

Teacher-Pupil Ratio.   A ratio of 1:3 to 1:6 was given for the majority of programs for pupils at ages 3 to 6; some programs (22%) had in excess of a 1:10 ratio.

Parental Participation.   84% of programs had parental participation for the 3-month to 3-year age group. This decreased to only 15% parental participation for the 5-year-olds.

Teacher Qualifications (Excluding Parents).   Virtually all programs claimed to require some sort of aquatic certification or training but not necessarily in the preschool specialty area.

Myths and Facts Concerning Preschool Swimming

The issue of preschool swimming continues to be controversial because the aquatic community has not reached consensus on several points. Many myths are perpetuated by both proponents and opponents (for a summary of these myths and an explanation of the facts that are known, see Appendix E).

Program Decisions

The facility manager and the supervisor of instruction are faced with a major question: What type of preschool swimming program will be offered? Programs for children at ages 3 to 6 are more apt to emphasize swimming skills, but baby classes might have noticeably different approaches. According to Kochen and McCabe (1986), the four most common types of classes for babies are those that emphasize drownproofing, recreation, competition, and tender loving care.

Drownproofing

Babies are taught to roll on their backs, extend their heads, and lift their faces out of the water. One trained instructor works with each baby, and parental attendance is discouraged because of much crying and screaming by the infants. The basic philosophy is that "learning to save oneself in a panic situation outweighs the benefits of feeling loved and secure in the water" (Kochen & McCabe, 1986, p. 22). This approach is the least popular with most experienced teachers, as they have found less harsh techniques to accomplish the same tasks.

Recreational

Emphasis is on water play with parents, with little or no instruction or direction from a teacher. Group games are played for entertainment value. In such a recreational program, children will learn to enjoy the water but little else. A more structured, disciplined approach is favored by most instructors.

Competitive

Stroke mechanics is the basis of this program, with the goal of performing in competitive situations. There is much peer pressure to excel. Such a program often frustrates those children who are not superior in motor development (and even frustrates the parent!). The dropout rate can be high, as the slower students become discouraged and the better ones bored with the emphasis on technique. In our opinion, this is also an undesirable approach to teaching the young child.

Tender Loving Care

This is similar to recreational programs, except that parents are to keep challenging babies to attempt increasingly difficult skills. Group games are used to reinforce new skills as well as for entertainment. This teaching method is used in most of the successful programs in the United States because it can accomplish the goals of the other three—safety skills, fun, and stroke work—in an atmosphere that is pleasing to everyone.

CNCA's Position

As might be expected, each type of program for the young child has advocates, accompanied by convincing examples of its superiority. Various individuals and groups have, over the years, used CNCA conferences as the vehicle to meet and discuss (and argue!) the merits of specific emphases. Because baby and preschool programs are still both universal and controversial, the advice given in a position paper by the CNCA (1985) is offered in Appendix F. In summary, the paper supports aquatic programs for the young child, provided that competent leadership is available, that children are physically able to benefit from such experiences, that parents or guardians are involved, and that certain health and safety practices are observed.

Management Suggestions

Because facilities and instructors vary, no two preschool swimming programs are the same. Nevertheless, certain items should be considered by those who would sponsor such a program.

Teachers

The chief instructor (a person with special training as an instructor of preschool children) guides parents or other care givers as they work with the child. Advanced Lifesaver, Lifeguard, or WSI certification is not sufficient.

The chief instructor must be knowledgeable about this particular age group and also supervise a parent training program that is held before the first in-water session. Shank (1986) outlined the content of such a program, which included (a) causes and prevention of the fear of water, (b) water safety, (c) preschool swimming programs, and (d) providing on-going water experiences.

Teacher-Pupil Ratio

In most infant (3 months to 3 years) programs, a parent is in the water with the child, thus achieving a 1:1 teacher-pupil ratio. In most preschool (ages 3 to 6 years) programs, usually only the chief instructor is in the water. For this age group, the recommended ratio is 1:4 in deep water and 1:8 in shallow water (American National Red Cross, in press).

Goals

The main goal is to have fun while making children safer in the water. Parents should not expect that children will develop formal strokes.

Skills and Techniques to Be Covered in Classes

These include water adjustment; survival and safety practices (such as bobbing and floating, and resuscitation and reaching assists if the age of the student permits); enjoyment (not fear) of water; education of parents concerning safety procedures and aquatic teaching techniques; and development of neuromuscular coordination and social skills.

Length of Program

Programs should be short (3 to 6 weeks) and frequent (2 to 3 sessions per week).

Environment

Bright, cheerful surroundings and high water temperatures are important. If possible, brightly colored suits should be worn by the instructor and participating persons.

Toys

Floatable and sinkable toys (which may be brought from home) are desirable.

Flotation Aids

Devices such as buoyant belts, small tubes, kick boards, and flippers are commonly used at least part of the time.

Water Sanitation

Thomas (1976) points out that there is no appreciable increase in water sanitation problems, but frequent checks are still desirable.

PROGRAM EVALUATION

Evaluation refers to the instructor's assessment of both the individual student's competence and the work of the class as a whole. In the first instance, individual instructors are responsible for accurate evaluation and for the subsequent awarding of certificates. The instructor must know what and how to test (measurable objectives are strongly recommended) and be able to determine correctly the skill level attained. In case of a disagreement, the instructor should be able to justify any evaluation made. Only in rare cases should the supervisor become involved with student evaluation.

The supervisor should, however, ensure that the instructor makes an evaluation of the class as a whole. The instructor can refer to the program's objectives to obtain a basis for judgment. In addition to discovering how well the objectives were met, the instructor will be better prepared to teach the next class by paying attention to the following:

1. The number of students enrolled and the number at the end: Why did some drop out?
2. The number of students passing the course and the number of these same students enrolling for subsequent classes: Why doesn't everyone continue?
3. The average daily attendance: Why were people absent?
4. What was your overall opinion of the class? Was it fun? Did students feel they were learning? Was time managed efficiently? What were the best parts of the class? How could the class be improved?

RECORD KEEPING

The paperwork involved in operating instructional programs is primarily the duty of the instructors, who may or may not perform this task meticulously. Because instructors come and go, and students lose certificates or move, a copy of the course-completion sheets must be filed in the office at the end of each class. To ensure that this is done, assign the job to one staff person.

Instructors do not realize that the office staff constantly receives such requests as "How many people took lessons last summer?" "Who was the instructor at 9 a.m. last spring for water exercises?" "Please send Joe Beaver another beginner card; the first one was lost." Facility managers and program supervisors must ensure the avail-ability of records that can provide answers to such questions.

SUPPLEMENTAL LEARNING ACTIVITIES

1. Visit a city, school, or aquatic facility's library. Make a reference list of all the aquatic instructional books you find.

2. Interview an experienced teacher or manager of an aquatic facility. Obtain the person's view on one of the following categories pertaining to the instructional program: planning, scheduling, enrollment details, or fees.

3. Observe a preschool swimming class. Focusing specifically on one child, describe how he or she becomes adjusted to the water, responds to comments by the instructor, responds to comments by the parent (if present), and reacts when water is splashed on his or her face.

4. Observe a swimming class. Focusing specifically on one child, describe the safety techniques used, the interaction between the instructor and the pupil, and the degree of attention being paid to the instructor by the student.

5. Interview an aquatic facility manager. How are instructional programs scheduled? Be specific.

6. Interview an experienced teacher. Find out his or her student evaluation techniques and the problems he or she encounters when evaluating.

REFERENCES AND SUGGESTED READINGS

American National Red Cross. (In press). *Infant/preschool aquatics*. Washington, DC: Author.

Council for National Cooperation in Aquatics. (1985). Aquatic activity programs for children under the age of three. *National Aquatics Journal* (Summer), **1**(2), 12-13.

Hicks-Hughes, D., & Langendorfer, S. (1986). Aquatics for the young child: A survey of selected programs. *National Aquatics Journal* (Spring), **2**(2), 12-17.

Kochen, C., & McCabe, J. (1986). *The baby swim book*. Champaign, IL: Leisure Press.

Langendorfer, S. (1987a). Swimming for children under three: A clarification. *National Aquatics Journal* (Fall), **3**(3), 8.

Langendorfer, S. (1987b). Separating fact from fiction in preschool aquatics. *National Aquatics Journal* (Winter), **3**(4), 2-4.

Langendorfer, S. (In press). Status of research in infant/preschool aquatics. *Research Consortium Newsletter*.

Langendorfer, S., & Willing, E. (1985). The impact of motor development upon issues of infant and preschool aquatics. *National Aquatics Journal* (Spring), **1**(1), 11-14.

McCabe, J. (1986). Training swimming instructors of young children. In L. Priest & A. Crowner (Eds.), *Aquatics: A changing profession* (pp. 80-84). Indianapolis, IN: Council for National Cooperation in Aquatics.

Shank, C. (1986). Parent orientation to aquatic programs for young children. *National Aquatics Journal* (Winter), **2**(1), 14-16.

Thomas, D. (1976). Pool chemistry and preschool swimming programs. In B. Empleton (Ed.), *Aquatics for all* (pp. 62-64). Indianapolis, IN: Council for National Cooperation in Aquatics.

Weber, E. (1987). Medical information related to aquatics for young children. In L. Priest & A. Crowner (Eds.), *Aquatics: A changing profession* (pp. 128-131). Indianapolis, IN: Council for National Cooperation in Aquatics.

RESOURCES

Swimming (Beginning, Intermediate, Advanced)

American National Red Cross. (1981). *Swimming and aquatics safety*. Washington, DC: Author.

Describes swimming strokes, related aquatic skills, diving fundamentals, safety, survival floating, and artificial resuscitation

Canadian Red Cross Society. (1977). *National instructor guide and reference* (5th ed.). Toronto, Ontario, Canada: Author.

Explains learning and teaching processes, physical principles applied to swimming, strokes and related skills, basic safety and emergency procedures, organization of programs, and evaluation standards

Clayton, R., & Hallett, B. (Eds.). (1980).

Swimming: A syllabus for the aquatic council courses "teacher and master teacher of swimming." Reston, VA: Aquatic Council of the American Alliance for Health, Physical Education, Recreation and Dance.

Explains the relationship of motor learning theories to the teaching of swimming, fundamental principles (anatomical, physiological, and hydrodynamic) involved in swimming, teaching methods and progressions, stroke mechanics, teaching preschool and adult groups, physical conditioning, safety, and aquatic references

Thomas, D.G. (1989). *Swimming: Steps to success.* Champaign, IL: Human Kinetics.

Serves as individualized learning guide for swimming; includes progressive steps and drills with goals and self-evaluation

Thomas, D.G. (1989). *Teaching Swimming: Steps to success.* Champaign, IL: Human Kinetics.

Shows how to organize, conduct, and instruct swimming classes using the individualized learning guide Swimming: Steps to Success

Torney, J., & Clayton, R. (1981). *Teaching aquatics.* Minneapolis: Burgess.

Describes the foundations of successful aquatic instruction, essential aquatic skills, intermediate and advanced skills, basic springboard diving, lifesaving, evaluation of performers, and sections on teaching preschoolers, adults, and the impaired

YMCA of the USA. (1986). *YMCA progressive swimming program instructor's guide.* Champaign, IL: Human Kinetics.

Contains skills for six levels of swimming plus teaching methods and lesson plans; Polliwog, Guppy, *and* Minnow Swim Books *are available for use with children ages 6 to 9*

Springboard Diving

Batterman, C. (1977). *The techniques of springboard diving.* Cambridge, MA: MIT Press.

Describes and illustrates in sequence photos the mechanics and general principles of all dives (forward, backward, spinning, reverse, inward, and twisting)

Personal Safety

American National Red Cross. (1984). *Basic rescue and water safety.* Washington, DC: Author.

Explains basic techniques (e.g., assists, PFDs, boating safety, etc., and rescue techniques, clothing inflation, survival floating, search and rescue, recovery of submerged victims) that nonswimmers and beginners or children over the age of 9 can perform

American National Red Cross. (1981). *Lifesaving: Rescue and water safety.* Washington, DC: Author.

Describes lifesaving skills and techniques for the advanced lifesaving course. (Note: The American National Red Cross plans to eliminate the Advanced Lifesaving course, replacing it with Emergency Water Safety, a course covering primarily swimming assists with emphasis on personal safety. A more elementary course, Basic Water Safety, is also new. This latter course focuses on accident prevention and personal safety and is designed for special groups such as families, backyard-pool owners, recreational boaters, etc.)

Smith, D. (1979). *Handbook of cold water survival.* Imperial, MO: Author.

The most complete and authoritative source on the practical aspects of cold-water survival, including reprints of articles, and a discussion of the problems, techniques, and survival skills for aquatic outdoorsmen (write D. Smith, 5163 Christy La., Imperial, MO 63052)

Lifeguarding

American National Red Cross. (1983). *Lifeguard training.* Washington, DC: Author.

A textbook that includes philosophy, responsibilities of guards, guard selection and training, preventive lifeguarding, emergencies, records and reports, equipment, health and sanitation, water rescues, search and recovery, weather and environment, and waterfront areas

Andres, F. (1980). *Lifeguarding: A syllabus for the aquatic council course "teacher and master teacher of lifeguarding."* Reston, VA: Aquatic Council of the American Alliance for Health, Physical Education, Recreation and Dance.

Discusses the history of lifeguarding and provides information about public safety, the aquatic environment, and the organization and administration of lifeguard services

Royal Life Saving Society Canada. (1985). *The Canadian Life Saving Program.* Toronto, Ontario, Canada: Author.

Contains accident statistics, description of lifesaving programs, and guidelines for the evaluation of candidates

United States Lifesaving Association. (1981). *Lifesaving and marine safety.* Piscataway, NJ: New Century.

Contains a history of lifeguarding and discussions of public relations, hazardous water and surf conditions, facilities and equipment, basic rescue techniques and special procedures, communication and backup systems, underwater search and recovery, legal ramifications of lifeguarding, special procedures and functions, and principles of organization and management

YMCA of the USA. (1986). *On the guard.* Champaign, IL: Human Kinetics.

The manual for the YMCA lifeguard training program, containing sections on personal safety, general aquatic information, aquatic rescues, special rescues, lifeguard responsibilities, and lifeguard administration

Programs for the Young Child

Note: Numerous "how-to" books attest to the popularity of preschool aquatics. The list that follows is representative of various approaches to teaching preschoolers; it is not an attempt to recommend only certain publications. In all cases, the authors describe techniques and procedures that have been successful in their situations.

The National Advisory Committee on Aquatics for the Young Child has been formed by CNCA to serve as a forum for practitioners and researchers in this area. For more information, contact CNCA, 1201 W. New York St., Indianapolis, IN 46223.

American National Red Cross. (In press). *Infant/preschool aquatics.* Washington, DC: Author.

Langendorfer, S., & Bruya, L. (In press).

Aquatic readiness for young children. Champaign, IL: Human Kinetics.

YMCA of the USA. (1987). *Y skippers.* Champaign, IL: Human Kinetics.

Kochen, C., & McCabe, J. (1986). *The baby swim book.* Champaign, IL: Human Kinetics.

Loman, D., McNichol, J., & Crowley, S. (1985). *The little guys.* Burnaby, British Columbia, Canada: Aquaventures.

Murray, J. (1980). *Infaquatics.* Champaign, IL: Human Kinetics.

Newman, V. (1967). *Teaching the infant to swim.* New York: Harcourt Brace Jovanovich.

Petzel, P. (1975). *Teach your tot to swim.* St. Petersburg, FL: Great Outdoors.

Prudden, B. (1977). *Your baby can swim.* New York: Reader's Digest Press.

Devices

Tot Docks are manufactured by Stadiums Unlimited, Grinnell, IA 50112.

Chapter 12

AQUATIC PROGRAMS FOR SPECIAL GROUPS

Assistance for Special Groups
Leadership Development
General Management Suggestions
Adult Aquatic Programs
Programs for Disabled Swimmers
Scuba Programs
Competitive Programs
Open-Water Programs
Supplemental Learning Activities

Special groups (adults, the disabled, and special interest groups such as scuba clubs, sailing squadrons, and so on) are found in almost every community. These groups create special demands on facilities because their numbers are small and they need space and equipment. Too often these groups are relegated to poor time periods simply because their attendance is small compared to that of instructional or recreational users. Although maximum attendance is desirable for the facility from a financial and public relations standpoint, each group deserves its share of prime facility time.

Figure 9.1 makes it obvious that such special groups do not receive much time, prime or otherwise. Although agency sponsors (e.g., YMCA and Boys Clubs) allot up to 30% of their time to these groups, the commitment from others can be as low as 5%. The adult groups, especially, will demand more and better time slots as they increase in number.

ASSISTANCE FOR SPECIAL GROUPS

Five special aquatic groups can be identified: (a) adults, (b) the disabled, (c) scuba clubs, (d) teams (swimming, diving, synchronized swimming, water polo), and (e) small-craft sailors. Other groups include water-skiers, canoeists, Hobie sailors, skin divers, spearfishermen, bodysurfers, snorkelers, and so on.

In keeping with the concept of a total aquatic program, all these groups should be supported in any way possible. At the very least, each group should have minimum access to space at a reasonable time period. Although it is recognized that the membership of some groups is small and that the facility must at least be self-supporting, the need for a financially sound operation must be balanced with the necessity to involve all segments of the population in aquatics.

LEADERSHIP DEVELOPMENT

In some cases, a person from the aquatic staff should be the catalyst in forming a special group, calling the initial meeting, arranging time and space, and contacting potential members. It is common to provide extra benefits (e.g., reduced rental charges, postage for flyers to a select mailing list, etc.) to help fledgling groups.

In those instances where the aquatic facility is helping to initiate the special group, the program content is tentatively determined by the aquatic staff. However, the leaders and/or the members should quickly assume this role, with a staff person serving as a facilitator. Outside organizations such as the YMCA, the National Association of Underwater Instructors (NAUI), and the Professional Association of Diving Instructors (PADI) have established excellent curricula and training programs of their own. In other situations, a local group organizes a program on the basis of the needs of its clientele, such as a swimming program for the disabled. In all cases, the aquatic facility manager is responsible for conducting the program and observing established safety regulations.

An ongoing problem with aquatic groups is leadership. Many groups began under the leadership of interested parents who were not employed by the aquatic facility. This can be a good arrangement if the leaders are qualified and conduct a superior program. Too often, however, the quality of leadership is uneven or deficient; proper safety precautions are not observed, substitute leaders are left in charge, and so on. Especially in smaller communities, leaders are thrust into responsible roles simply because they will serve rather than because they are qualified. Even more serious is the void that remains when the founding leaders leave the program. In addition, there are situations in which the leader is simply unqualified and will not voluntarily relinquish control.

All the preceding circumstances underscore the importance of assigning at least one member of the aquatic staff to each group that uses the facility. This person should assume a minor leadership role, ensuring that safety rules are followed and that the program is beneficial to the participants.

GENERAL MANAGEMENT SUGGESTIONS

Suggestions concerning planning, scheduling, enrollment, fees, and record keeping for these special groups follow.

Planning

Safety

Lifeguards should be supplied by the facility rather than by the group. If regular employees are not on duty, there is no assurance that facility regulations will be enforced.

Special Needs

Space and equipment needs must be known before permission to use the facility is given. For example, a synchronized-swimming group needs record players, but sometimes there are no safe electrical outlets available. Or, a Master's swim team needs a secure area in which to store its pace clock, fins, and so on. In other cases, insurance companies may require the sponsor of the facility to carry additional coverage if, for example, water skiing is permitted on a small lake. If so, costs should be borne by the special interest aquatic group.

Sharing Facilities

If the group is primarily recreational and space is not a problem, two or more groups might be able to share an area. For example, two lanes for lap swimmers can be reserved during general recreational swimming hours.

Entertainment, Fund-Raising, and Clinics

Many special groups wish to have one or two special programs a year (e.g., swimathons, clinics for coaches, and swim shows). If possible, the rental charge should be minimal (or even nonexistent) for one annual program by each group.

Instruction

If the group will provide the instruction, the facility administrators must know about and approve both the instructor's qualifications and the planned curriculum.

Scheduling

Inclusiveness

Advance contact with every possible group is necessary so that all can be included in the schedule.

Space Availability

Attempt to have one unassigned time period per week. This could be used by special groups (e.g., a water-survival session for fly fishermen) on a one-time-only basis.

Contract

The leader of each group should sign a contract for facility use. Contract details include time, equipment provided by the facility, assigned space, names of instructors, and rental fees.

Space Allotment

If special groups practice during recreational hours, they should have their own areas in which to do so.

Enrollment

Registration

If possible, let the group handle all enrollment details.

Participation

In some cases, the group becomes tightly organized and does not seek new members. It is debatable whether this is desirable at a public facility, where the goal should be maximum participation.

Skills

Standards for participation (e.g., minimum swimming skill to take part in a scuba club) should be established and checked by the group. Enforcement of such prerequisite skills could be a problem because some groups tend to invite everyone to participate. The absence of enforced standards may put the facility manager in a precarious legal position in case of an accident.

Fees

Rental Charges

Fees may vary, but it is a sound procedure to have at least a nominal charge for all groups. A flat fee for the use of the facility is preferable for highly organized clubs (e.g., scuba), whereas others (e.g., swimmers on a Master's team) may be charged on a per person basis.

Refunds

Discourage refunds but instead offer make-up sessions or enrollment in subsequent classes.

Amount

If the program is to be cost efficient, total hourly income must at least equal the hourly cost of operation (see chapter 7).

Record Keeping

Generally, the only records kept by the facility staff include a listing of the leader's name and the attendance at each session. If instruction is offered, details of the class (e.g., roster, the qualifications of the instructor, and the curriculum outline) should be kept for at least 1 year.

ADULT AQUATIC PROGRAMS

One of the major changes in aquatic recreation in the past decade is the great increase in the number of adults participating in swimming fitness and competitive programs. To participate, many had to be better swimmers, so they enrolled in instructional classes. They soon began to swim laps of various strokes; for some, the urge to compete led them to take part in adult competitive programs. Specific suggestions concerning the programs for adults follow.

Instructional Programs

Adults should (in theory) be able to learn to swim easily. They understand concepts, are motivated, and have a wealth of experience in all kinds of psychomotor tasks. However, it is common to find that their enthusiasm rapidly wanes because they fail to progress as fast as they wish. Generally, the dropout rate increases as the students become older, so effective organization and teaching strategies are a necessity.

The following considerations underlie a successful instructional program for adults (and for all swim programs).

Goals

In general, adults take lessons for personal enjoyment, to gain safety skills for themselves and to help others, and to improve personal levels of health and fitness. The instructor can help best when he or she is aware of each individual's personal goals.

Skills to Be Mastered

At a minimum, adults need to become adjusted to water and to reduce their fear of it. They also need to learn at least two effective strokes, survival floating, bobbing, turning over from the stomach to the back and vice versa, reaching assists, and resuscitation. Finally, adults must gain the ability to swim distances without undue fatigue.

Classes

These should be held during the less crowded and less noisy times, with short series (2 to 3 weeks with 3 to 4 sessions per week) and half-hour sessions.

Peer Groups

Participants prefer being with others of the same relative ages and general ability levels.

Individual Instruction

Free time (for supervised practice) before and after class is appreciated by students.

Safety

All instructors and lifeguards should be certified in CPR and first aid. A suggested teacher-pupil ratio is 1:10.

Facilities

If ladders or roll-out gutters are not available, entry and exit from the pool can be facilitated by using chairs in pool corners.

Water Temperature

Warmer water (84 °F to 86 °F) is preferred by learners.

Swim Aids

Flotation devices are useful but may cause embarrassment. Swim fins are excellent both for kicking practice and for swimming laps.

Water Exercise Programs

The current interest in physical fitness has offered adults another reason to use aquatic facilities. Water exercises can be defined as various aquatic conditioning movements that are designed to help the participant attain and maintain physical fitness. These techniques can be calisthenic-type exercises, "slimnastic" routines, games, or lap swimming.

Not everyone can swim lengths (or even widths), yet persons of all ages can move in the water. Water exercises have certain advantages over land exercises: Buoyancy puts less strain on the joints, there is no fear of falling to the ground, the heated environment can produce relaxation, and eccentric contractions (a major source of muscle soreness) are virtually nonexistent (Committee Report, 1986). In addition, the water offers a new and enjoyable environment in which to perform such familiar and traditional exercise movements as running, hopping, and twisting. The usual swimming movements (kicking, pulling, and bobbing) can be employed for conditioning as well as for skill development. Because water exercises can be either easy or vigorous, they must be adapted to the physical limitations of the individual to improve flexibility, strength, and circulatory endurance. In short, water exercise can increase the individual's physical condition, skill level, and self-confidence.

Leading a water exercise class entails more than directing calisthenics in the water. The most obvious suggestion is to have an enthusiastic leader participate while leading the group. Other suggestions follow.

Medical Permission

Water exercises can be rather vigorous. Everyone, especially senior citizens, should obtain a physician's permission before beginning. Physicians are more apt to approve if a prepared form that outlines the program is available for them to sign.

Warm-Up, Exercise, Cool-Down

Senior citizens, in particular, need planned warm-up and cool-down segments in an exercise program. The exercises should be invigorating and somewhat tiring but not exhausting.

Deep and Shallow Water

Because many members of an exercise group will be poor swimmers, the workout should be conducted primarily in shoulder-deep water. Restrict deep-water exercises to proficient swimmers who are in good physical condition.

Instruction

While skill development is not the primary purpose of a water exercise class, it is wise to include skills such as rotary breathing, arm strokes while standing, kicking lengths, and so on, which will help members improve their swimming ability.

Variety

Include different activities in classes: easier exercises with many repetitions, more difficult exercises with fewer repetitions, slimnastic-type exercise, occasional swimming or kicking laps, and water games.

Lap Swimming

Adults of all ages have discovered that lap swimming is an excellent way to achieve physical and mental exuberance. Permanent lap lanes (generally one-third of the pool) are common during recreational swimming hours. In some cases, taking reservations for 30-minute periods in a particular lane may be necessary. Swimming is done in the traditional circle pattern, with lanes designated as "fast," "medium speed," and "recreational laps" (do not use the phrase "slow lane").

Adults should view lap swimming as a long-term commitment and not only a monthly or a seasonal activity. The basic concept is to increase the yardage one swims gradually, preferably using a variety of strokes. The following advice should be prominently displayed in each locker room:

Adult Lap Swimming
- Obtain a physician's approval before beginning a program.
- Always warm up and cool down.
- Avoid all-out sprinting.
- Do not swim to exhaustion.

Adult Competitive Programs

Competitive swimming for adults is a recent phenomenon in the United States, having only begun in 1970. In 1980, there were about 1,000 competitors in the national Master's short-course meet; in 1987, there were over 2,400! A second competitive opportunity is the Senior Olympics, which includes swimming as one of its events. Thus, teams of men and women, ages 25 and over, are found in virtually every city that has an indoor pool. The proliferation of competitive swimming is a cause for concern among aquatic staffs because competitive swimmers want more water time and fewer people in their lanes. Fortunately, many adults are flexible in their workout hours, so mid-morning and late-evening hours are sometimes suitable.

Competitive swimmers have one essential need, namely, pool time. For the most part, they are former competitors who believe they can train themselves. If they have a coach, however, team membership may grow dramatically, causing even more pressure for pool time.

PROGRAMS FOR DISABLED SWIMMERS

Depending on the criteria used, there are approximately 50,000,000 Americans with some physical, mental, or emotional impairment. The term "handicapped" is commonly used in the United States; however, it is accurate to consider those with physical, mental, or emotional problems as disabled. This latter term will be used throughout this chapter to signify persons with various handicaps. "Adapted aquatics" is the term used to signify aquatic programs developed for the disabled.

The vast majority (90%) of disabled people have little or no difficulty participating in regular programs. However, until the last 20 years, the remaining 10% had limited opportunities to participate in any type of aquatic program. For the most part, the disabled were restricted to occasional special programs conducted by interested groups of volunteers.

Exactly what are the needs of this smaller group? Basically, their needs are not much different from those of the general population. Instruction obviously is important, and much adaptation is necessary. Recreational swimming and boating are most often done in conjunction with instructional periods. Annual Special Olympics meets are held on local, regional, and national levels. Practice time for these special events is usually held during instructional sessions.

Mainstreaming

With the passage of PL 94-142 and Section 504 of the Rehabilitation Act of 1973, special populations have been given the opportunity to participate in the "least restrictive environment" (i.e., the most regularly scheduled program from which the person can benefit). These laws do not prohibit special programs but encourage mainstreaming, that is, placing a person in a regular class until it is evident that a special class would be more beneficial.

Is mainstreaming in aquatics desirable? McIlwain (1978) found evidence that the handicapped will gain more if they are mainstreamed. In addition, proponents of mainstreaming feel that placing disabled persons with nondisabled persons increases awareness and concern of all participants and that the disabled encounter enough obstacles in life, so why segregate them unnecessarily?

Conversely, others feel that mainstreaming in general is not desirable because (a) working in the water with the disabled requires more staff (specially trained teachers sometimes in a 1:1 ratio), (b) it requires more time and more safety considerations, and (c) it often necessitates special equipment and facilities.

What is the solution to mainstreaming? We feel that society creates the handicaps and that very few persons are so disabled that they cannot learn to move through, be safe in, and enjoy aquatic sports. As more instructors become qualified (through certification with recognized training programs), mainstreaming will gain impetus in aquatic programs.

Aquatic Classes for the Disabled

Whether they are in separate classes or are mainstreamed, disabled persons will need some degree of special attention. It is advisable that most seriously disabled persons begin in separate classes (see following discussion) and then move into regular classes as their skill and your resources permit.

The operation of separate programs depends on volunteer helpers, cooperation with the facility staff, and community enthusiasm. Suggestions concerning such programs follow.

Overall Goal

As with the nondisabled, these persons want to enjoy aquatic activity regardless of their physical, mental, or emotional disability.

Specific Goals

Strokes and skills must be adapted to the capabilities of each person, keeping in mind the safety of the student (both currently and in the future). Equally important is to create positive attitudes and beliefs in both the student and the parents/guardians so that the person can be helped in both aquatics and other aspects of life.

Needs

Survey the community, determining the number of persons who would benefit from the program, the available facilities, and potential helpers.

Sponsors

To secure assistance, form an advisory council that represents every conceivable group. After selecting a director, assign tasks (e.g., transportation) to subgroups.

Personnel

Select and train master teachers, who in turn can provide in-service training to others. A long list of helpers must be developed, as volunteers tend to come and go quickly. An effective technique that is not as universal as it should be is to use instructors who are also disabled (Priest, 1982).

Funding

Although the program might eventually become self-supporting, it certainly will not be so during its formative period. Local service groups or the United Way are more likely to be the sustaining sponsors; government money cannot be depended on for support.

Public Relations

Designate a director of public relations, whose job it is to publicize the worthiness of the program through planned public relations efforts and cooperation with other agencies.

Beginning the Program

Start small, enrolling those with greatest chance of success at first (usually those ages 6 to 10). Be certain that all participants have obtained medical permission to participate.

Course Content

The references at the end of this chapter contain specific advice on skill development. Regardless of the disability, skills to be practiced include physical adaptation to water, mobility, floating, leg and arm propulsion, and deep-water mobility.

Safety

If the person cannot follow directions and/or cannot regain balance, never deviate from a 1:1 teacher-pupil ratio.

Facilities

All persons must have safe access to the facility and to the pool. A small pool with bright surroundings and warm water (85 °F to 88 °F) is desirable.

Dressing Area

The pool must be accessible to persons in wheelchairs, and it must have a nonslip floor and handrails. The dressing area must be on the same level as the pool.

Record Keeping

Make a daily record of each person's activity. But remember that records are confidential and should be viewed only by a physical therapist, a physician, and so on.

SCUBA PROGRAMS

For basic instruction, scuba clubs need deep-water time, which is usually obtained by renting the diving well of a pool. Open-water space is normally available in lakes and ponds, where a rental fee is seldom charged.

In some cases (primarily colleges) a certified instructor is employed by a facility to teach scuba classes. However, the large amount of money required to purchase insurance, diving gear, and audiovisual aids (to say nothing of the labor cost) has caused most facilities merely to serve as a landlord to scuba clubs and to various commercial diving shops. The responsibility falls on the facility manager to ensure that a competent instructor is present, that the equipment is safe, and that the instruction is given in a safe manner.

Regardless of which role the aquatic facility assumes, only instructors certified by national agencies such as the YMCA, NAUI, NAUIC, PADI, and SSI should be allowed to conduct classes (see the resource list at the end of this chapter).

COMPETITIVE PROGRAMS

Competition is a very visible part of a total aquatic program. Regattas, swim meets, canoe races, and novelty events receive much publicity because they involve a large number of participants. Unfortunately, competitive events bring at least two recurring problems: (a) They use prime facility time, thus crowding other activities and sometimes disrupting group use of the facility for several days; and (b) use of the facilities sometimes results in a loss of income that cannot be offset by admission fees or concession sales.

Basic Concept: Support of All Competitive Groups

Swimming teams (age group, high school, college, adult) are numerous and seek much pool time for practices and meets.

Diving teams, synchro teams, and water polo teams are less demanding but no less deserving. Regardless, competition is an essential part of a total aquatic program. To the best of its resources, the aquatic staff must support all kinds of competitive aquatic events. This means, at the very least, providing space and time to the various sponsoring groups and aiding in the management of events.

Aquatic Facility Relationship With Competitive Programs

There are two possible formats under which competitive programs can operate. One is when a private group rents the facility on a long-term basis, and the other is when the aquatic facility sponsors the team.

In the first situation, the facility manager essentially becomes a "landlord." The facility must be available at the specified time and under the agreed-on conditions. The aquatic facility staff acts cooperatively with the group, exercising only minimal control once it is apparent that proper safety measures are being followed.

In the second situation, the aquatic facility sponsors various teams. Because the coach will be an employee of the facility, the staff can emphasize consistent and proper goals as opposed to the inconsistency that is common when coaches are responsible to an outside group. Also, a team sponsored by the facility has a greater chance of receiving its fair share of time and resources.

Facility sponsorship does not imply that all costs be borne by the aquatic program. Actually, every competitive team (except those sponsored by schools) should be self-supporting. Parental and other outside aid should be encouraged when the facility sponsors a team, as it broadens the base of support.

Selection of Coaches

The selection of team coaches is a necessary task of the sponsor (either the private group or the facility staff). After an overall goal is determined, which can range from "fun and games" to domination at the national level, a job description should be written. The selection committee needs to consider the coaches' personal philosophies in addition to the obvious requirements (experience, maturity, consciousness of public relations, etc.). One coach might consider winning the only worthwhile goal, while another might consider participant enjoyment the primary goal. We are not advocating one goal over another but are pointing out only that the ideals of the coach must be compatible with the goal of the sponsor.

Management Suggestions

The material that follows will provide an understanding of the aid that must be given to competitive groups.

Time Provisions

Securing time for competitive groups is not difficult if it is considered when the quarterly or seasonal schedule is developed. On the other hand, freeing time for competitive events can be a problem. Good financial sense dictates that all prime time be scheduled (but this obviously leaves no unscheduled prime time). The usual solution is to cancel the regularly scheduled program to provide for competitive events, but this can be unpopular with the preempted group. In truth, there may be no satisfactory solution to this dilemma.

Fees

Because most facilities plan to operate at least to break-even, the rental fee for competitive teams is based on the true cost to operate the facility (or portion thereof) for the time period. It is common to give a 10% to 20% reduction in the standard fee if a certain number of hours in a month (e.g., 25) are contracted for. The rental fee for special competitive events is normally based on the income lost (because the facility is closed to general use) plus the wages of the workers during the event.

Indoor-Space Provisions

Competitive groups need storage space for record players, kick boards, hand paddles, lap counters, touch pads, and so on. The space must be secure from intruders yet accessible to the proper persons.

Weight-Training Equipment

The growing popularity of weight training in aquatic programs has added to space problems at indoor facilities. An accessible, secure room is essential, and use of the equipment should be permitted only when a coach is present.

Outdoor Storage Space

Sheds, boathouses, and canoe racks can be made easily, but making them secure from vandalism and theft will add to the costs.

Official Rules and Regulations

Each sport's national governing body has the ultimate authority regarding competition. Because of this power, each governing body has become the dominant force in its specialty. The national governing body should be consulted by coaches and facility managers for information of all types: program suggestions, rules interpretation, printed material, and so on (for a current listing, see the resources list at the end of this chapter).

OPEN-WATER PROGRAMS

Open-water facilities sponsored by public entities often serve many purposes. If resources and the environment permit, such activities as canoeing, waterskiing, sailing, snorkeling, scuba diving, fishing, and so on should be part of the total aquatic program.

Except for supervised swimming and boating areas, the amount of control over each group is minimal. The aquatic facility manager is concerned primarily that the facilities provided are free from danger and that one group does not infringe on the rights of others.

Facility needs vary according to the group. Moorage/storage space at the facility is apt to be assigned to each open-water group, with leaders being able to come and go as they desire. Special races or meets are sometimes held that bring occasional complaints from others who wish to use the facilities but who are not members of the group.

Ritz (1987) pointed out that the continued growth and prosperity of open-water recreation groups will not be easy. Merely offering the facilities is not enough. To be successful, three program techniques must be implemented:

1. *Measure levels of attainment:* Users must be educated so that they attain competence in both skills and knowledge; this motivates them to continue.
2. *Provide challenging activities:* Once the basics are mastered, motivate the members with techniques that are more challenging.
3. *Practice good safety habits:* Members will react negatively to unsafe practices and to peers who take undue risks. In addition, because much of the activity of these groups is out of sight of the main facility, good safety habits provide peace of mind for both the group leaders and the sponsor (and the insurance company).

SUPPLEMENTAL LEARNING ACTIVITIES

1. Interview an aquatic facility manager to discover the general philosophy of the sponsor on accommodating special groups.

2. Interview an aquatic facility manager concerning one of the following aspects of adult programs: planning, scheduling, enrollment, or fees.

3. Observe an adult swimming class. Discover the motivational techniques and the fear-reduction and teaching strategies used by the instructor.

4. Observe a swimming session for the disabled. What safety procedures are

being followed? How does the leader direct the learning environment? What stroke adaptations are seen?

5. Complete a Red Cross or a YMCA training course for working with the disabled.

6. Interview an aquatic facility manager concerning the competitive program. What exactly is the relationship (landlord or sponsor) with the team(s)? Is the relationship satisfactory?

7. Query the facility manager about the teams. Are there problems with time allotments for regular practice and for competition? Is there adequate storage space? Is the leadership adequate?

REFERENCES AND SUGGESTED READINGS

Adrian, M. (1985). Practical applications of research in teaching aquatics to the elderly. *National Aquatics Journal* (Summer), **1**(2), 2-4.

Committee Report. (1986). National advisory committee on aquatic exercise. *National Aquatics Journal* (Spring), **2**(2), 5-7.

Coughenour, C. (1986). Aquatic fitness for senior citizens. *National Aquatics Journal* (Winter) **2**(1), 6-7.

Council for National Cooperation in Aquatics. (1987). *What is aquatic exercise?* [Videotape by National Advisory Committee on Aquatic Exercise].

Crowner, F. (1986). Scuba programs in the university setting. *National Aquatics Journal* (Fall), **2**(4), 3-4.

Evenbeck, B. (1986). Aquatic exercise. *Journal of Health, Physical Education, Recreation and Dance* (October), 22-25.

Fitzner, A. (1986). Aqua-percept program. *National Aquatics Journal* (Spring), **2**(2), 8.

Gabrielsen, M. (Ed.). (1987). Pool facilities for impaired and disabled persons. In *Swimming pools: A guide to their planning, design, and operation* (pp. 131-140). Champaign, IL: Human Kinetics.

Heckathorn, J. (1985). *Strokes and strokes: An instructor's manual for developing swimming programs for stroke victims.* Reston, VA: American Alliance for Health, Physical Education, Recreation and Dance.

Johnson, R. (1978). Leadership in adapted aquatics. In B. Empleton (Ed.), *New horizons in aquatics* (pp. 40-45). Indianapolis, IN: Council for National Cooperation in Aquatics.

Kistler, B., & Espeseth, R. (1986). Water skiing—A rapidly growing aquatic activity. *National Aquatics Journal* (Fall), **2**(2), 2.

Krasevec, J., & Grimes, D. (1984). Water exercise takes on a new image. In L. Priest & A. Crowner (Eds.), *Opportunities in aquatics* (pp. 27-28). Indianapolis, IN: Council for National Cooperation in Aquatics.

LePore, M. (1987). Teaching aquatic activities to persons with head injuries. *National Aquatics Journal* (Winter), **3**(1), 8-9.

Lin, L. (1987). Scuba divers with disabilities challenge medical protocols and ethics. *The Physician and Sportsmedicine*, **15**(6), 224-235.

McIlwain, L. (1978, February). Speech given at "Operation Mainstreaming" conference, Denver.

Piper, C. (1987, April 11). *Aquatics for special populations.* Paper presented at the convention of the American Alliance for Health, Physical Education, Recreation and Dance, Las Vegas, NV.

Priest, L. (1982). Utilization of disabled instructors in adapted aquatic programs. In R. Clayton (Ed.), *Aquatics now* (pp. 96-102). Indianapolis, IN: Council for National Cooperation in Aquatics.

Priest, L. (1985). Diving for the disabled. *National Aquatics Journal* (Spring), **1**(1), 14-15.

Project Aquatic Mainstreaming. (1978). *Outline for a successful program for mainstreaming special populations through aquatic programs.* Longview, WA: YMCA.

Ritz, C. (1987, April 11). *Small craft programming.* Paper presented at the convention of the American Alliance for Health, Physical Education, Recreation and Dance, Las Vegas, NV.

Steinbrunner, R. (1982). Aquatics for the disabled. In R. Clayton (Ed.), *Aquatics now* (pp. 95-102). Indianapolis, IN: Council for National Cooperation in Aquatics.

White, S., & Landis, L. (1987). Aquatic exercise as an individualized self-testing aquatic fitness course. *National Aquatics Journal* (Winter), **3**(1), 5-6.

RESOURCES

Adapted Aquatic Programs

A starting point for information on adapted aquatics is the Computerized Information Retrieval System in Adapted Aquatics. For further information about their annotated bibliography, contact Sue Grosse, 7252 W. Wabash Ave., Milwaukee, WI 53223.

The source for information concerning competition for the mentally retarded is the Joseph P. Kennedy Jr. Foundation, 1350 New York Ave., NW, Suite 500, Washington, DC 20006.

A source for mainstreaming in aquatics is Project Aquatic Mainstreaming. Contact Grace Reynolds, Box 1781, Longview, WA 98632.

National agencies (most notably the Red Cross and the YMCA) have been the leaders in publishing reference material. The aquatic facility library should have the following references on hand:

American National Red Cross. (1977). *Adapted aquatics.* Washington, DC: Author.

Discusses the value of a swimming program for the impaired, the specific handicaps the instructor is apt to encounter, program organization and administration, teaching approaches, and special programs

American National Red Cross. (1977). *Methods in adapted aquatics.* Washington, DC: Author.

Text used when persons are taking the Red Cross instructor certification course

American National Red Cross. (1981). *Manual for the aide in adapted aquatics.* Washington, DC: Author.

Priest, L. (Ed.). (1985). *Adapted aquatic leadership development, and adapted aquatic teaching methods.* Indianapolis, IN: Council for National Cooperation in Aquatics.

A compilation of articles that first appeared in the proceedings of various CNCA conferences

YMCA of the USA. (1987). *Aquatics for special populations.* Champaign, IL: Human Kinetics.

Scuba Programs

Certifying Agencies

National Association of Underwater Instructors (NAUI), Box 14650, Montclair, CA 91763

National Association of Underwater Instructors Canada (NAUIC), 10 Monet Ave., Etobicoke, Ontario, Canada M9C 3N7

National YMCA Aquatic Program, Oakbrooke Square, 6083-A Oakbrooke Parkway, Norcross, GA 30092

Professional Association of Diving Instructors (PADI), 1243 East Warner Ave., Santa Ana, CA 92705

Scuba Schools International (SSI), 2619 Canton Ct., Fort Collins, CO 80521

Each of the preceding groups has its own text and audiovisual aids. The appropriate materials should be in the facility library.

Library Resources for Scuba Programs

Pierce, A. (1985). *Scuba life saving*. Champaign, IL: Human Kinetics.

"A compilation, consolidation and condensation of scuba lifesaving and self-rescue techniques developed by diving physicians, authors, instructors, divemasters, scuba divers, snorklers and other aquatic enthusiasts" (p. iii)

Robinson, J., & Fox, A.D. (1987). *Scuba diving with disabilities*. Champaign, IL: Human Kinetics.

Provides information for divers and instructors on the equipment and skills used by divers with a variety of disabilities

Smith, R. (Ed.). (1985). *The new science of skin and scuba diving*. Indianapolis, IN:

Council for National Cooperation in Aquatics.

The first publication in the United States on this topic and still the standard reference

Competitive Programs

National Governing Bodies

United States

U.S. Canoeing and Kayaking Association, Pan Am Plaza #470, 201 S. Capitol Ave., Indianapolis, IN 46225

U.S. Diving Association, Pan Am Plaza #430, 201 S. Capitol Ave., Indianapolis, IN 46225

U.S. Rowing Association, Pan Am Plaza #400, 201 S. Capitol Ave., Indianapolis, IN 46225

U.S. Swimming, 1750 E. Boulder St., Colorado Springs, CO 80909

U.S. Synchronized Swimming, Pan Am Plaza #510, 201 S. Capitol Ave., Indianapolis, IN 46225

U.S. Water Polo Association, 901 W. New York St., Indianapolis, IN 46223

Canada (All at 333 River Rd., Vanier City, Ontario, Canada K1L 8B9)

Canadian Amateur Diving Association

Canadian Amateur Swimming Association

Canadian Amateur Synchronized Swimming Association

Canadian Amateur Water Polo Association

Library Resources for Competitive Programs

Swimming

Colwin, C. (1977). *An introduction to swimming coaching*. Vanier City, Ontario,

Canada: Canadian Amateur Swimming Association.

Colwin, C. (1978). *Swimming coaching at the club level*. Vanier City, Ontario, Canada: Canadian Amateur Swimming Association.

Each book by Colwin is valuable to beginning coaches especially, as it contains organizational as well as technical information

Maglischo, E. (1982). *Swimming faster*. Palo Alto, CA: Mayfield.

Currently the definitive text for coaches; too technical for beginning coaches, but essential for those who aspire to develop swimmers for regional and national competition

Thomas, D.G. (1988). *Competitive swimming management*. Champaign, IL: Human Kinetics.

Offers time-tested management tips and forms, flowcharts, and cards that will aid the beginning or veteran coach in managing the competitive team

Synchronized Swimming

Forbes, M. (1984). *Coaching synchronized swimming effectively*. Champaign, IL: Human Kinetics.

Complete description and illustrations of strokes and skills used in the U.S. Synchronized Swimming's National Achievement Program

Lundholm, J., & Ruggieri, M.J. (1985). *Introduction to synchronized swimming*. (2nd ed.). Columbus, OH: R & R Sports Academies.

Concepts, body positions, strokes and variations, sculling, progressions and stunts, conditioning, routine development, and competitive meets

Diving

Batterman, C. (1968). *The techniques of springboard diving*. Cambridge, MA: MIT Press.

Still the basic reference for diving

Water Polo

Cicciarella, C. (1981). *The sport of water polo*. Boston: American Press.

A good introduction for beginning coaches and players

Cutino, P., & Bledsoe, D. (1976). *Polo: The manual for coach and player*. Los Angeles: Swimming World Publications.

Strategies and tactics for the experienced coach

Small Craft and Miscellaneous Programs

National Groups

American Canoe Association, Box 248, Lorton, VA 22079

American Water Ski Association, Box 191, Winter Haven, FL 33882

American Whitewater Affiliation, Box 321, Concord, NH 03301

Canadian Canoe Association, 333 River Road, Vanier City, Ontario, Canada K1L 8B9

U.S. Coast Guard Office of Boating Safety, USCG Headquarters, 400 Seventh St., SW, Washington, DC 20560

Publications

Performance techniques for these various activities

American National Red Cross. (1979). *Basic outboard boating*. Washington, DC: Author.

American National Red Cross. (1982). *Basic sailing*. Washington, DC: Author.

American National Red Cross. (1982). *Basic canoeing and kayaking*. Washington, DC: Author.

Boating safety guide (No. T31-3173). Available from Transport Canada officers or Royal Canadian Mounted Police detachments.

Pyle, B. (Ed.). (1980). *Flatwater canoeing: A syllabus for the aquatic council courses* *"teacher and master teacher of flatwater canoeing."* Reston, VA: American Alliance of Health, Physical Education, Recreation and Dance.

Information on instructor skills, practical knowledge, canoe racing and meets, canoe adaptations, kayaking, canoeing for the handicapped, organization and administration of programs, and teaching methods

AQUATIC-RELATED ORGANIZATIONS

Amateur Athletic Union of the USA, 3400 W. 86th St., Indianapolis, IN 46268

American Alliance for Health, Physical Education, Recreation and Dance, 1900 Association Dr., Reston, VA 22091

American Camping Association, Bradford Woods, Martinsville, IN 46151

American National Red Cross, 17th & D Sts., Washington, DC 20006

Boy Scouts of America, 1325 Walnut Hill La., Irving, TX 75261

Boy Scouts of Canada, Box 5151, Station F, Ottawa, Ontario, Canada K2C 3G7

Boys Clubs of America, 711 First Ave., New York, NY 10017

Camp Fire, Inc., 1740 Broadway, New York, NY 10019

Canadian Red Cross Society, 95 Wellesley St. E., Toronto, Ontario, Canada M4Y 1H6

Council for National Cooperation in Aquatics, 901 W. New York St., Indianapolis, IN 46223

Girl Scouts of America, 830 Third Ave., New York, NY 10022

International Association for the Advancement of Aquatic Art, c/o J. White, 2507 Carlisle Place, Sarasota, FL 33581

International Swimming Hall of Fame, 1 Hall of Fame Dr., Ft. Lauderdale, FL 33316

National Board of the Young Women's Christian Association, 726 Broadway, New York, NY 10003

National Council of YMCAs of Canada, 2160 Yonge St., Toronto, Ontario, Canada M4S 2A9

National Forum for the Advancement of Aquatics, Attn: A. McCloskey, 26 Channing Place, Eastchester, NY 10709

National Jewish Welfare Board, 15 E. 26th St., New York, NY 10010

National Recreation and Park Association, 1601 N. Kent St., Arlington, VA 22209

National Spa and Pool Institute, 12111 Eisenhower Ave., Alexandria, VA 22314

President's Council on Physical Fitness and Sports, Suite 303, Donahoe Bldg., 6th & D Sts., Washington, DC 20201

Royal Life Saving Society Canada, 191 Church St., Toronto, Ontario, Canada M5B 1Y7

Underwater Society of America, Box 628, Daly City, CA 94017

United States Lifesaving Association, Box 366, Huntington Beach, CA 92648

United States Professional Diving Coaches, c/o H. Billingsly, Athletic Department, Indiana University, Bloomington, IN 47405

YMCA of the USA, 110 N. Wacker Dr., Chicago, IL 60606

POOL OPERATION INFORMATION FORM

The information requested on this form is vital to the complete understanding of the operation of a particular swimming pool.

Date: _____

Pool name or identification: _____

Location or address: _____

Name of operator, or contact: _____

   Phone no.: _____

Dimensions and depth schedule (sketch):

Pool capacity in gallons: _____

  according to: _____

(Cont.)

Pool Operation Information Form (Cont.)

Circulation system type

Inlets—number and location: _____

Drains—number and location: _____

Type overflow trough: _____

Overflow water goes to: _____

Standard or reverse flow circulation: _____

Pump information

Make: _____   Model: _____

Serial no.: _____   Motor HP: _____

Pump capacity (gpm) in present situation: _____

Flow rate (typical)

Type flow-rate gauge: _____

Beginning of filter run (gpm): _____

End of filter run (gpm): _____

according to: _____

Turnover

1 turnover every _____ hours. Turnovers per day: _____

Filters operate _____ hours per day.

according to: _____

Average length of filter run: _____ (hours) (days) (weeks)

End of filter run determined by what? _____

Filters

Make: _____

Type: conventional sand and gravel, high-rate sand, vacuum diatomite, pressure diatomite, cartridge

Number of tanks: _____ Size of tanks: _____

No. filter elements per tank: _____

Filter surface area per element: _____ sq ft

Filter surface area per tank: _____ sq ft

Total filter surface area: _____ sq ft

Pool Operation Information Form (Cont.)

Filter design flow rate: _____ gpm/sq ft

Actual flow rate: _____ gpm/sq ft

   according to: _____

Filter pressure gauges

  At beginning of run—Influent: _____ Effluent: _____ (psi)

  At end of filter run—Influent: _____ Effluent: _____ (psi)

  Location of gauges: _____

Gauges at the pump

  Pressure: _____ psi Vacuum: _____ in. Hg

  Total operating head? _____ psi or ft

Chemistry

  At time of visit:

    pH: _____ Free residual: _____ Total residual: _____

    Combined residual: _____ Total alkalinity: _____ ppm

    Water temperature: _____ Air temperature: _____

    Water clarity (comment): _____

  Test kit

    Make: _____

    Type: _____

    Reagent used for pH test: _____

    Reagent used for bactericide test: _____

    Does it test for total alkalinity? _____

    Does it test for cyanurates? _____

    Other capabilities: _____

  Sanitation accomplished with

    Gas Cl_2: _____ NaOCl: _____ $Ca(OCl)_2$ _____ Cyanurates: _____

    Chlorine generator: _____ Bromine: _____ Ozone: _____

    Silver ion: _____ Silver and copper ion (Tarnpure): _____

    Iodine: _____ Ultraviolet: _____

    Specific product name: _____

(Cont.)

Pool Operation Information Form (Cont.)

Bactericide feeder

Make: _____ Model: _____

Type—Gas feeder: _____ Liquid pump: _____ Erosion type: _____

Capacity of feeder: _____ per hr/day

Average amount of bactericide used per day: _____

Applied before filter? _____ after filter? _____

pH control

Product used for pH control: _____

Average use per day/week: _____

Type feeder used: _____

Total alkalinity control

Product used for alkalinity control: _____

Average use per week/month: _____

Type of feeder used: _____

Alum

Is alum used? _____ How much per application? _____

When added? _____ Where added? _____

How added? _____ How fast added? _____

For what purpose is alum used? _____

Type of feeder: _____

Algaecide

What product is used? _____

Average use per week/month: _____

How added? _____

When added? _____

What type of feeder? _____

Other chemicals used

List all other chemicals used in treating the pool. For each chemical listed, state the purpose for its use, how much was used, and how often each was used.

SEASONAL TASKS FOR OPENING AND CLOSING AN AQUATIC FACILITY

TASKS: PRIOR TO OPENING THE FACILITY

Initial Preseason Tasks

1. Verify that all utilities have been connected (water, light, phone).
2. Check all parts of the purification and recirculation systems to make sure that they are ready to operate.
3. Make sure that all connections are tight, no gaskets are worn, no air locks exist, and no rust or corrosion has caused a dangerous condition.
4. Confirm that supplies of towels, suits, soap, toilet tissue, paper towels, and chemicals are adequate.
5. Be sure that all toilet, shower, fountain, and wash fixtures are operating properly and have been washed with disinfectant.
6. Make certain that an adequate supply of report forms, bottles for water samples, and chemicals for the water-testing kit is on hand.
7. Verify that there is an ample supply of mops, buckets, hoses, and disinfectants.

8. Clean away all dirt and sediment in the pool, deck, office, and locker room areas.
9. Remove all mold and algae growth.
10. Replace fuses, light bulbs and globes, reflectors, clocks, ladders, diving boards, and similar items removed when the facility was closed at the end of the previous season.

Preseason Preparation of Recirculation and Purification Systems

1. Examine the filter (top of each sand-and-gravel or high-rate sand filter, the cartridges of a cartridge filter, or the plastic cloths of the diatomaceous-earth filter) for defects.
2. Make certain that the chemical feed containers are filled.
3. Be sure that the pump is primed with water before starting.
4. Review the manufacturer's instructions for operation of the filtration and purification equipment.
5. Apply diatom precoat if diatomite filters are used. Turn on the water

slowly to minimize the amount of rust and sediment loosened by the flow. Fill the sand-and-gravel filter from bottom to top before beginning normal filter flow. The pool will be filled with cleaner water if the new water is routed through the filter rather than letting it flow directly from the city water main into the pool.

6. Start the chlorinator, or add bactericide to the water when the pool is about one-quarter full, and maintain a high residual (about 1.5 to 2.0 ppm for chlorine or 2.0 to 2.5 ppm if bromine is used) while the pool is filling. Then allow the residual to drop to normal operating level.

7. Test the pH of the water as soon as the pool is filled and add acid or soda ash as required to bring the pH within the range of 7.2 to 7.8. If gas chlorine is used, some soda ash must be added as the pool fills.

8. If city drinking water is used to fill the pool, about 24 hours of filtering will make it clear enough to swim in.

Last Preseason Tasks

1. Record the pH, clarity observations, and residual chlorine readings three times during the day prior to opening day. Record the amounts of chemicals used.

2. Take lifesaving equipment, clocks, diving boards, check-room bags, and other equipment from storage and install or station them in the proper places for use or issue.

3. See that warning signs, information posters, and regulations are posted.

4. Post duty assignments and schedules for lifeguards, filter operators, locker room supervisors, check-room workers, and other personnel.

CLOSING TASKS

Immediately on Closing

1. Tell the test lab to stop sending sample bottles.

2. Leave the air-relief valve open on sand-and-gravel filters. Be sure it is operating.

3. Open the manhole in the sand filter tank and inspect the top sand. Remove mudballs and other debris.

4. Drain the sand filters completely. Leave the cover off to permit filters to dry but cover the opening with screen to keep small animals out.

5. Leave the drain lines open.

6. Clean the diatomaceous-earth filter. Drain completely and leave drain line open. Remove the elements and wash with oxalic acid and muriatic acid and with detergent.

7. Inspect the filter cloths and discard those that require replacement before the pool is reopened.

Within a Week or So After Closing

1. Drain all lines at the lowest point.

2. Drain toilets and similar fixtures.

3. Put kerosene in pipe traps and goosenecks.

4. Confirm that all floor and deck drains are open and operating.

5. If the pool is to stand empty, drain the water and leave the drain lines open.

6. Place heavy screens over all drains and inlets to keep out rodents and trash.

7. Repair grouting to prevent seepage that may freeze and expand.

8. Inspect the outlet grating, remove rust spots, and apply rust inhibitor.

9. If an outdoor pool is not to be drained, set the water level 6 to 8 inches below the inlet level, chlorinate heavily, add an algaecide, and cover the pool with a pool cover that is strong enough to prevent children from falling through. This keeps debris, rodents, and small animals from getting into the pool during the winter and provides a measure of safety from liability.

10. Some pool operators now believe that it is unnecessary to float logs, tires, kegs, or other objects into the water to protect the pool walls from the effects of ice formation in the pool. Others believe that it is necessary. It is not a good idea to leave the water level at that of underwater lights or underwater windows. They should remain a foot or so beneath the surface and out of the danger of freezing.

11. Disassemble the chlorinator, drain it free of water, and clean and inspect all parts. Make necessary replacements of parts. Identify all parts, store in dry place, and protect with petroleum jelly.

12. Drain and disconnect other chemical feeders, leave lines open, and thoroughly wash off all chemicals.

13. Open the pump casing and drain it thoroughly.

14. Remove fuses from the motor switch and protect the starter against corrosion.

15. Grease the drain plug and identify it with a tag.

16. Have an electrician inspect the motor and wiring to determine repair or replacement needs.

17. Inspect the impeller and shaft. Replace warn parts. Protect unpainted surfaces with a rust inhibitor.

18. Clean and inspect the hair-strainer baskets and gaskets and make necessary replacements. Use a rust inhibitor on unpainted surfaces.

19. Disassemble valves, clean them thoroughly, use a rust inhibitor, and identify by number the parts for reassembly when the pool is reopened. Parts may be stored in a pan of oil or in oiled paper.

20. Disassemble gauges and flowmeter. Clean them thoroughly, use rust inhibitor, and replace parts as needed. Leave all openings open.

21. Brush all rust spots on piping, fixtures, and mechanical parts. Cover the metal parts of the recirculation system with petroleum jelly. Paint marred or chipped spots on equipment and structures.

22. Clean the vacuum cleaner and replace parts as needed. Store it in a safe, dry place.

23. Store the water-testing kit in a heated building. Discard all remaining test-kit chemicals and make a list of them to be reordered next season.

24. Remove remaining supplies of chemicals that may deteriorate while the building is unoccupied. Make a list of chemicals and all other items that must be ordered and delivered before the facility is reopened.

25. Confirm that roof drains are functioning properly.
26. Store or make nonfunctional any outdoor item that might be termed an "attractive nuisance" when left unsupervised (e.g., swing sets or spin wheels).
27. Store ring buoys, ropes, and similar items in a safe, dry place away from exposure to sunlight. Be sure they are completely dry before storing.
28. Remove springboards from stands and store away from heat and moisture. To prevent wooden boards from warping, lay them flat on two-by-four boards.
29. Pack suits and towels in rodent-proof containers and store them in a dry place.

Complete the Closing Process

1. Cover outside drinking fountains with inverted barrels or with 30-mil plastic sheeting for protection.
2. Remove all outside light bulbs and globes. Protect reflectors against weather and vandalism.
3. Bring lifelines, boundary signs from beach areas, and similar items inside for dry storage. Leave warning signs intact that indicate that the beach or pool is closed.
4. Store boats and outside guard stands.
5. Apply a rust inhibitor to gates, ladders, and other metal fixtures and equipment.
6. Clean up refuse and dirt. Leave the inside area spotless.
7. Remove all food, animal nesting materials, and other items that might attract and sustain rodents and insects.
8. Shut off the municipal water.
9. Discontinue gas and telephone services.
10. Disconnect electricity. Remove all fuses or open all circuit breakers except those that are needed for alarm systems and security.
11. Notify the police department of the closing and state how long the premises will be unoccupied and unsupervised.
12. Assemble all records, reports, and operating instructions and arrange for safe storage until the facility is reopened.
13. Install storm shutters or board up windows.
14. Lock all doors and windows. Secure all gates.
15. Submit to superiors a list of all repairs, improvements, and supplies that are needed to reopen the facility.

STANDARDS FOR AQUATIC FACILITIES

SAFETY STANDARDS FOR SWIMMING POOLS

Size and Slope

The maximum safe bather load varies from state to state. New York State's maximum limit is 25 square feet per bather. The U.S. Public Health Service's limit is 24 square feet per bather in water deeper than 5 feet and 15 square feet per bather in shallow water.

The slope of the bottom in shallow-water areas (less than 5 feet) should not be greater than 1:12 (U.S. Public Health Service) except in pools less than 50 feet in length, where 1:8 is acceptable. Slopes of up to 1:3 are acceptable in water areas deeper than 5 feet.

Depth for Diving

No diving should be permitted in water less than 5 feet deep.

The minimum depth for 1-meter board diving is 12 feet. Three-meter boards require a minimum depth of 13 feet (competitive starting blocks should not be installed in depths less than 5 feet).

Water Clarity and Purity

Standards of clarity and purity must meet or exceed the standards of the state and local health departments. New York State requires clarity such that a 4-inch black-and-white object in the deepest water is clearly visible from the pool deck. New York State also requires a pool water pH between 7.2 and 8.2 and a free residual chlorine count of 0.6 to 1.5 ppm, depending on the pH.

Lighting

Safe lighting requirements vary from state to state. New York State requires a minimum intensity of 50 footcandles over the pool to limit glare. Competitive swimming rules recommend 100 footcandles for indoor pools and no glare from windows reflecting on the water surface.

Drains

The U.S. Public Health Service requires two bottom drains in any pool that is more than 20 feet wide and specifies that the grate shall be four times the area of the pipe to reduce the effect of suction. Drains should not be placed directly under diving boards, should have grate openings between 1/2 and 1 inch in size, and must be fastened firmly.

Overflow Troughs

Continuous overflow troughs completely around the perimeter of the pool are required in pools larger than 1,600 square feet (New York State and others) and should be designed so that no swimmer may catch a leg or arm in them. They must provide handholds (U.S. Public Health Service) and should be of a color that contrasts with the deck and pool walls.

Ladders and Steps

All ladders should be recessed into the pool walls and should be nonslip with a wide tread. They should be placed at each pool corner and at the middle of large pools with deck levels above the water level. Handrails at ladders should not hang over the pool.

Obstructions

Underwater lights, drains, and so on should be flush with the pool walls or floor. If resting ledges are provided around the pool wall, they should be of the recessed type, which do not protrude into the pool.

Deck

The deck must be nonslip. Brushed concrete or 1-inch-square nonslip tiles are suggested.

Fencing

Outdoor pools should be securely surrounded by nonclimbable fence at least 4 feet high, with secure latches above the reach of toddlers.

Entrances

Entrances to the pool should be through the shower rooms and located at the shallow end of the pool with the depth clearly marked on the pool edge.

Safety Markings

Pool-depth markings must be placed on the edge of the deck at maximum and minimum depth points, at the break between shallow and deep portions, and at 2-foot-depth increments, not more than 25 feet apart around the perimeter of the pool (New York State Sanitary Code, a typical state regulation).

Safety Lines

A floating line must be provided at the 5-foot-depth mark or at the breakpoint between shallow and deep water. New York State requires a 4-inch stripe of contrasting color on the bottom at the breakpoint.

Outdoor Areas

Trees that shed (e.g., apple, coconut) must not be placed where fallout could injure a patron. Avoid planting shrubs that attract insects (e.g., bees).

Playing areas (e.g., volleyball) should be separated from the swimming area. The children's area (separated by a gate) should be separated from the deeper-water swimming area.

Furniture should be situated away from the pool edge.

Safety Sensors

Where unsanctioned nighttime swims are popular, automatic alarm systems (especially for outdoor pools) should be activated whenever the pool is closed.

SAFETY STANDARDS FOR BEACH FACILITIES

Shoreline

The shoreline must be free of rocks and weeds and preferably of piers and jetties. It must be open to provide easy visibility for lifeguards. Safety hazards must be clearly marked or covered (e.g., with docks). Access for emergency vehicles must be provided.

Bottom

The bottom must be free of rocks, weeds, ledges, drop-offs, mud, glass, and so on.

Water Quality

Water quality must meet state and local health department standards (generally, a total coliform count under 1,000 per 100 milliliters of water and a fecal coliform count under 100 per 100 milliliters of water). "A pH within the range of 6.5 and 8.3 is required except that it may be between 5.0 and 9.0 when due to natural causes" (State of New York, n.d.).

Sun, Wind, and Temperature

The direction of the sun and prevailing winds must be considered when decisions are made for the location of docks, sailing areas, and swimming beaches.

Docks should be located to minimize wave action in the swimming area. Sailing areas should be located where novice sailors cannot enter the swimming area. Lifeguards should not be forced to look into the sun or to become chilled.

Depth

Depth should be clearly marked wherever diving or dropoffs occur. Seasonal changes in depth should be posted. Maximum recommended depth is 15 feet, depending on water clarity.

Currents and Tides

Signs should be posted that indicate the probable consequences of currents and tides.

Special Activities

Clearly marked areas should be designated for swimming, boating, scuba diving, waterskiing, and other activities.

Equipment

Rafts, docks, and ladders must have non-slip surfaces. Rafts must be securely anchored to prevent drifting. Diving boards should not be mounted on rafts. Floats should be connected with safety lines to the shore or dock.

Entrance

The entrance to the waterfront area should be restricted to one or two well-controlled gates. Where strict bather control can be exercised, a check-in or "buddy board" is advisable.

Safety Lines and Buoys

Swimming and danger areas should be clearly marked with safety lines or buoys at all times.

Safety Flags

Flags on the beach should mark the boundaries of the swimming area.

SAFETY STANDARDS FOR DIVING BOARDS, MINITRAMPS, AND SLIDES

Diving Boards

Construction

The board surface must be of a nonslip material. The adjustable fulcrum must be easily moved, with gears guarded to prevent injuries to the toes and fingers. Boards must be checked regularly for wear, cracks, and other defects.

Diving Stands

A safety net should be slung underneath the board to prevent a diver from falling from the stand to the deck. Side rails with canvas panels should extend at least 2 feet over the water. If no side panels are used, center rails should permit no opening greater than 12 inches in the side rails. Steps rather than ladders are desirable. Stands must be regularly checked for loose bolts, etc.

Installation

Installation must conform to accepted standards as defined in the manufacturer's instructions and in competitive-diving rule books. The board must be mounted level with correct fulcrum placement and extend at least 6 feet over the water. The board should be placed so that the sun is behind the diver.

Depth Under the Boards

Although health department regulations in many states permit mounting a 1-meter board over 9 feet of water, a study by Gabrielsen (1984) showed that this depth is not sufficient to prevent injury. A 1-meter board requires 12 feet of water, and a 3-meter board requires 13 feet of water to be reasonably safe. Because divers do not enter the water directly under the tip of the board, competitive-diving rules require that the safe water depth must extend at least 16 feet beyond the end of the board, at least 8 feet on either side, and at least 5 feet under the board for safety.

Boards on Rafts

Diving boards on rafts are not safe because of the motion of the raft during diving and because they seldom meet the correct length and mounting standards.

Minitramps and Jump Boards

These items are even more dangerous to the unskilled diver than is a diving board. Their use should be discouraged and should be restricted to experienced divers who are under constant, qualified supervision.

Water Slides

Signs that prominently disclose the danger and the accepted method of sliding must be clearly visible. Only feet-first entries may be permitted in shallow water (under 5 feet). The end of the slide should be only 6 inches above the water. Persons should leave the slide at a 0° angle. An unobstructed space of 16 feet in front and 8 feet to either side must be provided.

REFERENCES AND SUGGESTED READINGS

Gabrielsen, M. (Ed.). (1984). *Diving injuries: A critical insight and recommendations.* Indianapolis, IN: Council for National Cooperation in Aquatics.

Gabrielsen, M.A. (Ed.). (1987). *Swimming pools: A guide to their planning, design, and operation* (4th ed.), pp. 97-120. Champaign, IL: Human Kinetics.

Palm, J. (1974). *Alert: Aquatic supervision in action,* pp. 29-50. Toronto, Ontario, Canada: The Royal Life Saving Society Canada.

Pantera, M. (1977). The design of public swimming facilities. In J. Borozne (Ed.), *Safety in aquatic activities,* (pp. 13-21). Reston, VA: American Association for Health, Physical Education, Recreation and Dance.

State of New York. (n.d.). *New York State sanitary code,* Chapter 1, Part 6. Albany, NY: Author.

U.S. Department of Health, Education and Welfare. Public Health Service. Center for Disease Control. (1976). *Swimming pools, safety and disease control through proper design and operation.* Washington, DC: Author.

PRESCHOOL SWIMMING: MYTHS AND FACTS

Myth: Young children can be made "water safe" (i.e., drownproofed).

Fact: Regardless of age or skill, no person is completely water safe.

Myth: Young children cannot really learn to swim. (Corollary: Due to developmental considerations, young children under 3 years of age should not be in organized programs.)

Fact: Swimming can be defined as voluntary locomotion through the water, and young children can do this. Developmentally, children use different movements in the water, but they are able to swim and benefit from organized programs.

Myth: The swimming reflex helps infants learn to swim.

Fact: The swimming reflex is a primitive, involuntary reflex seen only in newborns. Its purpose is unknown. A child does not and cannot breathe during reflexive swimming.

Myth: The epiglottal reflex keeps infants from drowning or from developing hyponatremia (water intoxication).

Fact: The epiglottal reflex keeps fluids and food from the lungs and prevents choking. It does not prevent swallowing (it actually assists it), and it certainly cannot prevent drowning (which is suffocation, not the lungs filling up with water).

Myth: Infants and young children must not be submerged. (Corollary: Submersion of infants and young children is risky.)

Fact: Submersion itself does not produce hyponatremia, but excessive fluids, lack of sodium, or both do. (Hyponatremia is a condition in which an electrolyte imbalance results from the loss of electrolytes or rapid ingestion of fluids or both.) Normally, the kidneys balance blood sodium levels. Too little is known about the incidence and contributing factors of hyponatremia to ignore the potential dangers. The CNCA guidelines suggest limiting the number of submersions and the length of time in the water for young children. [Note: Langendorfer (in press) reports that "No epidemiologic or empirical research has substantiated the extent of the danger to young children. Whether hyponatremia is a significant threat to aquatic programs who allow young children to submerge is unknown at present."]

Myth: Swimming causes ear infections in young children.

Fact: The incidence of ear infections in young children is high due to their short eustachian tubes (from the middle ear), which prevent adequate air and fluid exchange during periods of congestion when mucous membranes are swollen. Ear infections occur in many young children regardless of whether or not they swim.

Myth: Children absolutely cannot swim with ear tubes.

Fact: Although many pediatricians forbid swimming for patients with ear tubes, others permit it. Except during deep submersion, little water is likely to be forced into the middle ear with casual wetness. [Note: Langendorfer (in press) cites evidence that swimmers with ear tubes had no greater incidence of inner-ear infections than had swimmers without tubes.]

Myth: Swimming lessons for young children should be "work" and not play and fun.

Fact: The work of childhood is play, not adult-oriented work and structured teaching situations.

Myth: Children's aquatic skill acquisition should be all fun and play.

Fact: Children learn through play and fun, but they also need guidance. Play leaders can guide play and learning rather than use formal command and lecture methods.

Myth: Only proper techniques and programs permit young children to learn advanced strokes and water safety. In particular, operant conditioning and behavior modification techniques are considered to be the best ways to condition children and infants to be safe or to swim. (Corollary: Instructors teach children to swim, or children must be taught to swim.)

Fact: There are many ways to encourage swimming, including play and structured lessons. Children learn to swim in spite of, not because of, the teacher and the teaching techniques. Learning is the active domain of the learner. A child (or adult) can learn proper swimming strokes without formal teaching. They learn through imitation, play, and exploration.

Myth: The standard multiuse swimming pool is the best place to teach young children to swim and to be safe in and around the water.

Fact: The standard multiuse swimming pool is usually too cold, deep, noisy, and crowded for effective instruction to be given.

Myth: Infants and young children contaminate swimming pools and throw off the chemical balance.

Fact: The total output of urine and feces by even up to 30 infants barely influences the chlorine levels of pools.

Myth: Infants and young children can contract serious diseases from swimming pools.

Fact: Properly maintained pools do not normally transmit diseases. Chlorine is an effective disinfecting agent. Most diseases are passed from person to person in pools, not through the water. Open bodies of water, however, have been found to transmit diseases. [Note: Langendorfer (1987b, p. 8) affirms that, "Contrary to rumors, giardia parasites are adequately controlled by normal chlorine levels in pools and NO pools have been closed down".]

Myth: Infants and young children should not use flotation devices, which they become dependent on.

Fact: A young child's preference for (not dependence on) a flotation device is transitory and demonstrates that the child does not yet trust his or her own body's ability to float.

Myth: Infants and young children should always wear flotation devices.

Fact: Programs that advocate the constant use of flotation do not allow the child to learn the body's inherent floating ability. It also can provide parents with a mistaken notion of water safety and discourage constant vigilance around the water.

Myth: Toys and equipment are distractions that are unnecessary in swimming lessons.

Fact: Toys and equipment are often valuable sources of distraction (to help the fearful child overcome reluctance) and familiarity (to encourage exploration of new ways to move in the water). Schmidt's schema theory of motor learning even suggests that broader experiences (e.g., toys, equipment, and exploration) can build a superior foundation for later learning and performance.

Myth: Infant swimming promotes superior child development (''superbaby'').

Fact: Few studies have focused on the results of infant swimming. Those that have been conducted produced conflicting results. There is, at present, no compelling evidence that infant swimming or other early aquatic experiences enhance the otherwise normal infant. There have been studies in child development that demonstrate that handicapped infants can benefit from early aquatic experiences to help remediate the effects of the handicapping conditions.

Myth: Infant swimming does not promote child development.

Fact: Early aquatic experiences can produce some results. The child and parent share important learning time while the child explores and learns new skills in a novel environment.

Myth: There is presently a scientific basis for aquatics for the infant and young child.

Fact: There are inadequate informed judgments about many practices in aquatics for the young child.

REFERENCES AND SUGGESTED READINGS

Langendorfer, S. (1987a). Separating fact from fiction in pre-school aquatics. *National Aquatics Journal* (Winter), **3**(4), 2-4.

Langendorfer, S. (1987b). Swimming for children under three: A clarification. *National Aquatics Journal* (Fall), **3**(3), 8.

Langendorfer, S. (in press). Status of research in infant/preschool aquatics. *Research Consortium Newsletter*.

Appendix E is adapted from Langendorfer (1987a). Adapted by permission of Council for National Cooperation in Aquatics.

CNCA STATEMENT AND RATIONALE REGARDING AQUATIC ACTIVITY PROGRAMS FOR CHILDREN UNDER THE AGE OF 3

1. Aquatic programs for children under the age of three years most appropriately should be promoted, described, and conducted as water "adjustment," "orientation," or "familiarization" programs. Emphasis should be placed upon the need for young children to explore the aquatic environment in enjoyable, non-stressful situations that provide a wide variety of games and experiences.

Rationale: Other terms, such as "drownproofing," "waterproofing," and "water safe," often can suggest to parents and the general public that children can be safe in and around the water without careful supervision. In addition, the developmental literature supports the primary role of play activities and movement exploration in the acquisition of movement competence by young children.

2. Water experience/orientation programs should have the in-water participation of a parent, guardian, or other person who is responsible for and trusted by the child.

Rationale: The parent is the first and primary teacher of the young child. As such, the parent must assume actual responsibility for the supervision and learning of the child. Aquatic programs, when properly structured, can provide an excellent type of parent-child learning environment. Programs conducted without parents in the water should be limited in size and make every consideration for the safety and psychological comfort of the child.

3. The participating parent, guardian, or other responsible adult assumes primary responsibility for monitoring the child's health before, during, and after participation in aquatic programs. All children, especially those with known medical problems, should receive clearance from the physician prior to participation in the aquatic program.

Rationale: The child's parent and physician are the persons who can best judge the child's medical developmental readiness for exposure to a public swimming pool at an early age. There is disagreement among professionals about the benefits and detriments of the child's early exposure to the aquatic environment. The potential benefits of enhanced movement, socialization, and parent-child interaction must be weighed against problems such as possible increased susceptibility to eye, ear, respiratory, and bacterial infections. More definitive research evidence is needed to assist parents and physicians in evaluating the child's readiness.

4. Personnel directing and operating aquatic programs for children under three years of age should have training in child development and parenting as well as aquatics, or have consultants who have been trained in these areas. Fully trained and qualified lifeguards must be on duty at all times during programs.

Rationale: Because of the developmental differences in cognitive, psychomotor, and affective domains between the young child and older children, the directors and teachers of these programs must have a well-founded understanding of child development. Because the programs usually involve both the parents and the children, a further understanding of parenting principle also is necessary. Finally, in spite of the presence of parents in the pool, it must be recognized that the instructor cannot assume lifeguarding responsibilities while teaching. A certified lifeguard in addition to the instructor is needed.

5. Participation in aquatic programs by neonates and by young children lacking prone head control should be limited. [Note: Not a part of the CNCA statement is Langendorfer's assertion (1985) that the onset of independent walking, usually at ages 12 to 18 months, is a logical starting time for aquatic instruction.]

Rationale: While there is general disagreement among professionals and practitioners regarding the youngest age at which children should begin water experiences, there is some evidence suggesting that until the child can voluntarily control the head by lifting it 90 degrees when prone, they probably will gain little from the water experience and may be more at risk of accidentally submerging or swallowing water. Certain aquatic skills can successfully be introduced when the child demonstrates rolling over, crawling, and creeping. Due to individual differences among young children, behavioral, rather than strict age, criteria are usually the most valid way to evaluate children for program participation.

6. Certain teaching techniques, such as dropping a child from a height, should be strictly prohibited. Other procedures such as face submersions, especially those which are controlled by an adult, must be limited both in duration and in number for the young child.

Rationale: Dropping a child from any height is unnecessary and serves no reasonable purpose. In fact, it is extremely dangerous, as it may produce head, neck, or organ damage to a young child, as well as introduce water and bacteria into the nose, ears and sinuses. There is also potential for psychological trauma in such an activity.

A growing number of recent clinical reports have implicated the practice of repeated hyponatremia, or "water intoxication" in young children. Hyponatremia is a condition in which an electrolyte (especially sodium) imbalance results from the loss of electrolytes or rapid ingestion of fluids or both. The symptoms include such "soft" signs as irritability, crying, and fussing, as well as more serious signs of vomiting, convulsions, and coma. Despite claims that a young child has a "breathholding" or epiglottal reflex, both children and adults can swallow significant amounts of water while learning to swim. Due to the small body size and large skin area to body weight ratio of most children under 18 months of age, water ingestion can produce symptoms of hyponatremia, some of which may be going unnoticed by parents and teachers. Therefore, submersions by young children must be brief (one to five seconds), and few in number (less than six per lesson) while the child is initially learning. Once the child can initiate the submersions AND can demonstrate competent breath control, submersions can become longer and more frequent. However, the parents and teachers still must be alert to bloated stomachs and "soft" signs that may indicate excessive water ingestion and incipient problems.

The conditions of hyponatremia must be the focus of a concerted research effort to discover the extent and scope of its presence in infant swimming classes. Clinical and empirical evidence would be the basis for subsequent amendments to this guideline.

7. Maximum in-water class time for infants and very young children must not exceed 30 minutes.

Rationale: Most children benefit from shorter, but more frequent, learning experiences. Limiting in-water time to less than 30 minutes should maximize the learning and enjoyment of children while avoiding fatigue, hypothermia, and possible hyponatremia. One of the constant factors discovered in each clinical hyponatremia case was that children had been in the water far in excess of 30 minutes. Apparently, fatigue, chilling, and excessive submersions all may contribute to hyponatremia.

8. Water and air temperature must be maintained at sufficient levels and in proper proportion to one another to guarantee the comfort of young children.

Rationale: Young children can become chilled more easily than adults and may have immature thermal regulatory systems. They also cannot enjoy the experience or learn optimally if chilled. There is no general agreement as to the proper level of water temperature in indoor pools. However, experience suggests that water temperature should be a *minimum* of 82° Fahrenheit (86° is preferable) and that air temperature should be at least 3° higher than the water temperature. Locker and changing room temperatures also should be maintained at warm levels. Failure to achieve these minimum standards should be a strong factor in cancelling or shortening classes.

9. All laws and regulations pertaining to water purity, pool care, and sanitation must be carefully followed.

Rationale: Young children are extremely susceptible to disease. Utmost care in maintaining facilities in accord with bathing codes and water purity standards can prevent unnecessary outbreaks of disease and infections. Locker rooms and pool decks must be clean and free of clutter. Slippery surfaces and impeded walkways can be very dangerous to beginning and inexperienced walkers. Proper facilities for the changing and disposal of diapers and soiled clothing must be provided.

10. Appropriate, but not excessive clothing should be worn by young children to minimize the spread of body wastes into the water.

Rationale: Fecal matter is aesthetically unattractive and potentially hazardous to other swimmers. Children should wear some type of tight-fitting but lightweight apparel, perhaps covered by rubber pants. Heavier diapers can be both a health and a safety hazard and should not be worn. Parents and instructors should monitor young children and remove them from the water if a bowel movement is apparent.

REFERENCES AND SUGGESTED READINGS

Council for National Cooperation in Aquatics. (1985). Aquatic activity programs for children under the age of three. *National Aquatics Journal*, **1**(2), 12-13.

Langendorfer, S., & Willing, E. (1985). The impact of motor development research upon issues in infant and preschool aquatics. *National Aquatics Journal* (Spring), **1**(1), 11-14.

Appendix F is adapted from Council for National Cooperation in Aquatics (1985) and Langendorfer and Willing (1985). Adapted by permission of Council for National Cooperation in Aquatics.

INDEX